Treading on Hallowed Ground

Treading on Hallowed Ground

Counterinsurgency Operations in Sacred Spaces

Edited by
C. Christine Fair and Sumit Ganguly

OXFORD
UNIVERSITY PRESS
2008

OXFORD
UNIVERSITY PRESS

Oxford University Press, Inc., publishes works that further
Oxford University's objective of excellence
in research, scholarship, and education.

Oxford New York
Auckland Cape Town Dar es Salaam Hong Kong Karachi
Kuala Lumpur Madrid Melbourne Mexico City Nairobi
New Delhi Shanghai Taipei Toronto

With offices in
Argentina Austria Brazil Chile Czech Republic France Greece
Guatemala Hungary Italy Japan Poland Portugal Singapore
South Korea Switzerland Thailand Turkey Ukraine Vietnam

Published by Oxford University Press, Inc.
198 Madison Avenue, New York, New York 10016

www.oup.com

Library of Congress Cataloging-in-Publication Data

Treading on hallowed ground : counterinsurgency operations in
sacred spaces / edited by C. Christine Fair and Sumit Ganguly.
p. cm.
Includes bibliographical references and index.
ISBN 978-0-19-534203-1; 978-0-19-534204-8 (pbk.)
1. Counterinsurgency. 2. Insurgency. 3. Counterinsurgency—Case
studies. 4. Sacred space—Political aspects. 5. Shrines.
I. Title: Counterinsurgency operations in sacred spaces.
II. Fair, C. Christine. III. Ganguly, Sumit.
U241.T74 2008
355.02'18—dc22 2008007789

1 3 5 7 9 8 6 4 2

Printed in the United States of America
on acid-free paper

Acknowledgments

This project was notionally conceived while one of the editors was conducting research on urban operations undertaken by South Asian security forces under the direction of Dr. Russell Glenn at the RAND Corporation. However, it came to fruition through the collaboration of the editors, who initially organized a panel at the annual conference of the International Studies Association in 2007. That panel formed the cornerstone of this volume. The editors are appreciative of the efforts of each of the authors, without whose contribution this book would not be possible. Special thanks are owed to Manjeet Pardesi, who provided invaluable assistance in tracking down errant references.

Contents

Contributors

Editors

C. Christine Fair is a senior political scientist with the RAND Corporation. Prior to rejoining RAND, she served as a political officer to the United Nations Assistance Mission to Afghanistan in Kabul and as a senior research associate in USIP's Center for Conflict Analysis and Prevention. Prior to joining USIP in April 2004, she was an associate political scientist at the RAND Corporation. Her research focuses upon the security competition between India and Pakistan, Pakistan's internal security, the causes of terrorism in South Asia, and U.S. strategic relations with India and Pakistan. She has authored and co-authored several books including *The Madrassah Challenge: Militancy and Religious Education in Pakistan* (2008), *Fortifying Pakistan: The Role of U.S. Internal Security Assistance* (2006); *Securing Tyrants or Fostering Reform? U.S. Internal Security Assistance to Repressive and Transitioning Regimes* (2006); *The Counterterror Coalitions: Cooperation with Pakistan and India* (2004); *Urban Battle Fields of South Asia: Lessons Learned from Sri Lanka, India and Pakistan* (2004); and numerous peer-reviewed articles covering a range of security issues in Pakistan, India, Sri Lanka, and Bangladesh. She is a member of the International Institute of Strategic Studies, London, and is the managing editor of *India Review*.

Sumit Ganguly is a professor of Political Science, holding the Rabindranath Tagore Chair in Indian Cultures and Civilizations, and is the director of research of the Center on American and Global Security at Indiana University, Bloomington. He is also an adjunct fellow of the Pacific Council on International Policy in Los Angeles. Professor Ganguly has previously been on the faculty of James Madison College of Michigan State University, Hunter College of the City University of New York, and the University of Texas at Austin. He has also taught at Columbia University in New York City. He has also been a fellow and a guest scholar at the Woodrow Wilson International Center for Scholars in Washington, D.C., and a visiting fellow at the Center for International Security and Cooperation at Stanford University. His research and writing focused on South Asia has been supported by grants from the Asia Foundation, the Ford Foundation, the Carnegie Corporation of New York, and the W. Alton Jones Foundation. He serves on the editorial boards of *Asian Affairs*, *Asian Survey*, *Current History*, the *Journal of Democracy*, the *Journal of Strategic Studies*, and *Security Studies*. He is also the founding editor of both the *India Review* and *Asian Security*, two refereed journals. Professor Ganguly is the author, editor, or co-editor of 15 books on South Asian politics. His most recent book is *The State of India's Democracy* (edited with Larry Diamond and Marc Plattner). He is a member of the Council on Foreign Relations in New York and the International Institute of Strategic Studies in London. He is currently at work on a book, *India Since 1980*.

Contributors

Nora Bensahel is a senior political scientist, RAND Corporation, and adjunct associate professor in the Security Studies Program at the Edmund A. Walsh School of Foreign Service at Georgetown University. She specializes in military strategy and doctrine. Her recent work examines stability operations in Iraq and Afghanistan, post-conflict reconstruction, military coalitions, and multilateral intervention. Her recent publications include "Mission Not Accomplished: What Went Wrong with Iraq Reconstruction," *The Counterterror Coalitions*, and *The Future Security Environment in the Middle East*. She has held fellowships at the Center for International Security and Cooperation at Stanford University and the John M. Olin Institute for Strategic Studies at Harvard University. She is currently a member of the executive board of Women in International Security and is a past term member of the Council on Foreign Relations.

Ron E. Hassner is an assistant professor of political science at the University of California, Berkeley. He is a graduate of Stanford University with degrees in political science and religious studies. His research revolves around symbolic and emotive aspects of international security with particular attention to religious violence, Middle Eastern politics, and territorial disputes. His publications have focused on the role of perceptions in entrenching international disputes, the causes and characteristics of conflicts over sacred places, the characteristics of political-religious leadership and political-religious mobilization, and the role of national symbols in conflict. In 2007–2008 he was a visiting professor at the Center for International Security and Cooperation, Stanford University.

Joseph Chinyong Liow is an associate professor and head of research (IDSS) at the Rajaratnam School of International Studies, Nanyang Technological University, Singapore. His research interests include Muslim politics in Malaysia and Malay-Muslim resistance in Thailand. He is the author of *The Politics of Indonesia-Malaysia Relations: One Kin, Two Nations* (2005) and *Muslim Resistance in Southern Thailand and Southern Philippines: Religion, Ideology, and Politics* (2005).

Pascal Ménoret is a Ph.D. candidate at the University of Paris-Sorbonne. He has authored *The Saudi Enigma: A History* (Zed Books, 2005), as well as several publications about the Saudi Islamic movements.

Manjeet S. Pardesi is a Ph.D. student at the Department of Political Science at Indiana University-Bloomington. His research interests include war and strategy, great power politics, and India's foreign and security policy. He obtained his M.S. in Strategic Studies in 2002 from the Institute of Defence and Strategic Studies (IDSS, now called the S Rajaratnam School of International Studies), Singapore. After completing his M.S., he worked as an associate research fellow at IDSS, where he focused on the institute's projects on the Revolution in Military Affairs (RMA). He has lectured, conducted tutorials, and led discussion groups of the Tri-Service Staff Course and the Command and Staff Course at the SAFTI Military Institute, Singapore.

David Siddhartha Patel is an assistant professor of government at Cornell University. His research focuses on Islamic institutions and collective action in the Middle East. In 2003–2004 Patel conducted independent research in Iraq on the role of mosques and clerical networks in creating social order post-invasion. He has also conducted research in Jordan, Syria, and Yemen on state oversight of Islamic institutions, information dissemination through mosques, and Islamist movements. Before joining the Cornell faculty, Patel was a pre-doctoral fellow at the Center on Democracy, Development, and the Rule of Law and a post-doctoral fellow at the Center for International Security and Cooperation, both at Stanford University. He received his B.A. from Duke University in Economics and Political Science and his Ph..D.. from Stanford University in Political Science.

Treading on Hallowed Ground

Introduction

Sumit Ganguly and C. Christine Fair

In the aftermath of the U.S.-led interventions in both Afghanistan and Iraq there has been a renewed interest in the study of counterinsurgency. Classic works on the subject have been reissued,[1] the U.S. Marine Corps has produced a new counterinsurgency manual,[2] and a spate of academic articles have appeared in important professional journals.[3] Despite this understandable academic and policy interest in the subject, the bulk of the scholarship has been focused on the *general* problems of conducting counterinsurgency operations. Two *specific* problems of counterinsurgency, however, have received inadequate attention in the scholarly literature.

The first such problem addresses the challenges of military operations in urban environments. There is a considerable body of policy analysis and military treatments of conducting operations in urban environments. However, academic treatments of this subject are scarce.[4] The rural bias in the literature is understandable. The vast majority of insurgencies during the Cold War era, with the possible exception of some operations in Northern Ireland, were in rural areas, and so much of the relevant literature focused on the problems that would be encountered in such a milieu.[5] At the same time, counterinsurgency operations in urban terrains pose very specific problems because they dramatically raise the risks and dangers of unwitting harm to civilian populations. Such harm, however inadvertent, can inflict significant costs on counterinsurgent forces and can easily result in widespread violation of human rights, alienate an already distrustful population, and help bolster the standing of the insurgents.

Additionally, in highly congested urban areas, counterinsurgent forces may face significant difficulties in ferreting out insurgents who, in all likelihood, will be intimately familiar with particular localities, with the geographic layouts of neighborhoods, with the physical features of buildings, and with the demography of the their inhabitants. These forms of local knowledge are likely to confer significant tactical advantages to the insurgents. Consequently, the demand for local knowledge and intelligence about prevailing conditions may tax the resources of most counterinsurgent forces unless they can swiftly elicit the cooperation of the local populace.

While the urban dimension of insurgencies has attracted some—albeit inadequate—attention, another more important lacuna exists in the literature concerning the conduct of counterinsurgency operations in sacred places (e.g., shrines, mosques, temples, synagogues, churches). In several insurgencies in the Middle East as well as South and Southeast Asia, sacred spaces have become major, perilous sites of conflict. The exploitation of sacred spaces confers on insurgents a patina of religious sanction, provides access to ready recruits who visit such spaces, affords insurgents secure logistical bases, permits secure venues for weapons accumulation and other fortifications, and offers sanctuaries for the groups' leadership and cadres.

Counterinsurgency forces are hesitant—or should be hesitant—to operate against insurgents based in sacred spaces, because such operations may expand popular local support for the insurgents, swell the recruitment market for insurgents, and even galvanize support beyond the particular theater of operation. The Indian Army operation against the most sacred Sikh shrine (the Golden Temple in Amritsar) in 1984 bolstered the insurgency in the Punjab and, equally important, motivated a substantial number of Sikhs throughout the global diaspora to support the demand for an independent Sikh state by sending funds, weapons, and even fighters. Similarly, U.S. operations on the significant Shi'a shrines in Najaf and Karbala in Iraq outraged Muslims of all interpretative traditions from Morocco to Malaysia. Recently Pakistan's operations against the Red Mosque in Islamabad succeeded in ferreting out militants but likely galvanized a wider Islamist militant resurgence in key areas in Pakistan.

Thus security forces and operational planners face a challenging dilemma: do they avoid "desecrating" sacred space to accommodate the religious sensibilities of the enemy and the population of adherents writ large, *or* do they pursue military operations as required by the tactical demands of the battle? While the tactical and operational challenges of counterinsurgency operations in such spaces may seem apparent, operational planners have failed to account for the strategic import of these operations. As a result, they have made inadequate efforts to manage the public perceptions of the operations through the effective use of strategic communications.

Unfortunately, the religious spaces that are often exploited by insurgents have tended to be located in urban or urbanized areas. As was noted above, urban environments pose unique operational challenges for even the most capable counterinsurgency forces, because they afford the adversary numerous advantages such as a diverse and poorly characterized social landscape, anonymity, in-place logistical support infrastructure, and large audiences for their actions. Insurgents may deliberately seek to engage security forces in urban areas to vitiate the former's conventional advantages. Thus, dealing with insurgents in sacred space often requires counterinsurgency forces to contend with the vicissitudes of urban combat.

Widespread failure to identify the problem of conducting counterinsurgency operations on sacred space has obviously precluded analysis of such operations and the determinants of their operational and strategic success or failure. This lacuna in military planning has proven deadly. U.S. operations in important mosques in Iraq likely have made winning the hearts and minds of Iraqis difficult and have inflamed the sentiments of Muslims throughout the world. Of course, there are numerous other reasons for popular disaffection with the United States and the failure to win the support of Iraqis and others in the Muslim world. These include military operations in Iraq and Afghanistan and widespread distrust about the official U.S. justification for these interventions , U.S. commitment to maintaining military bases in the Middle East, U.S. championing of undemocratic governments in Muslim states, unstinting U.S. support for Israel, and an inadequate U.S. commitment to the establishment of a viable Palestinian state.

Given current U.S. and British operations in Iraq and the centrality of mosques to that conflict—often mosques that are highly esteemed throughout the Muslim world—understanding the factors that account for successes and failures of counterinsurgency operations on sacred space is of paramount importance. The importance of this query is buttressed by the important examples of such operations beyond Iraq waged by police and by paramilitary and regular military forces against religiously motivated insurgents in numerous countries.

This volume addresses these various gaps in several important ways. First, it explains why sacred space is important both to insurgents and to counterinsurgency forces. Second, it presents a series of case studies evaluating the most important counterinsurgency operations on sacred space in the Middle East and South and Southeast Asia. These cases include operations involving the deployment of security forces against religious sites within the state's own sovereign territory, within "occupied territories" or areas where sovereignty is contested, and within states where foreign armed forces are invited by the government to fight insurgents. Also the adversaries in these cases vary in their capabilities and commitment, in their ties to the locality, in their veneration and respect for the space in question, and in the degree of support they enjoy within the local populace and beyond. Third, drawing from the insights of the significance of sacred space as well as the detailed case studies, this volume will conclude with an important set of propositions for successful counterinsurgency operations on sacred space.

This volume begins with Ron Hassner's attempts to carefully spell out the key problems that counterinsurgency operations pose in sacred places. At the outset, Hassner delineates the concept of a "sacred space" and explains the key features that grant such spaces a sacral quality. He then examines how insurgent groups can usefully occupy and exploit sacred places. Hassner contends that insurgents can mingle with pilgrims and worshippers and can also use the sacredness of shrines, mosques, and temples as sanctuaries from counterinsurgent forces who may be understandably loath to offend local religious sensibilities by using force against such locales. Next he outlines possible strategies and potential pitfalls for security forces when they are seeking to flush out insurgents who have taken refuge in sacred arenas.

Finally, Hassner briefly examines some of the lessons derived from the Israeli siege of the Church of Nativity in Bethlehem, where several Palestinian militants retreated in 2002. Hassner selects this case because of its novelty and importance. The Church of the Nativity was held sacred by a group that was distinct both from the religious identity of the Palestinian insurgents ensconced at the site and from the ethnic and religious majority represented by the Israeli government. As Hassner notes, despite the peculiarities of this case, it exhibits "many of the arguments, challenges and possible solutions" detailed in his introductory essay.

C. Christine Fair deals with two operations conducted in the course of the Khalistani insurgency in the Indian state of Punjab which resulted in markedly different outcomes. Her two case studies focus on the operations of the Indian security forces against Sikh insurgents who had occupied the Golden Temple, the holiest Sikh shrine in the city of Amritsar. The first operation, as Fair shows in considerable detail, was a military as well as a public relations debacle. The Indian Army had inadequate and flawed intelligence about the strength and capabilities of the insurgents who had entered and occupied the Golden Temple, and they failed to forge a viable public relations strategy and ultimately used excessive force to prevail.

Fortunately, she also shows that the Indian state was capable of learning from its initial errors. When Sikh militants again attempted to use the temple as a sanctuary, the Indian security forces launched a second assault which involved a prolonged siege, but one marked by careful attention to the sentiments of religious authorities and by a deft public relations strategy. The two contrasting episodes underscore how the same regime, under different circumstances, can cope with and respond to the requirements of a counterinsurgency operation in a sacred site.

Sumit Ganguly next attempts to explain the dramatically different outcomes of two sieges conducted in the course of combating India's Kashmir insurgency: one of a historic mosque in urban setting and the other of an ancient shrine in a rural milieu. The first siege, that at the Hazratbal mosque in the capital city of Indian-controlled Kashmir, ended peacefully. The siege of the shrine of Sheikh Nooruddin Noorani, a Sufi saint, however, ended in a bloody conflagration culminating in the destruction of the shrine. Ganguly argues that the markedly different locations of the two religious sites partially explains the different outcomes of the two sieges. The Hazratbal mosque located in the heart of Srinagar promptly attracted the attention of the national government in New Delhi, which granted an able civilian administrator to handle the negotiations while allowing the military to maintain a vigilant posture.

The Charar-e-Sharief shrine, on the other hand, was located near the Line of Control (the de facto international border) in Kashmir and therefore was at some remove from significant political attention. This situation led the military and local police forces to adopt a more unyielding posture toward the insurgents. Additionally, and perhaps more importantly, the demographic composition of the insurgents in the two sites played a vital role in shaping the final outcomes. The insurgents at the Hazratbal mosque were mostly native Kashmiris and thereby more amenable to negotiations. The militants who had occupied the shrine were all foreign insurgents with no particular affinity for Kashmir and therefore were less willing to compromise.

Manjeet Pardesi focuses upon the July 2007 Pakistan military operation against the Lal Masjid (Red Mosque) in Islamabad, the capital of Pakistan. Pardesi demonstrates that while the operation was a tactical success, it was a strategic failure. The Lal Masjid, long a seat of radical Islamist and even militant activity, became the site of a siege after several of its acolytes carried out a series of abductions and vigilante attacks on persons and institutions in Islamabad that the militants deemed to be "un-Islamic." Initially the Pakistani regime of General Pervez Musharraf granted the denizens of the mosque considerable leeway because of their close ties with a key Islamist party, the Jamiat-ul-Ulama-i-Islam (JUI). The JUI was a critical component of a coalition of Islamist parties called the Muttihida-Majlis-Amal (MMA). President Musharraf was forced to appease various members of the MMA since he required the support—or at least diminished opposition—of the MMA to push through a number of controversial policies, including remaining as Pakistan's president beyond 2007.

In addition, the Pakistani military had been courting radical Islamists and their militant offshoots as part and parcel of state strategy since the time of General Zia ul Haq. While the activists associated with the mosque had engaged in a number of provocations, including seizing police officers and Pakistani women alleged to be prostitutes, the Musharraf government at last was compelled to confront the Red Mosque militants when the extremists seized several Chinese women whom they claimed were prostitutes. While Beijing remained silent about the deaths of Chinese workers at the Gwadar port in remote Baluchistan, it was unwilling to countenance such lapses in governmental authority in the capital city.

The operation was carried out quite deftly. When initial appeals for a peaceful surrender failed, the military was given the authority to attack the mosque. Their use of force was calibrated and the number of casualties was limited. Despite the tactical success of this operation, it nevertheless inflamed the sentiments of a range of radical Islamist groups across Pakistan. The adverse political fallout raised significant questions about the wisdom of the regime's strategy of cultivating radical Islamists to pursue other strategic goals.

Pascal Ménoret deals with the 1979 siege of the Grand Mosque in Mecca. This case also came to a sanguinary close with the Saudi regime seeking the assistance of French commandoes to bring an end to the occupation. The insurgents who entered the shrine were members of a Salafi sect which were in violent opposition to the Saudi monarchy. They had chosen to enter and occupy the Grand Mosque in Mecca because of its extraordinary significance to Sunni Islam. The response of the Saudi authorities was one of panic. They imposed a complete news blackout, imposed a curfew in Mecca and neighboring cities, arrested political activists, and disarmed regular police and military personnel in the area. After taking these steps, they sought publicly to discredit the occupiers through a propaganda barrage.

Because of the paucity of reportage, it is unclear whether the Saudi regime even contemplated a viable, negotiated solution to this crisis. What is known, however, is that initially Saudi royal forces refused to attack the mosque because of its paramount religious significance. After considerable pressure was exerted on them, they did resort to the use of considerable but crude force. After their failure to accomplish much other than inflict widespread damage to the mosque, the Saudi authorities sought and obtained the assistance of French commandoes. Though these commandoes prevailed in a two-week siege of the mosque, the loss of life and damage to the edifice was considerable. The operation, which was costly in both human and material terms, revealed the obvious inability of Saudi security forces to cope with a well-organized group of religiously motivated insurgents and the possibilities of a dangerous armed insurrection within this citadel of Islam.

David Patel focuses upon two uprisings in 2004 in Najaf, one of the holiest cities in Shi'ite Islam and home to the revered Imam Ali shrine. In the first uprising, in April 2004, U.S. army forces immediately attacked insurgents elsewhere in Iraq but deferred significant offensive operations against those in Najaf by four weeks. During those operations, they did not pursue insurgents into Najaf's Old City or the shrine.

The second uprising occurred in August in 2004 and was put down by U.S. Marines. In contrast, the Marines immediately attacked insurgents throughout Najaf, reducing their exclusion zone around the shrine and around abandoned no-fire zones. Marine and Army units advanced deep into Najaf's Old City and held positions near the shrine while air assets and tanks struck targets adjacent to it. When Grand Ayatollah Ali al-Sistani intervened in late August, most observers anticipated an assault on the shrine by Iraqi security forces working with U.S. forces.

Patel asks why, despite similar risks, did U.S. forces aggressively pursue insurgents in Najaf's sacred spaces in August but not in April? He argues that the most important variable explaining the two different outcomes was the nature of the government at the time of the operations. In April, Iraq was governed by Paul Bremer, III, who was the administrator of the Coalition Provisional Authority (CPA). In contrast, by August the CPA had been dissolved and "power" was transferred to an appointed Iraqi Interim Government with Iyad Allawi as the prime minister. Allawi's government vociferously supported decisive action against insurgents in Najaf in August. The support of this nominally sovereign Iraqi government, Patel argues, may explain the later U.S. willingness to assault Najaf's sacred sites. Earlier in the year, U.S. planners were unwilling to do so because they were uncertain about how Iraq's Shi'ites would respond.

Joseph Liow focuses on the Thai military's complete mishandling of a counterinsurgency operation at the Krue Se Mosque in southern Thailand. Liow argues that the Thai military violated some of the most basic principles of counterinsurgency operations and demonstrated a profound lack of both tactical and strategic awareness. Specifically, their security forces had lacked adequate intelligence on the insurgents operating in the region where the mosque was located, there were problems in the chain of command, and there was no clear blueprint for the operation barring the use of force. Not surprisingly, this operation ended in considerable bloodshed at a mosque that was fraught with a history and myth of local resistance. As a consequence of this botched operation, the insurgency received a substantial boost because the harshness of the military's tactics alienated much of the local population.

Nora Bensahel concludes this volume with an instructive analysis across the various case studies. She draws out a number of operational lessons to be learned from the cases, including an assessment of the degree of sacredness of a site, the level of support that insurgents enjoy within the local population, and the relative strengths of direct and indirect strategies. Bensahel observes that counterinsurgency operations rarely succeed or fail solely because of the sacredness of the site on which they take place. Rather, counterinsurgency is inherently difficult, and the presented cases demonstrate the numerous other factors that affect success, including differences in terrain and geography, tactical choices, the legitimacy of the national government, and the training and capabilities of both the insurgents and the counterinsurgency forces. However, the cases in this volume demonstrate that counterinsurgency in sacred spaces presents a number of special concerns that operational planners must address to ensure success.

Some of these concerns are worth highlighting. When military strategists plan operations, they must attempt to assess the degree of sacredness that is attached to a particular site. Not all shrines are equally consecrated. Consequently, they must take special precautions when dealing with sites that are of critical significance to believers. Adopting such strategies obviously requires a keen attention to local customs, beliefs, and mores.

As with all counterinsurgency operations, it is critical that military planners try to elicit the support of the local community. Once again, though this task is exceedingly difficult, small gestures—such as restraints on the use of force and consultation with local religious notables—may contribute much to win a modicum of support.

Finally, Bensahel argues that force should be used only when initial attempts to bring about a negotiated solution fail. Resorting to the use of force in the absence of any attempt at mediation is almost invariably a recipe for disaster.

Notes

1. See, for example, David Galula, *Counterinsurgency Warfare: Theory and Practice* (Westport, Conn.: Praeger Security International, 2008); Alastair Horne, *A Savage War of Peace: Algeria 1954–1962* (New York: The Viking Press, 1978); and Thomas Edward Lawrence, *Revolt in the Desert* (New York: G. H. Doran, 1927).

2. The United States Army Marine Corps, *Counterinsurgency Field Manual* (Chicago: University of Chicago Press, 2007).

3. See *inter alia* Colin Kahl, "COIN of the Realm: Is There a Future for Counterinsurgency," *Foreign Affairs* 86, no. 6 (2007), 169–76; Alexander Downes, "Introduction: Modern Insurgency and Counterinsurgency in Comparative Perspective," *Civil Wars* 9, no. 2 (2007), 313–23; James S. Corum, "Rethinking US Army Counter-Insurgency Doctrine," *Contemporary Security Policy* 28, no. 1 (2007), 127–42; Walter C. Ladwig III, "Training Foreign Police: A Mission Aspect of U.S. Security Assistance to Counterinsurgency," *Comparative Strategy* 26, no. 4 (2007), 285–93; Frank G. Hoffman, "Neo-Classical Counterinsurgency," *Parameters* 37, no. 2 (2007), 71–87; John Arquilla, "The End of War as We Knew It? Insurgency, Counterinsurgency and Lessons from the History of Early Terror Networks," *Third World Quarterly* 28, no. 2 (2007), 369–86; Mark T. Berger and Douglas A. Borer, "The Long War: Insurgency, Counterinsurgency and Collapsing States," *Third World Quarterly* 28, no. 2 (2007), 197–215; Daniel L. Byman, "Friends Like These: Counterinsurgency and the War on Terrorism," *International Security* 31, no. 2 (2006), 79–115; Bruce Hoffman, "Insurgency and Counterinsurgency

in Iraq," *Studies in Conflict and Terrorism* 31, no. 2 (2006), 103–21; Ian Beckett, "The Future of Insurgency," *Small Wars and Insurgencies* 16, no. 1 (2005), 22–36; Thomas Marks, "Ideology of Insurgency: New Ethnic Focus or Old Cold War Distortions," *Small Wars and Insurgencies* 15, no. 1 (2004), 107–18.

4. One of the most renowned analysts of warfare on urbanized terrain is RAND's Russell Glenn, who has authored a number of treatments on the subject from a variety of vantage points. See, for example, Russell W. Glenn et al., *Preparing for the Proven Inevitable: An Urban Operations Training Strategy for America's Joint Force* (Santa Monica, Cal.: RAND, 2006). See also C. Christine Fair, "Military Operations in Urban Areas: The Indian Experience," *India Review* 2, no. 1 (2003), 49–76; Robert Warren. "Situating the City and September 11th: Military Urban Doctrine, 'Pop-Up Armies and Spatial Chess,'" *International Journal of Urban and Regional Research* 26, no. 3 (Sept. 2002), 614; Ralph Peter, "Urban Planning, the Army Way," *Harper's* (August 1996), 12–14; Robert Leheny, "Addressing the Challenges of Urban Operations," *Military Technology* 30, no. 11 (2006), 81–88. Wayne A. Bryden, "Assured Urban Operations," *Military Technology* 30, no. 3 (2006), 72–76; Mark Hewish and Rupert Pengelley, "Facing Urban Inevitabilities—Military Operations in Urban Terrain Are a Classic Resort of Asymmetric Warfare," *International Defense Review* 34 (August 2001), 39–48; John R. Groves, Jr., "Operations in Urban Environments," *Military Review* 78, no. 4 (1998), 31–51; Mark Hewish and Rupert Pengelley, "Warfare in the Global City," *International Defense Review* 31, no. 6 (1998), 32–44; Marshall V. Ecklund, "Task Force Ranger Vs. Urban Somali Guerrillas in Mogadishu: An Analysis of Guerrilla and Counterguerrilla Tactics and Techniques Used During Operation GOTHIC SERPENT 1," *Small Wars and Insurgencies* 15, no. 3 (2004), 47–69; A. Hills, "Hearts and Minds or Search and Destroy? Controlling Civilians in Urban Operations," *Small Wars and Insurgencies* 13, no. 1 (2002), 1–24.

5. See, for example, Bard E. O'Neill, *Insurgency and Terrorism: Inside Modern Revolutionary Warfare* (Dulles, Va.: Brassey's, 1990).

1

Counterinsurgency and the Problem of Sacred Space

Ron E. Hassner

On April 2, 2002, a clash between the Israeli military and Palestinian gunmen that began like so many other violent encounters in the West Bank took a decidedly odd turn when the gunmen, 39 in all, sought refuge in the Church of the Nativity in Bethlehem, revered by Christians as the birthplace of Jesus.[1] There they remained, relatively safe from harm, for the next six weeks. Although the gunmen were Muslim, the Christian clergy inside the church offered them sanctuary from the Israeli soldiers outside as well as food and shelter. The Israeli military, under international scrutiny for besieging such an important sacred site, refrained from attacking the building or apprehending the gunmen. Instead they attempted, with some success, to snipe at the gunmen through open windows, taking particular care not to damage the structure itself. Despite the danger, the priests refused to leave when given the opportunity to do so yet also insisted that they were not hostages. The gunmen, on the other hand, accepted various strictures on movement and behavior dictated by their hosts, even when these encumbered their survival during the siege. This unusual state of affairs ended with the safe conducting of the surviving gunmen out of Bethlehem.

How can we explain the seemingly strange behavior by various parties to this incident? The answer, in large part, has to do with the sacred character of the building in which the gunmen sought refuge. Asked later about the unusual standoff, the mayor of Bethlehem explained: "It is an unusual situation that required exceptional decisions. The Church of the Nativity demands this exception. If it were not for the church, we would not have agreed to this."[2] Yet attributing the idiosyncrasies of this particular incident to the religious importance of its setting seems to raise more questions than it can resolve: Why should Israeli soldiers and Palestinian gunmen care about the sanctity of a Christian holy place? What makes a place sacred in the first place? What sort of restrictions does this religious status place on insurgents and on counterinsurgency forces? Do these strictures apply to all sacred places equally or are some sites more important than others? Underlying these queries are two fundamental policy riddles that echo throughout this volume: Why are insurgencies drawn to sacred sites? What can counterinsurgency forces do in such cases?

This chapter offers some answers to these questions by focusing on the three actors involved in any counterinsurgency effort at a sacred site: believers to whom the site is sacred, insurgents, and counterinsurgency forces. I begin with a functionalist definition of sacred space that focuses on the services such space performs for believers. I show that sacred sites are places for communicating with the divine, receiving divine gifts, and gaining insight into greater religious meanings.

In the second part of the chapter I show that the ability of sacred sites to perform one or more of these functions determines their importance to members of a religious movement. The relative significance of a sacred site is a useful predictor for public responses to counterinsurgency operations at such a site. At its essence, the function of sacred places in counterinsurgency operations is to enhance audience costs. Audience costs are the penalties imposed on an action by spectators.[3] Audiences can penalize decision makers for failure to secure beneficial outcomes, for neglecting to abide by prior promises, or for committing actions from which the decision makers had promised to refrain. During counterinsurgency operations at sacred places, sites *deepen* audience costs by adding a religious dimension to a conflict that an audience might otherwise judge on its political, ethnic, or moral merits. These sites *widen* audience costs by drawing the attention of a national, regional, or even global community of believers to an event that might otherwise attract local observers only.

In the third part of this chapter I focus on insurgents and examine the multiple advantages that the functions of sacred space and the rules that govern that space offer to insurgents. Sacred sites offer a convenient place of refuge and a logistical hub because of their location at the heart of population centers, their layout, and the presence of unarmed worshippers that can be used as decoys or hostages. These sites offer access to potential recruits, temporary reprieve from security forces that are often reluctant to enter sacred sites, as well as basic needs such as food, water, and shelter.

More important, insurgents can rely on the local population's sensitivities toward the sacred site to level the playing field with counterinsurgency forces, particularly when insurgents share a religious affiliation with the community worshipping at the site. When this happens, the community tends to interpret rules and restrictions to the advantage of the insurgents inside the shrine and the disadvantage of the counterinsurgency forces on the outside.

In the fourth part of this chapter I turn to the challenges facing counterinsurgency forces at sacred sites, in particular the adverse consequences of destroying sacred sites and the costs of desecrating these sites. Failure to meet these challenges will further alienate the local population, potentially increasing local support for the insurgents. Managing counterinsurgency operations that involve sacred sites thus requires not merely a knowledge of the specific site, its design, and the rules that regulate access and behavior within it, but also a familiarity with the relevant audiences observing the operation.

By taking the religious dimensions of these disputes seriously, decision makers can access "religious intelligence": religious experts and community leaders who can provide information about the relevant parameters of a given site and can attempt to negotiate these parameters so as to facilitate military operations. To conclude this chapter, I highlight some of these arguments with a brief examination of the siege at the Church of the Nativity in Bethlehem in April 2002.

What Is Sacred Space?

Sacred sites are prevalent, varied, and complex enough a phenomenon to allow for multiple definitions, approaches, and theories. Because I am interested in the effects of counterinsurgency operations on those observers who revere the relevant sacred site, this chapter espouses a functionalist approach that defines sacred space from the point of view of the worshipper.[4] For the believer, geography is not uniform in its religious significance. Sites that facilitate access to the divine are more important than those that do not. At these locations, the gods break through to the human realm and become accessible. Sacred places are bridges, connecting the mundane and the divine, turning these sites into religious centers for adherents of the faith.

As far as worshippers are concerned, sacred places fulfill three types of needs. First, they are places in which worshippers can communicate with the divine by means of prayer and ritual. Second, sacred places contain a permanent divine presence. Worshippers thus approach such places with the expectation of receiving blessings, healing, forgiveness, spiritual merit, or salvation. Finally, in their layout and design, sacred places provide meaning to the faithful. They evoke passages from history, social structures, or religious precepts and, ultimately they hint at the underlying order of the cosmos through architecture, decoration, and rituals.

The ability to communicate with the divine, to receive gifts, and to gain insight into greater meanings turns all sacred spaces, irrespective of size or importance, into religious centers for believers. This is true of primary sacred sites, such as Mecca, Amritsar, and the Temple Mount, which form historical, spiritual, and cosmological centers for Muslims, Sikhs, and Jews respectively. Believers often associate such places with the act of creation, the end of days, or the timeless authority of God over man. The same holds, on a smaller scale, for minor sites such as local mosques, shrines, temples, churches, or synagogues. By facilitating group ritual and communication with the divine, these sites also act as two-way channels between the present world and a world removed. They are world axes that connect heaven and earth but also function as spiritual pivots around which the believers' world revolves.[5]

Pilgrims who journey to sacred places thus travel toward the center, seeking in the sacred space a microcosm of the universe and of the specific religion it represents. Consider three of the cities that loom large in this volume: Mecca in Saudi Arabia, Amritsar in India, and Najaf in Iraq. These sites attract pilgrims who wish to come into closer contact with their god by accessing sites of religious history and geography. In all these cases the pilgrims' journey to the sacred site is also a journey to the center of the universe, where they can expect to see a representation of their spiritual world and to conduct exchanges with the divine. It is toward such centers that synagogues, mosques, shrines, temples, and churches are oriented and that prayer is directed.

Muslims worldwide pray toward the Black Stone, a meteor embedded in the *Ka'ba*, the large cuboid structure in the center of the Grand mosque in Mecca.[6] This stone is said to mark the very first place of prayer, erected by Adam and later rebuilt by Abraham. It is here that an angel saved the lives of Hagar and her son Ishmael, patriarch of all Arab peoples. It is here that the Prophet Muhammad founded the Islamic movement, and it is from here that the he embarked on his miraculous night flight to Jerusalem, from whence he ascended to heaven. The pilgrimage to Mecca, the *hajj*, is a sacred duty for all Muslims. Once the devout complete their pilgrimage and arrive in Mecca, their directed prayer is translated into circumambulation of the stone, followed by a series of group rituals designed to symbolically reenact key events in Islamic cosmology.

The Harimandir Sahib in Amritsar (colloquially known as "the Golden Temple") was founded by Guru Arjun, the fifth leader of the Sikh movement. The Temple complex, known as the Court of the Lord, is made up of several ornate structures arranged around a large, rectangular reflecting pool, the Pool of Nectar. These structures include the *Akhal Takht*, the Throne of the Ever-Living God, several guest houses, fruit gardens, pavilions, and a 130-foot domed tower. The centerpiece of the complex is the Golden Temple itself, the *Harimandir*, the most sacred shrine in the Sikh religion. Here the representation of sacred space as center takes the form not of a stone but of a sacred text, the *Guru Granth Sahib*. The book, a collection of poems, prayers and hymns composed by the first ten gurus of Sikhism, contains the tenets of the faith. The tenth and last leader of the faithful bestowed the title "guru" onto the text itself, at which point it became the eternal guide for all Sikhs. The *Guru Granth Sahib* is placed in the heart of the Harimandir Sahib, verses from it are sung continuously from dawn to sunset, to the accompaniment of flutes, drums, and strings. Pilgrims can cross the causeway to circumambulate the text or hear its verses while encircling the pool.

Like Mecca, Najaf is a Muslim sacred site. Yet whereas Mecca can claim the position of the very center of the religious universe for all Muslims, Najaf and its twin city of Karbala are of religious significance for Shi'a Muslims only. It is in Najaf that the Imam Ali, cousin and son-in law of the Prophet Muhammad, is buried. His shrine, in the center of the city, adorned by a magnificent gilded dome, is the destination for Shi'ite pilgrims from across the globe. They revere Ali as a martyr, last of the righteous successors of the Prophet and first of the *imams*, the spiritual leaders of the Shi'a faith. Many who visit the shrine do so toward the end of their lives with the intention of being interred in the large cemetery nearby, thus ensuring themselves a resurrection with Ali on the Day of Judgment.

Estimating the Importance of a Sacred Site

Despite their attachment to Najaf, Shi'a Muslims rank Mecca, Medina—where the Prophet Muhammad is buried—and Jerusalem as more significant sacred sites than Najaf. And yet Shi'a Muslims pay reverence to their local mosques as well. This phenomenon raises the problem of ranking sacred sites by significance. How do believers prioritize sacred sites? An answer to this question holds the key to determining how believers might respond to military operations at their sacred sites. How might Thai decision makers have estimated, ex ante, the public response to the military incursion of the Krue Se mosque in Pattani (analyzed here by Liow in chapter 7)? How might the Indian government have predicted the response by Kashmiri Muslims to the counterinsurgency operation at the Charar-e-Sharief shrine, given its experience with counterinsurgency at the Hazratbal Mosque (both examined by Ganguly in chapter 3)?

The religious significance of a sacred site depends on its relative ability to fulfill the three crucial functions listed earlier: communication, divine gifts, and insight. The stronger a group's belief that a site provides communication with the divine, a sense of divine presence and meaning, the more important the site is for believers. At the most central of sacred sites, the believer can hope for the clearest and most unmediated exchange with the gods.

Sites of primary importance are constructed on sacred ground on which some divine revelation or a founding moment of a religious movement has taken place. Mecca is the most revered site for Muslims because Allah manifested himself there to the patriarchs and to Muhammad and because He decreed that this be the focus of all Muslim prayers. Christians revere the Church of the Nativity in Bethlehem as the site of several incidents related to the birth of Jesus Christ. They attach similarly primary importance to the Church of the Annunciation in Nazareth and the Church of the Holy Sepulcher in Jerusalem, purported to be the site of the crucifixion and resurrection.

Sacred sites of secondary importance are located on consecrated ground, that is, at locations chosen not by the gods but by religious actors. Their importance is elevated by the presence of a relic or some divine gift that bestows healing, miracles, and intercessions to the faithful. Muslims in Kashmir revere the Hazratbal Mosque in Srinagar because it contains a precious relic, a hair of the Prophet Mohammad. The *Moe-e-Muqqadas* (sacred hair) draws pilgrims from across Kashmir to the seventeenth-century shrine, hoping that proximity to this relic will provide a more immediate experience of God and a more effective answer to prayers. Shi'a Muslims revere the twin shrines of Abbas and Hussein in Karbala, not far from Najaf, because they contain the tombs of these two leaders of the early Shi'a movement, sons of Ali and martyrs for the faith.

Most sacred places, however, neither are located on sites of religious-historical importance nor do they contain relics. These places of tertiary importance account for the vast majority of sacred sites. The town or village mosque, church, synagogue, gurdwara, and the like are designed for routine use by a community that cannot access a primary or secondary shrine. Many of these tertiary sites emulate the primary shrine in layout and orientation. For example, just as the synagogue recalls the design and functions of the Temple in Jerusalem, so are Sikh Gurdwaras worldwide modeled after the Harimandir Sahib in Amritsar, similarly mosques face Mecca and derive their layout from the first mosque in Medina. The link between the tertiary site and the relevant primary site is constantly underscored in prayers, rituals, and invocations.

Because there are no relics to desecrate or sacred soil to defile at these tertiary sites, the rules designed to protect the sacred there can be relaxed. Nonetheless, these sites can come to acquire increasing significance over time, as the religious community celebrates its sacred rituals there, introduces sacred artifacts, and begins accepting the place as a suitable substitute for the primary sacred site. This process grants even tertiary sites, such as the Krue Se mosque in Thailand or the Lal Masjid in Pakistan, a significance that is sensitive to desecration.

Most religions, then, offer a hierarchy of sacred sites (see table 1.1). This ranking affects the depth and width of public responses to attacks and thus has two implications for counterinsurgency operations. First, the more significant a shrine, the stronger the public response to damage or desecration. At the same time, more important shrines will elicit such responses from a broader spectrum of observers, reaching, in the case of primary sites, to members of the religious community worldwide. Thus the audience to a counterinsurgency operation at an important sacred site can expand to include co-religionists in far reaches of the globe that have little else in common with the militants in terms of ethnic, national. or political aspirations.

Table 1.1 A Ranking of Sacred Sites by Significance

	Christianity	*Islam*			*Sikhism*
Primary	**Church of the Nativity** (and others, e.g., Church of the Holy Sepulcher, Church of the Annunciation)	**Mecca** Medina Jerusalem			**Harimandir Sahib**
		Sunni	*Shi'a*	*Sufi*	
Secondary	Cathedral with relic Miracle site (Lourdes, Fatima, etc.)	Mosque with relic (e.g., **Hazratbal**, Damascus, Cairo)	Mosque with Imam's tomb (e.g., **Najaf, Karbala**)	Saint's shrine (e.g., **Charar-e-Sharief**)	The five Takhts
Tertiary	Local church	local mosque (e.g., **Krue Se, Lal Masjid**)	Local mosque	Local mosque	Local *gurdwara*

Note: Sites listed are provided as examples only; sites highlighted in this volume appear in bold print.

Although the ranking of sacred places within a given religion is often quite clear and explicit, caution is required when one is prioritizing sacred sites in order to assess public responses to counterinsurgency operations. The typology suggested here cannot provide more than a rough heuristic. For one thing, different religious movements have radically diverging conceptions of sacred space, its importance, and its vulnerability to desecration. Comparisons of ranking across religious groups or even subgroups are thus of limited utility. Second, ranking within any one religious movement is often more continuous than dichotomous, with multiple intermediary stages blurring the boundaries between categories.

Finally, a community's local-patriotic, emotional, or political attachment to a shrine can elevate the value of even the most insignificant of sacred places. Believers might express a strong bond with a minor site for a host of reasons: because it is associated with a beloved local saint, because the community relates its own identity and history to that of the site, or because the institutions surrounding the site provide crucial economic, political, or social services to the community. Indeed, local political events, such as discriminatory policies toward a community and its sacred site or—at the extreme—government-sanctioned violation of the site during counterinsurgency operations, can all increase the significance of a sacred place, thus complicating the calculation significantly.[7]

Insurgency and the Utility of Sacred Space

Why are insurgents drawn to sacred places? The answer has to do with both the physical features of sacred sites and the rules imposed on these sites by the community of believers. The location, the layout, and the presence of unarmed worshippers at these sites offer insurgents an opportunity for leveling the playing field with the counterinsurgency forces outside the shrine. More important, the rules governing access to the shrine and the behavior within it tend to play to the insurgents' advantage. All these factors can be derived from the three functions that sacred space performs for believers: communicating with the divine, receiving divine gifts, and gaining insight into greater religious meanings.

Because sacred places provide these critical functions, they symbolize the very essence of the religious movement, both to its members and to members of other faiths. They represent the religious movement at its most splendorous, displaying the power and wealth of the religious community even to those barred from access. Many of the great religious shrines around the world, such as the Grand Mosque in Mecca, the Harimandir in Amritsar, or the mosques in Najaf and Karbala, have in popular perception become synonymous with the religions they represent. Believers are drawn to sacred places not only because of the religious functions these sites perform but also because these places assume particular social roles. Shrines that occupy a prominent place in a society's religious landscape are likely to assume a central position in its social, cultural, and even economic and political sphere as well. Sacred places have doubled as courts, schools, marketplaces, and royal residences.

As a consequence, insurgents who occupy a sacred place can expect to find cover among the crowds attending the site. This cover can be exploited for obtaining hostages, as occurred in the Meccan insurgency in 1979 (examined by Ménoret in chapter 5) and in the Bethlehem siege (discussed in this chapter). In these cases, worshippers who happened to be at the sacred site when the crises erupted became unwitting human shields for the insurgents. Alternatively, insurgents can use the constant flow of worshippers, religious rituals, and tacit or explicit consent from the shrine managers as a cover for establishing a permanent base for their operations. Such was the case during the Shi'a insurgency based in Najaf and Karbala (examined by Patel in chapter 6). In some cases insurgents are able to capitalize on both options: Sunni insurgents based their activities in the Lal Masjid but also exploited the presence of worshippers to their own advantage during the ensuing siege (examined by Pardesi in chapter 4). By locating his headquarters in the Harimandir, the leader of the Sikh insurgency, Sant Jarnail Singh Bhindranwale, was able to use the flux of Sikh pilgrims as a cover for his fortification of the temple. The presence of hundreds of worshippers at the shrine during Operation Blue Star (examined by Fair in chapter 2) also complicated matters significantly for the Indian government. The location of many of these shrines in city centers, often surrounded by labyrinthine bazaars, makes for quick and convenient ingress and egress at times of need, sheltered by a dense urban environment that further hampers counterinsurgency operations.

The design of sacred sites provides further advantages to insurgents. The layout of a shrine employs architecture to represent the rules governing behavior and access. The structure channels and constrains movement around the sacred site by means of barriers, gateways and passageways. It also creates the necessary spaces and facilities for performing rituals such as group worship, ablution, baptism, confession, or sacrifice. The more familiar the insurgents are with the shrine, the easier it will be for them to gain advantage over their opponents by sheltering in hidden rooms, passageways, and subterranean vaults. Insurgents have also used minarets (during the Lal Masjid and Mecca sieges, for example) or tall structures such as guest houses and water towers (during Operation Blue Star) to snipe at counterinsurgency forces.

Older shrines, particularly those designed to house and protect a religious elite or to harbor the faithful during attacks by outsiders, tend to resemble veritable fortresses. They are often characterized by tall and thick walls, narrow windows and doors, and a self-sufficient design that may include gardens, wells, and stores of provisions. The broader the scope of social functions that the shrine performs, the better the odds that insurgents will find food and water at the site, supplies that will prove useful for surviving a prolonged siege.

More troubling yet, from the counterinsurgents' point of view, is the tendency of religious communities to locate the most valuable element of their sacred sites in the center of their shrine. The *Ka'ba* at the center of the Grand Mosque in Mecca, the Golden Temple in the middle of the Harimandir, the tombs of saints or imams in the heart of mosques, all these encumber counterinsurgency operations that seek to expel insurgents from a shrine without damaging the most sensitive aspect of that shrine. In most cases it is impossible to conduct offensive operations inside the shrine without severely damaging these crucial sites in its center.

The strongest factor that favors insurgents seeking refuge at a sacred site, however, is unrelated to the physical appearance of the site. This factor is the set of religious rules governing access to the site and behavior in it. Because these sites constitute ruptures in the ordinary realm, worshippers have to abide by specific rules designed to protect the divine presence from desecration, to protect humans from overstepping dangerous limits as they approach the divine, and to distinguish the sacred space from the surrounding secular area. Transgressing these rules is tantamount to sacrilege. One of a religious group's most important tasks is therefore to enforce these limits on access and conduct.

These strictures advantage insurgents, provided they share a religious affiliation with the community that guards the sacred site. Some of the rules governing a sacred site explicitly discriminate between members of the faith and outsiders. As members of the faith, the insurgents will enjoy a freedom of movement and access that may be unattainable to their adversaries. Other directives, such as those banning weapons or prohibiting the use of force within a sacred place, might apply equally to members of the faith and outsiders. Worshippers are nevertheless likely to show lenience in applying these rules to members of their own religious community, particularly if insurgents can persuade worshippers that they are acting in defense of the faith and in defense of the sacred site.

Finally, positioned inside the shrine, insurgents are less likely to cause offense by inflicting damage on the structure during fighting than would the troops opposing them. As long as insurgents are shooting out and counterinsurgency forces are shooting in, much of the responsibility for damage to the shrine will be placed squarely on the latter's shoulders. Insurgents have even willfully desecrated sites in preparation for and also in the course of fighting, perhaps in the expectation that the counterinsurgency forces would be blamed for the destruction. As Fair makes clear in her study of Operation Blue Star and as Ganguly suggests in his analysis of the Charar-e-Sharief crisis, this insurgent strategy often succeeds in directing observer wrath toward the counterinsurgents. Even though insurgents are usually complicit in any damage or desecration that occurs at a sacred site by virtue of having drawn the fighting there, counterinsurgency forces must take care to manage media depiction and public perceptions of the conflict lest they find themselves bearing the brunt of believers' anger.

Counterinsurgency and the Challenge of Sacred Space

Counterinsurgency forces conducting operations at a sacred site thus face a twin challenge that mirrors the advantages enjoyed by insurgents. First, they must overcome the obstacles posed by the physical features of the site without antagonizing the population that holds the site dear. This first challenge is beyond the scope of this chapter and is addressed in detail by other contributors to this volume. The second challenge requires a familiarity with the idiosyncrasies of a given sacred place. In particular, counterinsurgency forces need to be both clear about the audience that will be scrutinizing violations of the sanctity of the sacred site and aware of acts that might constitute violations thereof. Three possible violations merit particular attention: infringements on rules regulating access and behavior, damage to the structure of a sacred site, and transgressions of the right of sanctuary.

When confronting insurgencies at sacred sites, counterinsurgency forces must contend with enhanced audience costs. In drawing combat to a sacred place, insurgents *deepen* the normal public relations costs associated with counterinsurgency operations by adding a religious dimension to the conflict. Although counterinsurgency operations at temples, mosques, or churches involve some of the same difficulties as operations at other public sites, such as schools or hospitals, they are likely to evoke a more visceral reaction in a religious audience concerned with desecration. At the same time, combat at these sites *widens* the observing audience by appealing to members of the relevant religious community across a particular nation, region, or even the globe. The Pakistani and Thai government, for example, broadened the potential audience of their respective counterinsurgency operations to include all Muslims in their country, across Asia, and even worldwide when they chose to confront insurgents in the Lal Masjid and the Krue Se mosque.

The likelihood of a vehement response from a broad audience is proportionate to the significance of a shrine, as was discussed earlier. Primary shrines are esteemed by the global religious community. The sieges in Mecca, Amritsar, and Bethlehem thus unleashed angry responses from Muslim, Sikh, and Christian communities far beyond the location of the actual operations. Transgressions committed at secondary shrines will enrage a somewhat narrower audience: the two sieges in Kashmir affected Muslims in South Asia primarily, just as operations in Najaf and Karbala disturbed Shi'a communities in the Gulf region primarily. Muslims outside these particular communities would have limited knowledge of the sites involved or the significance of their desecration. Attacks on tertiary sites might draw the attention of a still narrower community, though their impact should still exceed in both intensity and scope that of a counterinsurgency operation at a "secular" site.

To minimize these costs, decision makers must familiarize themselves with the precise implications of their future actions in the religious realm. Desecration, meaning the transgression of the boundary between the sacred and the profane, is more than just an offense to the sensibilities of those who revere a sacred site. It is understood by these practitioners as a tangible assault on the status of the site that, if successful, can strip a site of its sanctity. As a consequence, believers will go to extremes to prevent the desecration of their holy places or to avenge such transgressions. Leaders concerned with the desecration of a sacred site must therefore obtain answers to three questions. First, what are the restrictions that the local religious community places on entry into this site? Second, how will this community respond to destruction of some or all of the shrine? Third, to what extent does this community envision the insurgents as protected by the right of sanctuary?

The first of these questions has to do with rules delimiting who may approach the sacred site and how such admission is to be performed. These rules are designed to uphold the distinction between profane and sacred space. They include gestures of approach that occur at the threshold of a sacred site, such as ablution or the removal of shoes before entering a mosque, the removal of headdress upon entering a church, or the covering of one's head upon entering a gurdwara or synagogue. Additional codes may prohibit a range of activities within the sanctuary or forbid all but a narrow range of behaviors. The use of force and shedding of blood are strictly prohibited within a mosque, for example. Upon entering the Grand Mosque in Mecca or the Harimandir in Amritsar, worshippers are expected to perform circumambulations of the central shrine (the *Ka'ba* and the Golden Temple, respectively) before engaging in a series of prescribed rituals. Yet while the carrying of weapons, for example, is strictly prohibited in Mecca, no such prohibition exists in Amritsar, since all baptized Sikhs are expected to carry a *kirpan*, a short ceremonial dagger, at all times.

These two sacred places also exemplify extreme positions regarding restrictions on entry. Members of all faiths are welcome at the Harimandir; its four gates facing the cardinal directions represent accessibility to all. Churches, mosques, temples, and synagogues display varying degrees of openness to outsiders, though most communities require that visitors seek their permission before entering their sacred space. Access to the Grand Mosque in Mecca, on the other hand, is prohibited to non-Muslims, who cannot even come within a 20-mile radius of the city.

Given these restrictions, it is incumbent upon decision makers to assess the right of access for counterinsurgency forces in each case, to learn the appropriate gestures of approach, and then, most challenging of all, to determine the costs and benefits of abiding by these rules. One cannot expect counterinsurgency forces to remove their shoes during hot pursuit into a mosque but one might expect them to do so before conducting a routine search in a mosque. In either case, the effect of their failure to do so at a local mosque would be negligible compared with the repercussions of doing so at a more significant mosque. The more important the site, the greater the likelihood that a transgression will be viewed as an unforgivable act of desecration. Once inside the sacred site, military or police personnel can trigger indignation in an endless variety of ways, such as acting or talking inappropriately, handling items considered sacrosanct, consuming prohibited food or drink, spitting, smoking, or even posing irreverently for the media.

The second question decision makers must answer before engaging insurgents at a sacred site concerns the consequences of damaging the sacred structure. Unlike the sacred place, which is perceived as divinely ordained, the sacred structure is usually understood as man-made: consecrated by human hand, it can also be repaired or rebuilt. How a religious community will respond to damage caused to that structure during combat thus depends on how it views the relationship between the underlying site and the structure that towers above it. The more significant the site below, the more likely that the structure above has absorbed its sanctity, incorporated the religious functions that the underlying site provides, and merged with the site to become one sacred space. For believers, then, damage caused to a local church, for example, is qualitatively different from damage caused to a cathedral or a primary shrine, such as the Church of the Nativity in Bethlehem. Religious movements have established clear rules that dictate the conditions under which a sacred structure is considered salvageable, requires reconsecration, or needs to be demolished and totally rebuilt.

Complicating matters further, the offense taken by believers in response to damage to their shrine depends not only on the rules pertaining to a particular scenario, but also on the subjective interpretation of these rules by observers. This interpretation may depend on the extent of the damage, the significance of the part of the structure that was damaged, the imputed intentionality of the act, or the number of casualties caused by the attack. For example, the most visible elements on a sacred site's exterior, such as domes, bell towers, or minarets, often play a relatively minor role in the rituals performed in its interior. Yet, insignificant as their formal function might be, believers are likely to take grave offense at damage to the outward appearance of their shrine. This reaction is particularly likely if, as in both Sunni and Shi'a mosques in Iraq, these domes and minarets have become symbols not only of the shrines they adorn but of the very community that worships there.

Timing is another significant parameter that can affect how a community responds to an incursion that destroys or desecrates a shrine. Such assaults will be viewed with greater hostility if they coincide with significant dates in the religious calendar. Attacks on mosques on a Friday (the Muslim Sabbath), during Ramadan (the holy month), or on the memorial day of a saint entombed in a mosque suggest callous opportunism and convey disrespect toward the community and its values. Operation Blue Star, unfortunately timed to take place during the fifth day of the lunar month—an auspicious time for Sikh pilgrimages—and on a date marking the martyrdom of the constructor of the Harimandir, who had been executed under religious persecution, represents the epitome of this type of insensitivity.[8]

A third obstacle facing counterinsurgency forces contemplating an attack on insurgents in a sacred place is the right of sanctuary. This right rests on the belief, common in some religious movements, that the persecuted are immune from seizure inside a sacred place.[9] The right of sanctuary has undergone varying degrees of development across religious traditions, with some movements denying the right altogether while others differ on the justification for the right and the conditions under which it is extended.

In biblical Judaism, for example, the right of sanctuary rested on the assumption that particular sites, enumerated in the scriptures, were protected by divine sanction.[10] The practice of sanctuary achieved its fullest development in Roman and Christian law, which derived the right from the inherent inviolability of all sacred sites. In medieval Christianity, this right detailed the crimes for which a felon might obtain sanctuary, the locations at which sanctuary was available, the duration and conditions of the felon's tenure at the sacred site, and mechanisms for escorting him out of the sacred place to beyond the reach of the persecuting authorities. The right of sanctuary continues to be practiced and respected with astonishing frequency, such as by illegal immigrants seeking refuge in churches to avoid deportation.[11] The right of sanctuary as understood in Sunni Islam applies not to protection from criminal prosecution or arrest, as it does in Christianity, but to an absolute prohibition on violence inside a mosque, as spelled out in the Qur'an.[12] The Shi'a practice, on the other hand, developed in a manner reminiscent of the Christian and Jewish practice; Shi'a mosques can provide criminals with a temporary sanctuary from arrest (*bast*), particularly if the mosque contains the tomb of a saint (*wali*) who can extend a divine protection over the refugee.[13] All of these traditions, with their varying interpretation of the right of sanctuary, must grapple with the difficult question of whether this right should be extended to armed insurgents.

The preceding discussion does not exhaust the universe of rules, norms, and expectations attached to the conduct of counterinsurgency operations at sacred sites. The conclusion from this brief survey is simple: Decision makers must take the religious dimension of operations at sacred sites seriously and acquaint themselves with the religio-legal minutiae that determine how a religious community will respond to an attack involving a sacred site. Given variations within as well as across religious movements, with changes often depending on the idiosyncrasies of a particular site or the local preferences of a particular community, there remains only one reliable means of accessing the "religious intelligence" required for the successful completion of such an operation: decision makers must consult with religious experts who can provide information about the implications of using force at a sacred site. If no such experts are available, the decision makers will have to acquire this intelligence from the community itself, such as by conferring with community leaders or the religious elites.

Religious leaders are likely to hesitate to cooperate with secular authorities that are planning an attack on their sacred site. At the same time, these leaders should be willing to provide information that can help minimize damage to its most important elements, keep believers out of harm's way, and reduce the risk of sacrilege and desecration. Religious elites can provide key facts about the targeted site, its meaning to worshippers, existing restrictions on access and behavior, and crucial information about sensitive times and dates. They may be able to predict, explain, and even influence public perceptions of operations in sacred space. Finally, if they have gained the trust of both insurgents and counterinsurgents, they may be willing to act as go-betweens during a standoff.

Because insurgents are aware that their legitimacy can be undermined by religious authorities, they are likely to threaten these authorities into compliance. Faced with intimidation, death threats, or even the murder of an outspoken associate, religious leaders have often chosen to overlook militant excesses and the desecration of sacred sites. Properly manipulated, religious actors may even choose to direct the responsibility for the desecration onto the counterinsurgents. To avoid this danger, counterinsurgency forces would do well to conceive of religious authorities as assets that need to be protected before they can be expected to cooperate.

The Bethlehem Siege, April 2002

The Israeli siege of the Church of the Nativity in Bethlehem offers an intriguing example for counterinsurgency operations involving sacred space, because the site was sacred to a religious group that was distinct from the ethnic majority represented by both the Israeli government and the Palestinian insurgents. The gunmen were thus unable to capitalize on many of the advantages usually offered by sacred places during insurgencies. Nonetheless, this case exhibits many of the arguments, challenges, and possible solutions proposed in the preceding pages.

The site itself displays many of the characteristics of a sacred space. For nearly two millennia, Christians have revered this site as the location of various key events related to the founding of their religion. A grotto under the sanctuary marks the site at which Mary and Joseph spent the night; a silver star set into the floor of the grotto (engraved *Hic de Virgine Maria Jesus Christus natus est*) marks the precise location of Christ's birth. Nearby, worshippers show where Mary first set her child down in his crib and, elsewhere, where an angel warned Joseph to flee to Egypt. The adjacent Chapel of Saint Jerome is said to be the location at which that Church Father translated the bible into Latin. Near the church is the Shepherd's Field, the tomb of the matriarch Rachel, and a second grotto, known as "the Milk Grotto," where Mary is said to have nursed her son.[14]

Believers come to this church and to the adjacent sites in order to witness the evidence for these events and envision them more vividly. It is one of the most popular pilgrimage sites in the Holy Land and one of the most important holy places in Christendom. Pilgrims, many of whom frequent the church every year, come here in the expectation that their prayers will be more efficacious than at their home churches. At the yearly Christmas Mass, the birth of Christ is ritually commemorated and reenacted. Nursing mothers or barren women in hope of children visit the Milk Grotto nearby, marvel at its miraculously chalk-white walls, and pray for intercession by the Virgin.

The design of the church matches its function as a primary pilgrimage target. The church above the grotto is a simple Byzantine basilica, with stairs leading down into the grotto at its center. Adjacent to the basilica is a gothic church as well as Franciscan, Greek, and Armenian convents, yielding a single compound 130,000 square feet in area, surrounded by tall walls.[15] The exterior is fortress-like, with thick Byzantine walls further bolstered by buttresses. The only access into the basilica is through the "Door of Humility," so called because its diminutive height forces visitors to bow upon entering. Over the centuries, this layout proved ideal for protecting the small Christian enclave of monks and pilgrims from attacks by Persian and Muslim forces.[16] This sturdy design also proved instrumental for the survival of 39 insurgents during a month-long siege in 2002.

In March 2002 Israeli Defense Forces (IDF) troops entered Bethlehem as part of "Operation Defensive Shield," a large-scale military effort to capture Palestinian militants throughout the West Bank. Several units of armed Palestinians, cornered in Bethlehem, sought refuge at sacred sites in the city: one group escaped to an Assyrian church, another to the Roman Catholic convent of Santa Maria.[17] The third and largest group, composed of members of the Al Aqsa Martyrs' Brigade, among them a dozen men on Israel's "most wanted" list, found refuge in the Church of the Nativity.

The clergy inside the basilica complied fully with the insurgents' demand for asylum. Brother Parthenius, the priest who interacted most frequently with the insurgents inside the church, later claimed that he had "felt obligated by his Christian vows to offer the gunmen sanctuary now that they had entered the church."[18] Michel Sabbagh, the Latin Patriarch of Jerusalem, explained: "The basilica, a church, is a place of refuge for everybody, even fighters, as long as they lay down their arms...in such a case, we have an obligation to give refuge to Palestinians and Israelis alike...once inside, any human being—whether Palestinian or Israeli, armed or not—who asks for protection will receive sanctuary. A basilica cannot give up people to be killed or made prisoners."[19] The Palestinian governor of Bethlehem, trapped with the insurgents inside the church, thanked the Greek Orthodox archbishop of Bethlehem for "providing the church as a haven for the persecuted."[20]

Israeli decision makers realized early on that the public relations costs of a hot pursuit into one of Christianity's primary sacred sites would be prohibitive. Then Prime Minister Ariel Sharon, keenly aware that Christian audiences worldwide were observing the crisis, promised that Israeli forces would not "defile" the church.[21] Despite pressure from hawks in the military to launch an assault on the church, the Israeli colonel in command ordered a siege, realizing the risk in turning "a symbol of peace for all the Christian world into a place of blood."[22] The presence of some 150 unarmed civilians in the church, who had happened to be in and near the church when the conflict began, placed additional limits on the military's freedom of action.

The military isolated the church from the surrounding houses and cut off water, food, and electricity supplies. Although the church had been stacked with provisions at the outset of the crisis, intended for consumption by the monks, all inside were reduced to squalor and starvation by the time the siege ended.[23] The IDF also broadcast loud sounds at the church and deployed stun grenades, expecting this psychological warfare to increase pressure on the gunmen.[24] Israeli snipers used cameras mounted on several cranes and one blimp as well as remote-control-operated rifles to pinpoint and kill seven insurgents in the church and wound seven others without harming the hostages or the structure. The exchange of fire between the besiegers and the besieged caused extensive damage to various structures in the church compound, but it did not harm the church itself.[25]

The fact that the insurgents were Muslim complicated matters further, because it led to the imposition of various restrictions by the priests, constraints that would not have been imposed had the insurgents been members of the Christian community. The priests prohibited them from interring their dead on church grounds, prevented them from leaving the church structure and entering the adjacent monasteries, restricted their movement within the church, and prohibited other activities, such as smoking and consuming alcohol.[26] By preventing the insurgents from entering the sacred grotto, the priests inadvertently increased their exposure to sniper fire aimed at the ground floor of the basilica. The priests even attempted, albeit in vain, to convince the insurgents to disarm.[27]

The sacred setting for this siege influenced not only the choices made by both parties but also the outcome of the conflict. The standoff ended, after forty days, in a compromise very much patterned after the practices used for concluding a traditional sanctuary episode. Under the supervision of a neutral party, the security staff of the American embassy, the insurgents surrendered their weapons, left the church, were taken by American diplomatic vehicles to an airport, and boarded a British military airplane to Cyprus, from where they were later dispersed throughout Europe.[28] This solution was reached after intense contacts between the Israeli government, the Vatican, and the Greek Orthodox Church, as well as the United States and the European Union. Remarkably, and in spite of the local Christian population's natural sympathy for the gunmen's cause, the restraint exhibited by the Israeli military as well as government contacts with religious elites in Israel and abroad ensured that much of the ill will associated with the incident was aimed at the Palestinian leadership. When the gunmen finally surrendered, members of the Arab Christian community castigated their armed presence in the church and their cynical use of this sacred site for publicity purposes.[29]

Conclusion

Resolving the standoff at the Church of the Nativity required significant sacrifices from all parties involved. The Israeli government wished to try the insurgents for acts of violence against Israeli citizens yet saw them escape to safety. The insurgents were forced to suffer the harsh fate of exile. Once the doors of the basilica were reopened, the Christian community returned to find their sacred site in a sorry state: filthy, bullet-pocked, and partially charred.

Yet, as the case studies in the chapters to come demonstrate, all sides to this conflict could have fared a great deal worse. The Bethlehem standoff sets a high standard for counterinsurgency operations at sacred places due to a series of exceptional circumstances that do not usually hold in conflicts of this sort. Because the sacred site was associated with a party neutral to the Israeli–Palestinian dispute, both rivals respected the site, restrained their use of force, and were able to rely on various Christian actors to broker an agreement. The priests inside the church chose to extend to the insurgents the protections that were due to refuge seekers, but they did not collude with them, lest they surrender the sacred site to the insurgents' whims or discredit themselves in the eyes of the Israelis.

The more common ending to sieges on sacred sites is an all-out attack on the site by counterinsurgency forces, either because the government identifies with the religious community that worships at the site or because it associates the insurgents with that community. In the first case, decision makers may feel unimpeded in using force or they may even feel compelled to use force to evict the insurgents from the sacred site. In the second case, perhaps realizing the difficulty in sustaining a prolonged siege and the futility of the limited use of force, decision makers often opt for the one course of action that maximizes their control over the situation. Either scenario is likely to end with the routing of the insurgents, troop losses, "collateral" civilian casualties, damage to the shrine, and significant political repercussions for the government that ordered the assault.

Managing counterinsurgency operations at sacred sites thus requires striking a delicate balance between political and religious interests as well as a fortunate confluence of variables that is beyond the immediate control of the decision maker. By taking the religious dimensions of these operations seriously and by consulting with religious experts and, if need be, with local religious elites, decision makers can stack the deck in their favor. Doing so may improve the odds of a desirable outcome, but it cannot ensure success. Ultimately, there is a limit to the extent to which violence in sacred space can be managed.

Notes

1. Joshua Hammer, *A Season in Bethlehem: Unholy War in a Sacred Place* (New York: Free Press, 2003).

2. Joel Greenberg, "Palestinians Prepare Exit from Church," *New York Times*, May 9, 2002, p. A22.

3. The term "audience costs" gained prominence through James Fearon's discussion of democratic audiences and their impact on dispute escalation by democratic regimes. James D. Fearon, "Domestic Political Audiences and the Escalation of International Disputes," *American Political Science Review* 88, no. 3 (Sept. 1994), 577–92. I use the term more broadly here to denote the costs imposed by any audience on counterinsurgency forces operating in sacred space.

4. Though this is the most dominant approach in the study of sacred space among sociologists of religion, drawing on work by Mircea Eliade, it is by no means superior to alternative approaches that problematize the social construction of sacred space or focus on religious elites and their use of sacred space to consolidate their power. Mircea Eliade, *Patterns in Comparative Religion* (New York: New American Library, 1958). See also Joel P. Brereton, "Sacred Space," in Mircea Elidea, ed., *The Encyclopedia of Religion*.12 (New York: Macmillan, 1987); A. Morinis, ed., *Sacred Journeys: The Anthropology of Pilgrimage* (New York: Greenwood Press,1992).

5. Eliade, *Patterns in Comparative Religion*, p. 375.

6. Here and throughout the chapter I have relied on a variety of public sources for empirical information about these sacred places. They include Norbert C. Brockman, *Encyclopedia of Sacred Places* (New York: Oxford University Press, 1997); James Harpur, *The Atlas of Sacred Places* (New York: Henry Holt, 1994); Colin Wilson, *The Atlas of Holy Places and Sacred Sites* (Toronto: Penguin Studio, 1996); Susan Hitchcock, *Geography of Religion: Where God Lives, Where Pilgrims Walk* (Washington: National Geographic Society, 2004); and Martin Gray's *Places of Peace and Power* website at http://www.sacredsites.com/.

7. Chidester and Linenthal elaborate this argument in the context of legal disputes over the ownership of sacred space. See David Chidester and Edward T. Linenthal, eds., *American Sacred Space* (Bloomington: Indiana University Press, 1995).

8. Mark Tully and Satish Jacob, *Amritsar: Mrs. Gandhi's Last Battle* (London: Jonathan Cape, 1986), p. 146.

9. See, for example, Christian Traulsen, *Das Sakrale Asyl in der Alten Welt: Zur Schutzfunktion des Heiligen von Koenig Salomo bis zum Codex Theodosianus* (Tuebingen: Mohr Siebeck, 2004); and G. Cyprian Alston, "Sanctuary," *Catholic Encyclopedia* 13 (New York: Robert Appleton, 1912). I examine this issue in depth in "At the Horns of the Altar: Counterinsurgency and the Religious Roots of the Sanctuary Practice," *Civil Wars*10, no.1 (March 2008), 22–39.

10. This practice is mentioned in Exodus 21:12–15, Numbers 35:13–15, Deuteronomy 4:41–43, Deuteronomy 19: 4–7, and Joshua 20:7.

11. See, for example, Randy K. Lippert, *Sanctuary, Sovereignty, Sacrifice: Canadian Sanctuary Incidents, Power and Law* (Vancouver: UBC Press, 2005); "Hundreds Have Taken Refuge," *The Gazette* (Montreal), August 2, 2003, A4; Jason Bennetto, "Judge Rules Deportation of Afghan Family Illegal," *The Independent* (London), September 12, 2002, p. 8.

12. These passages are Sura 2:125 and Surah 2:192.

13. Gordon B. Newby, "Bast," in *A Concise Encyclopedia of Islam* (Oxford, U.K.: OneWorld, 2002), p. 42.

14. Edward Arbez, "Bethlehem," in *The Catholic Encyclopedia* 2 (New York: Robert Appleton, 1907); James Harpur, *The Atlas of Sacred Places*; Colin Wilson, *The Atlas of Holy Places and Sacred Sites.*

15."A Church and a Site Revered by 3 Faiths," *New York Times*, April 4, 2002, p. 11, citing *Agence France-Presse*; Arbez, "Bethlehem."

16. Steven Erlanger, "Under Siege, Fiercely Longing for Peace," *New York Times*, May 8, 2002, p. 15.

17. Anton La Guardia, "Bloody Siege of Bethlehem: Surrounded by Israeli Troops and Tanks, Palestinian Gunmen Seek Refuge in the Church of the Nativity," *Daily Telegraph (London)*, April 4, 2002, p.1.

18. Hammer, *A Season in Bethlehem*, p.194.

19. "A Church and a Site Revered by 3 Faiths," *New York Times*, April 4, 2002, p. A11, citing *Agence France-Presse*; Alan Philips, "Survivor's Tale of the Siege of Bethlehem," *Daily Telegraph (London)*, April 20, 2002, p. 15.

20. Hammer, *A Season in Bethlehem*, p. 197.

21. David Rhode, "Church of Nativity Damaged and a Monastery Is Scorched," *New York Times*, April 9, 2002, p. A11; Philips, "Survivor's Tale of the Siege of Bethlehem; Hammer, *A Season in Bethlehem*, p. 205.

22. Philips, "Survivor's Tale of the Siege of Bethlehem," p. 15, citing Latin Patriarch Michel Sabbah.

23. Justin Huggler, "Middle East: Freed Youths Tell of Hunger and Death in Church of the Nativity," *Independent (London)*, April 27, 2002, p. 14; Paul Adams, " 'I Got Out for the Sake of My Family': Tired and Weak, Nine Young Palestinians Allowed to Leave Church of the Nativity," *Globe and Mail (Canada)*, April 26, 2002, p. A1.

24. Philips, "Survivor's Tale of the Siege of Bethlehem."

25. Joel Greenberg, "Israeli Snipers Play Cat to Palestinians' Mouse at Church of Nativity," *New York Times*, April 24, 2002, p. 10.

26. Alan Cowell and Joel Greenberg, "In Church of Nativity, the Refuse of a Siege," *New York Times*, May 11, 2002, p. A1; Hammer, *A Season in Bethlehem*, pp. 209 and 212.

27. Hammer, *A Season in Bethlehem*, p. 195.

28. Joel Greenberg, "Palestinians Prepare Exit from Church," *New York Times*, May 9, 2002, p. A22; Hammer, *A Season in Bethlehem*, pp. 251–60.

29. Hammer, *A Season in Bethlehem*, pp. 249–50.

2

The Golden Temple

A Tale of Two Sieges

C. Christine Fair

This chapter examines two important operations waged by Indian security forces to counter Sikh insurgents operating in India's northern state of Punjab, from the late 1970s to the early 1990s. In the early years of the movement, various Sikh militant groups waged an ethno-religious campaign to establish an independent Sikh state (Khalistan). By 1988 the ideological commitment of the various militant groups dissolved and their ranks became increasingly swollen with criminal elements and militants seeking to establish their own spheres of influence. Equally problematic for the Khalistan movement was the pervasive internecine fighting that developed in the same period as militant groups splintered, formed alliances, and developed deeply hostile rivalries. Consequently, while the various militant groups claimed to be fighting the Indian state on behalf of Indian Sikhs, Sikh villagers overwhelmingly comprised the victims of these proliferating and murderous groups.

In the course of India's sustained counterinsurgency campaign in the Punjab, Indian security forces conducted two important operations on the most significant temple in Sikh sacred cartography, the Golden Temple in Amritsar. The first, Operation Blue Star, was led by the Indian Army in June 1984 and was an unequivocal disaster that inflamed Sikh sentiment throughout India and the world and, by any measure, galvanized the insurgency and support for it. In contrast, Operation Black Thunder—fought in May 1988—was a police operation with support from the antiterrorist National Security Guards. Operation Black Thunder was a tactical success in that it was concluded within a week and resulted in the arrest of 12 hardcore militants and 160 other supporters. While the operation was in many ways minor, its impacts were critical and in some important measure contributed to the eventual defeat of the insurgency by 1992.

This chapter exposits the main factors that accounted for the dramatically different outcomes of these two operations. It poses several clusters of empirical questions, including the following: What were the circumstances by which security forces were drawn into operations on such sacred space? What security forces were used and with what motivations and with what outcomes? How did the forces' rules of engagement account for the sacredness of the battle space? How did the security forces manage public opinion about their operations through use of the media, community leaders, and religious authorities to mitigate the negative consequences of the operations or to generate support for their actions?

Before approaching the two case studies, the first two sections of the chapter provide a basic history of the insurgency. This is not meant to be exhaustive; rather it will provide only a cursory narrative of the conflict and its key protagonists. Because of the focus here upon counterinsurgency operations on sacred space, the third section of the chapter details the ways in which the Sikh insurgents manipulated Sikh religious symbols, institutions, history, and shrines to endow their movement with religious authority and legitimacy. The next two sections detail the two cases of Operations Blue Star and Black Thunder, addressing each of the above empirical questions. The final section presents a discussion of the factors that likely account for the very different outcomes of these two operations. As that discussion will illuminate, the outcomes are in good measure related to the operations' planning and execution, but their longer-range impacts are equally linked to larger issues such as state policies toward counterterrorism, police resources and training, interagency coordination, the changing nature of the militant groups themselves, and the evolution of public support away from the militants.

The Khalistan Movement

The Punjab insurgency was exceptionally brutal and claimed the lives of 21,000–40,000 persons before the movement was decisively defeated by 1992. The insurgency claimed more lives than the combined wars with Pakistan, in which 2,700 army personnel perished, yet this conflict has not drawn the attention of scholars and analysts.[1] It merits further study not only because of the scope and lethality of the movement, but because it was one of the few insurgencies that has been systematically defeated. Indian counterinsurgency efforts routinely struggled with the challenge of engaging militants in Sikh religious space, because the insurgents were very adept at appropriating these spaces as well as intimidating and co-opting major Sikh religio-political institutions and personages, as will be discussed below.

Although the concept of a separate Sikh state emerged in the early twentieth century, it was not until the late 1970s and early 1980s that proponents of an independent Sikh state took up arms for the cause.[2] The timing was due in part to the Indian government's systematic mismanagement of Sikh political and ethnic concerns over successive decades.[3] Sant Jarnail Singh Bhindranwale, as his followers refer to him, was the charismatic leader who initially led the call for Khalistan. He began his career as the head of the Damdami Taksal, a teaching and exegetical institution that claims direct connection to the tenth and last living Sikh guru, Gobind Singh. This purported—but perhaps not entirely legitimate—connection to Gobind Singh is important, because this guru is strongly associated with Sikh martial history and consolidation of Sikh political power.[4] Bhindranwale's affiliation with this respected institution gave him a substantial degree of credibility as a pious Sikh religious and political authority.

Bhindranwale emerged as a high-profile leader of the Sikh militancy in the early 1980s and cultivated many allies in the quest for Khalistan, including the All India Sikh Students Federation (AISSF), important Sikh religious and political leaders, and also personalities within the Shiromani Gurdwara Prabandhak Committee (SGPC), which is the management body that overseas the vast majority Sikh gurdwaras (Sikh places of worship) throughout India.[5] However, Bhindranwale did not rise to prominence solely by his own efforts. Prime Minister Indira Gandhi chose to buttress his political following in an effort to split the Akali Dal (the most prominent Sikh political party in the Punjab), which was the most viable opposition to her Congress Party. In hindsight, this support was a tremendous miscalculation, as Bhindranwale, with his developing separatist political objectives, gained popularity within segments of the Sikh population (e.g., the traditional agricultural caste, the *Jats*). His vociferous and militant position illuminated the comparatively moderate position (at least initially) taken by the Akali Dal.[6]

On December 15, 1983, Bhindranwale and several like-minded militants (e.g., members of the Babbar Khalsa) entered the Akal Takht, one of the most significant structures in Amritsar's Golden Temple complex, in order to avoid being arrested. Bhindranwale believed that the sacredness of the shrine would afford him some immunity and anticipated that the state would be hesitant to extract him forcefully from the complex. With the military assistance of a battle-hardened former major general of the Indian Army, Shahbeg Singh, he prepared an elaborate network of fortifications inside the complex, including stockpiles of arms, ammunition, and rations. Bhindranwale took over and subsequently occupied the Akal Takht, the apex structure that signified Sikh spiritual and political authority. In June 1984 Prime Minster Gandhi ordered the army into the temple complex to wrest it from the militants in an operation that was named "Operation Blue Star."[7] This action was followed by Operation Woodrose, the army's "mopping up" exercise that took place throughout the Punjab in effort to capture Bhindranwale's activists and to clear all gurdwaras in the state of militants.

Bhindranwale perished in this operation, but the militancy was not crushed. Mrs. Gandhi's Sikh bodyguards assassinated her in revenge, after which thousands of Sikhs perished in Hindu-led attacks upon them and their communities throughout India. Operation Blue Star and the ensuing massacres of Sikhs fostered a wider-spread militancy among the Sikhs in the Punjab by legitimizing the separatists' claims that India could not and would not protect Sikh interests. Operation Blue Star and its sanguinary sequelae also moved sections of the Sikh diaspora to espouse this cause.[8] Underscoring how divisive the operation was, numerous Sikh officers deserted the Indian Army in the wake of Operation Blue Star.[9] Doyen of Indian counterinsurgencies, K. P. S. Gill, declared this constellation of events to be the most "significant victories for the cause of 'Khalistan'... not won by the militants, but inflicted by its own Government."[10] In the absence of the operation and the ensuing massacres, Gill believed the movement could have easily been contained in 1984.[11]

Khalistani Groups: An Overview

While one may frequently hear the term "a Punjab insurgency," by 1988 there were actually several competing so-called "Khalistani" groups that committed acts of terrorism ostensibly in the name of

Khalistan. Few of these groups maintained their ideological coherence, and most began to criminalize as early as 1988, if not earlier. Furthermore, many of these groups were not actually working for a Khalistani state per se. For example, the Akhand Kirtani Jatha came into being in the late nineteenth century as an anticolonial revivalist movement. The organization came under the leadership of Bibi Amajrit Kaur when her husband was killed in 1978 in clashes between the Nirankaris, a Sikh sect considered by some Sikhs to be heretical, and Akalis. After his death, she directed the organization to focus upon isolating and even killing the Nirankaris. Other groups, such as the Babbar Khalsa, were less motivated by notions of Khalistan but rather sought to enforce a rigid code of behavior similar to Shari'a and used excessive violence (including murder) to achieve compliance.

All the major groups quickly factionalized and indulged in a wide array of criminal activities and internecine conflict, and many individual militants left their parent groups to work as mercenaries who moved between groups. This entrepreneurial status left these mercenaries without protection either from predation of other militants or from the state and therefore vulnerable to co-option by the authorities. The tendency toward intergroup conflict also permitted the state to infiltrate groups more easily, thereby obtaining better actionable intelligence. As a consequence of these various factors, the Sikh population increasingly bore the brunt of the violence. By the early 1990s militants enjoyed little support in the Punjab, at least in part because they lost their patina of being ethno-religious warriors and increasingly were regarded as criminal outfits.[12]

Some of the key insurgent cum criminal groups included the following:

- **Babbar Khalsa**. This organization came into prominence in 1981 and emerged as an offshoot of the Akhand Kirtani Jatha with the support of Bibi Amarjit Kaur. Its members maintained a low level of activity until 1983. It drew its membership from ex-servicemen, policemen, and particular Sikh religious organizations. While the organization fell into disarray after Operation Blue Star, it remained active.[13] Curiously, this group was *opposed* to Bhindranwale and was less committed to Khalistan than they were sectarian violence and enforcing Sikh personal law.[14]
- **Khalistan Commando Force** (KCF). The KCF was founded in August 1986 under the leadership of Manbir Singh. It broke into several factions. The KCF (Zaffarwal) retained the rump

of the organization, while smaller splinters joined other militant alliances. The KCF targeted principally the Indian security forces such as the Border Security Force (BSF), the Central Reserve Police Force (CRPF), and other police forces. It targeted Hindus as well as Sikhs who opposed the Khalistan movement. The KCF funded itself through looting, bank robberies, and extortion.[15] It also engaged in large-scale smuggling of weaponry from Pakistan. It was well organized, equipped, and trained and operated in coordination with other Sikh militant groups to enlarge the scope of its operations. The organization's ability to conduct operations was seriously degraded during Operation Black Thunder (to be described below).[16]

- **Khalistan Liberation Force** (KLF). Aroor Singh formed the KLF in 1986. It used small arms in its operations, which it obtained principally through theft. It operated in the Punjab city of Amritsar as well as other localities. The KLF, like the other Khalistani militant organizations, financed itself through criminal activities. By 1990 its stature was significantly degraded because of loss of important leadership.[17]

Insurgents' Appropriation of Sikh Religious and Political Authority

The sacredness of the Golden Temple is universally acknowledged. It is located in the city of Amritsar in the northern Indian state of Punjab. Amritsar was the site of important events throughout the history of the Indian independence movement (e.g., the Jallianwala Bagh massacre) and was, along with Lahore (now in Pakistan), considered to be an important center for Sikh political activity long before independence. Amritsar persists as the focal point for Sikh politics in Inda. For these and other reasons, Amristar was a prized theater to dominate for insurgents and counterinsurgency forces alike.

The Golden Temple is a rectangular complex organized around a sacred reservoir and surrounded by a fortified wall with eighteen gates, the main entrance being on its north side. The temple's inner sanctum is the Harimandir Sahib, located in the middle of the reservoir and accessed by a bridge that links the Harimandir with the rest of the temple. This three-story structure houses the Sikh sacred text, the Guru Granth Sahab, during the day when it is venerated by worshippers. (This text is considered to be the "eleventh and ultimate Guru," since Guru Gobind Singh declared that after him there would be no living Gurus.) There is a walkway (Parikrama) that maps out a rectangular path around the reservoir. The Akal Takht (timeless throne), located across from the Harimandir Sahib on the Parikrama, is the second most important structure in the complex and represents Sikh political and religious authority. At night the Granth Sahab "rests" within this structure. The sixth guru, Hargobind, built the Akal Takht to symbolize Sikh political and military resistance to the Mughal Empire. Hargobind is important to those who value Sikhism's martial aspect, because he is responsible for initiating it. In response to the capital punishment of his predecessor Guru Arjan, Guru Hargobind donned two swords (*miri* and *piri*), representing temporal and spiritual authority respectively.[18] These two swords are important symbols within Sikhism and emblaze the saffron Sikh flag (Nishan Sahab), which marks all gurdwaras.

Several other multistory buildings and passageways are located off of the Parikrama, including numerous rooms and offices which were taken over by the militants. Outside of the main temple area but well within the temple complex houses, there are several serai (residential buildings for pilgrims and temple staff, a kind of rest house) and a communal kitchen (langar). The langar is important in Sikh religious practice because Sikhism eschews commensalism (rules that govern who can eat with whom) and caste. The langar requires all persons, regardless of caste, to eat together and is a reminder that all are equal before God. Before or after revering the Guru Granth Sahab and venerating the various shrines in the temple complex, many Sikhs go to the langar to partake of a communal meal, which is considered to be an important element of their religious observance. Service (seva) in the langar is considered to be of utmost importance, and this seva includes purchasing foodstuffs for the langar, preparing and distributing the food, and cleaning the langar dishes and facilities.

The massive Golden Temple complex houses several important Sikh political and religious organizations, including: the headquarters of the Shiromani Akali Dal (a.k.a. the "Akali Dal," which is the most prominent and organized political party representing Sikh corporate interests); the afore-noted SGPC, which oversees the vast majority of the thousands of Sikh gurdwaras and shrines throughout India and the lucrative donations that they receive from worshippers; and the All India Sikh Students Federation, among other groups.[19]

Outside of the temple complex are several multistory hotels, restaurants, crowded and winding bazaars, and other buildings affiliated with the temple. Throughout the surrounding countryside and urban environs there are numerous other important Sikh historical gurdwaras, many of which were used by the militants. Finally, Amritsar is located very near the Pakistan border, which allowed Pakistan to provide the militants with small arms and even training in Pakistan.[20]

The ability of insurgents to base themselves within the precincts of the golden temple was facilitated by the fact that key Sikh religious institutions and leaders such as the SGPC, AISSF, and the Jathedar (leader) of the Akal Takht, in whole or in part, supported them. Sometimes this support was given voluntarily by key leaders, and in other cases it was coerced through the use of violence or threat of violence. The willingness to resort to violence became apparent after Operation Black Thunder, when security forces found the bodies of hundreds of slain and tortured opponents and competitors that were buried beneath the Akal Takht and other places.[21]

The ability of the militants to base themselves in the Golden Temple afforded them the façade of fighting a "holy war." It provided them with easy access to potential recruits whom they could impress with their presence in the most sacred of Sikh spaces. Operating in the Golden Temple also offered logistical advantages in that it consolidated their cadres and provided easy access to food, water, and communication lines. From within the Golden Temple complex, militants were able to control their operations from a central location.[22] While their ability to reside in the temple lent them religious sanction, it also conferred some protection from the security forces. Indian security forces were and indeed are loath to operate on sacred space, and militants exploited this fact. Ironically, as will be discussed, even though the Golden Temple was open and frequented by hundreds or even thousands of visitors each day, security forces chose not to send operatives into the complex to collect information for fear that they would be tortured and killed.[23]

In addition to appropriating Sikh institutions and religious structures, the militants also manipulated the corpus of Sikh hagiography and the Sikh martyr tradition. The latter Sikh gurus and their followers were hunted down and subjected to various forms of torture under various Mughal rulers, and tales of these form the basis of the Sikh martyr tradition and hagiography of Sikh heroic fighters known as "Singhs." The torments inflicted upon the gurus and their followers are graphically depicted in mass-produced paintings that figure in most gurdwaras, are enshrined in stories that are recounted to children, and are retold in countless Sikh songs and other forms of popular culture. The Sikh militants adeptly cast their causes and their dead into this rich martyr tradition and augmented the hagiographic traditions with their own "heroes." Notably, Sikh militants called themselves "mujahadeen" and their slain martyrs "shaheeds."[24] These efforts to appropriate Sikh history were very successful: pro-Khalistan gurdwaras featured photos of slain and often disfigured militants alongside the portraits of slain Sikh leaders from the past. Khalistani songs and folk dances performed to Khalistani lyrics became popular in this period.[25]

There is equally little doubt that the behavior of the militants who episodically seized the temple defiled it. They committed brutal acts of murder in the temple, disposed of the dead in and around the complex (e.g., in the gutters outside of the complex, underground in the temple, etc.), and destroyed parts of the temple to build fortifications. Amassing arms and using the temple as a center for waging war can be justified in some sense through the fact that most historical gurdwaras display massive weapons caches used by the gurus, depicting the centrality of Sikh sites to their struggles. Interestingly, while such historical arguments could be made for the temple's being used as a garrison, this author has found no evidence that such arguments were marshaled. Indeed, the prevailing opinion seems to be that Sikhs and non-Sikhs alike considered these actions to be defiling the temple, which is held in esteem by Hindus as well as Sikhs. Bhindranwale himself violated a number of important Sikh tenets, acts that came to represent his own spiritual and temporal hubris. Within the precincts of the temple, no one is to be higher than the Guru Granth Sahab, but during Bhindranwale's occupation of the Akal Takht, he slept in the upper floors of the structure above the floor where the holy book was kept. Needless to say, his very occupation of the Akal Takht—the site of Sikh political and spiritual authority—for these purposes underscores his temerity.

Despite actions that clearly would undermine support from pious elements of the Sikh community, in the early years of the violence the Indian counterinsurgency forces (police, army, paramilitary) failed to develop a systematic information offensive to publicize these misdeeds and to counter the militants' claims to religious sanction. Worse yet, the images of the destruction they wrought upon the temple during Opeartion Bluestar outraged Sikhs within India and beyond and did much to foster support for the militants in the aftermath of the operation. In the end, it was the militants' own behavior that persuaded Sikhs that these militants were not the "Singhs" of Guru Gobindh Singh; rather, they were rapists, extortionists, robbers, and murderers.

In contrast to the disastrous Operation Blue Star, the media management strategy of Operation Black Thunder facilitated the development of this perception by televising in real time the operation and the various offensive actions taken by the militants.

Operation Blue Star

Bhindranwale did not believe that Prime Minister Gandhi would employ the army to dislodge him. He did anticipate that she would employ the police or, at worst, the paramilitary forces (e.g., BSF and Central Reserve Police Force) into the temple and expected that the central government would mobilize the police to lay siege to the temple complex. In anticipation of this event, Bhindranwale tried to marshal support from Sikhs in and around Amritsar by distributing throughout the Punjab cassettes that had a threefold message. First, they explained that an operation against him and the temple was imminent. Second, they pointed out that such an operation constitutes a direct assault on the Sikh community. Third, they directed those committed to his cause to remain alert and prepared to act in the event of action against him in the temple. Bhindranwale believed that thousands of supporters would flood into Amritsar to swarm the police in the event of such an attack.[26]

Blue Star's primary objective was to wrest the temple complex from the various militants ensconced there with Bhindranwale.[27] In Lieutenant General K. S. Brar's authoritative account of the operation, there is no evidence that the operation took any particular account of the sacredness of the shrine, with the one notable exception that they wanted to avoid damage to the inner sanctum (Harmander Sahab) if at all possible. There were numerous problems that both necessitated Operation Blue Star and compromised its execution. First, the police forces (e.g., Central Reserve Police Force, the Punjab police) and paramilitary organizations (e.g., the BSF) had been unable—or unwilling—to control the growing militarization at the Golden Temple complex in Amritsar.

The reasons for this failure are numerous and include the insurgents' successful infiltration of these institutions (especially the police) and effective use of threats to dissuade the local security forces from acting against them. In hindsight it is clear that few within the security establishment and even fewer within the Punjab police understood the nature of the threat. Prior to 1984 the Punjab police kept no records on militant activities, did not carry out investigations of militant events, and did not record what—if any—action they took. K. P. S. Gill opined that while the Punjab police force was "no doubt stupefied by the sheer unfamiliarity of the challenge, it not permitted to act; nor did it dare to act on its own against the manifest intent and strategems of the political powers."[28] While the police were woefully ill prepared, they also were underresourced and lacked training for counterterrorism operations. In 1980 there were 28,853 sanctioned billets for the civil police in the state. (By1990 billets had increased to 53,325.)[29]

While having few human resources, they also lacked modern munitions, communications equipment, and even vehicles in adequate quantity and quality. The police were badly organized, with no clear chain of command, and they interacted ineffectively with other security agencies. In addition to these pervasive and debilitating problems, the police were poorly utilized: at any given time between 40 and 50 percent of the force were involved in static and unproductive duties (e.g., manning barricades that had little counterterrorism value). The police were also infiltrated by militant sympathizers, and there were communal rifts both within and between the police and paramilitary organizations. The police—given their various problems—were hesitant to act against militants because of the swift and often lethal punishment that the militants delivered to them and their families.[30] All of these problems were compounded by the policies of the central government, which patronized and protected Bhindranwale and his militants in order to erode the Congress Party competitor Akali Dal. By the time Bhindranwale turned on the state, it was too late for containment efforts. Moreover, the center's policy had alienated and even radicalized the mainstream Sikh political party.[31]

As a consequence of the systematic failure of several civil and military institutions to deal with the emergent situation, militants had forcibly occupied up to 17 three- and four-story buildings within the built-up area around the temple (within a 500- to 800-yard radius of the temple complex). These buildings were generally well fortified, had good fields of observation and fire, incorporated early warning posts, and were manned by militants equipped with light machine guns and other automatic weapons. Militants were able to monitor activities in and around the temple from these locations. Astonishingly, the police had not ordered the destruction of these posts and the army subsequently paid heavily for this lack of action. The failures of this operation underscored the necessity for effective coordination of civil and military institutions in counterinsurgency efforts.[32]

Despite the fact that the temple complex was completely open to visitors and could be observed from buildings on the perimeter, security forces and intelligence organizations failed to determine how many militants were in the complex, the extent of their fortifications, the number of worshippers in the temple, the number and types of weapons in the complex, or the pattern of defenses established by those in the compound.[33]

In these unfavorable circumstances, Brar launched Operation Blue Star, employing the Indian Army augmented by key police and paramilitary organizations such as the Central Reserve Police Force. All police and paramilitary forces were placed under the army's command. Additionally, a curfew was imposed throughout the state from the night of June 3, 1984, onward, and the army sought to ensure that the Punjab was effectively cut off from the rest of the nation by stopping all transportation into or out of the state, expelling all journalists, and denying all phone communications.[34]

Brar planned the operation on the (erroneous) assumption that there were 1,500 militants in the complex, of which 500 were assumed to be highly trained and motivated. Upon considering the strength, dispositions, fortifications, and fire power of the militants, it was assessed that that the mission would require four infantry battalions and specialist commandos of an equivalent strength of two companies. In addition, one squadron of Vijayanta tanks were allotted in order to minimize Indian Army casualties at the commencement of operations. Brar avers that these tanks initially were to be used only to serve as a protective shield for the leading infantry elements and to neutralize rooftop defenses in order to provide further immunity for the advancing troops. It was also hoped that the tanks would exert psychological influence on the militants in order to precipitate a hastened surrender.[35]

The operation was to be launched in three aggressive phases preceded by a preliminary operation that was to be launched late in the evening of June 5, 1984, in order to eliminate observation posts held by militants. These preliminary efforts were to employ the BSF and Central Reserve Police Force. It was anticipated that Phase 1 would be completed by 1:00 A.M. on June 6. The objectives of this first phase included, among other goals, securing the northern wing of the temple complex and lodgments within the Akal Takht and the Harimandir Sahib. Phase 2 was planned to conclude by 4 A.M. on June 6 and primarily aimed to complete "mop up" operations. Phase 3, which would extend operations to the remaining hostel complex, was to conclude by 8 A.M. on June 6.[36]

The operation called for the use of mechanized elements. Three tanks were grouped with the ten Guards in support of the approach to the main entrance. Upon reaching the entrance, they were to provide protection and support by eliminating militant fortifications with machine gun fire. Three tanks were also grouped with the 26 Madras, which entered the complex from the east, to neutralize militant fortifications and to provide close fire support to the assaulting infantry with machine gun fire. In addition, four BMPs (a Russian-produced infantry fighting vehicle capable of carrying a squad of soldiers) were assigned to the ten Guards to transport Para Commandos and divers. Four additional BMPs and three armored personnel carriers (APCs) were initially grouped with 26 Madras and would subsequently serve as a reserve.[37]

Only the preliminary operations were executed on schedule.[38] Phase 1 was launched at 10:30 P.M. However, by early morning of June 6 the Akal Takht had still not been taken. The eastern assault by the 26 Madras was seriously retarded by militant fire; the SFF and commandos were consistently beaten back by the militants. In light of the prevailing conditions, the decision was made to bring three tanks into the complex as well as an APC. A rocket-propelled grenade (RPG) immobilized the latter. (Indeed, the Indian Army did not know that the militants had antitank weapons, later discovering that they had two Chinese-made RPG-7s.) By 5:10 A.M. clearance was given to use the machine gun fire of three tanks to bring down Akal Takht defenses. Nevertheless, the fortifications and positions of the militants' automatic weapons enabled them to withstand the firepower of the tanks. The Indians launched a commando operation to take out the machine guns that were exacting a heavy price on their force. The operation failed and cost the security forces many additional casualties. At 7:30 A.M. the Akal Takht remained in the militants' control and the decision was undertaken to use the 105- mm squash head shells to neutralize the Akal Takht.[39] In total, it took some 12 hours to clear the Akal Takht of the militants and three more days to clear the remaining part of the complex of suicide squads and hidden militants.[40]

Both Brar and Dar suggest that there were some shortcomings of the night attack. Dar suggests that despite the Indians' overwhelming firepower and end strength, the night attack was unlikely to succeed in this heavily built-up area. First, the Indian forces were unable to assess the extent of fortifications of the Akal Takht. The peculiar nature of combat in built-up areas (e.g., narrow streets, restricted deployment area that impacts the number of troops that can be employed, domination of upper floors by the enemy) hindered the ability of Indian forces to make headway. Fighting in the rest of the complex took place under very stressful conditions, exacerbated by the cover of darkness as terrorist squads occupied rooms, halls, and balconies of the large multistoried buildings about the complex. Troops tasked with clearing these rooms often entered hand-to-hand combat in the darkness. Yet another problem that confronted those trying to clear the temple of militants was the difficulty of distinguishing the worshippers trapped in the temple complex from the militants, a task rendered even more difficult by the absence of light. One of the lessons that Dar extracts from this operation is that night attacks in built-up operations simply may not be effective.[41]

Brar and Dar are also critical of deficiencies in the Indian preparations for the operation, in particular the lack of intelligence about the militant's fortification. One of the numerous problems encountered by the Indian Army was the effective use of underground positions by the militants. Troops were trying to clear the rooms along the Parikrama while under heavy fire. Occasionally, militants would retake an area by exploiting concealed underground passageways that connected various rooms and even outside verandas. The Indian Army was not aware of this infrastructure.[42]

When the operation was complete, damage to the temple complex was extensive. The library, housing priceless and unique manuscripts, was burned. The Akal Takht was destroyed, and the Harmander Sahab was defaced with bullet holes. Dead bodies littered the sacred tank, and the structures along the Parikrama were destroyed during the course of hand-to-hand combat and the use of heavy vehicles.

In hindsight another deficiency of the operation was the media blackout—exacerbated by the fact that the operation was launched at night. Despite the state's efforts, media coverage continued to the extent possible, but the insurgents' supporters outside of the temple were in a better position to shape the media message. Because the army had no proactive media management campaign to shape the information offensive, the army had no capabilities to regain media dominance and thus ceded the information ground to Bhindranwale's supporters. When the international and domestic media finally entered the temple precincts, the massive damage to the temple was nearly universally depicted as the army's doing. By the time the army tried to describe the depravity of the militants who turned the temple into a fortress, it was too late. Despite the numerous photos of the recovered arms caches and preponderant evidence of the dissoluteness and sacrilegious conduct of Bhindranwale and his supporters, it was the image of the army's excess that spread throughout India and the world and inflamed Sikh sentiments everywhere.

Operation Black Thunder

In 1986 and 1987 the government was very keen to find a political solution to the crisis and began a process of engaging the militants. In 1986 law and order in Punjab was the direct responsibility of the government in New Delhi. The central government pursued what Gill called "two-faced tactics," whereby it would attempt to strike deals with some militant factions while simultaneously putting pressure on them with enhanced police action. The government granted "selective immunity" to some militants, including associates of Bhindranwale who were taken into custody during Operation Blue Star. These varied tracks of dealing with militants created confusion for the police regarding the type of action that they should pursue.[43]

Gill writes that the Punjab police, despite this political disarray, committed itself to what had become a drawn-out war with the militants. Between May 1987 and April 1988 the militants were killing on average 127 persons per month. The central government continued to search for political solutions despite the intensity of the violence and the extent of the lawlessness. As a part of this strategy they released 40 high-profile prisoners in March 1988. These prisoners walked into the Golden Temple without hindrance, and one of them even became the head priest of the temple. The militants once again began fortifying the temple with internal defensive structures. The Golden Temple's management committee (the Shiromani Gurdwara Prabandhak Committee, or SGPC) was both passive and active in its support: some members were afraid of the terrorists and therefore did little to prevent their actions while others directly assisted them.[44]

The government's strategy of negotiation with the militants did not mitigate the bloodshed. In March 1988 an unprecedented 288 people were slain, including 25 police personnel. In April 259 persons were killed, 25 of them policemen. The central government finally reversed its policy of political accommodation and again returned to a law enforcement approach.[45] The authorities once more concluded that some sort of action had to be taken to oust the militants from the temple. The government did not employ the army as it did earlier; rather, it mobilized the police, with backup from the National Security Guards (an antiterrorist force) and other paramilitary forces.[46] It was hoped that this police action could be accomplished without the inflammatory consequences of the army-led debacle Operation Blue Star. The optimism regarding the use of police derived in part from the fact that Punjab police personnel tend to be local and connected to the community. The Punjab police are overwhelmingly Punjabi and the majority are themselves Sikh. (Senior police leadership may not be from the area, however.) In contrast, army and paramilitary forces come from all over India. While the army and paramilitary personnel all speak Hindi, their mother tongues vary and their confessional identities are diverse. It was hoped that the Punjab police, with their local ethnic and religious ties, could be an effective counterinsurgency force without rekindling the belief that the central government was using non-Sikh forces to occupy an important Sikh shrine. This was an important lesson learned from Operation Blue Star.

There were other reasons for optimism as well. Since the debacle of Blue Star, a number of changes had been initiated within the police. While the police arguably lacked an ideological commitment to fighting the insurgency, this attitude began to change in 1986 with the appointment of police chief Julio Ribeiro, who served in that capacity until 1988. He implemented a "bullet for bullet" policy to counter militant violence with full force. K. P. S. Gill replaced him in 1988 and continued and indeed strengthened this policy until the central government became uncomfortable with this approach and again sought a political solution. However, by 1988 a political solution was no longer feasible, because the militant groups had become factionalized, criminalized, ensnared in internecine conflict, and unable to engage in any sort of dialogue, and the primary political party, the Akali Dal, had long become ineffective.[47]

Operation Black Thunder's objective was simple: to clear the temple of militant forces. The operation succeeded on many fronts: It was economical, nearly bloodless in execution, and conducted with full media attention. Unlike Operation Blue Star, Black Thunder focused upon controlling peripheral sections of the temple for reasons outlined below. It also sought to prevent food and water from reaching the militants and to deny them essential services such as electricity. The entire operation was completed within a week.[48]

K. P. S. Gill explained to this author some of the features of this successful operation. Unlike in Operation Blue Star, which made little effort to contend with the sacredness of the shrine once the decision to act was taken, the police now appraised the temple and environs and considered how operating in particular parts of the complex would resonate among the Sikh community. The Golden Temple compound could be divided into three rectangular areas: the serai (residential buildings for pilgrims and temple staff, a kind of rest house), the langar (a communal kitchen), and the temple (which included the inner sanctum, the Harminder Sahab). The police judged that they could enter the serai with very little protest. The langar is considered to be a very important institution in the Sikh religion, and action there was assessed to be more inflammatory than action within the rest house. Entering the temple, particularly the Harminder Sahab, would be the most provocative act. It is important to note that both the serai and the langar are outside the main temple structure. Taking into consideration these sensibilities, Gill proposed to take over the serai and the langar. The police would then conduct short and very limited attacks within the temple if needed. In the end, this contingency was not executed for reasons described below.[49] Gill also ensured that the entire operation would take place with full media coverage, in contrast to Operation Blue Star, which was conducted in a media blackout.

The police offered periodic cease-fires during which militants could give themselves up without fear of being fired upon. This technique was generally successful and several militants took advantage of these offers. However during one such cease-fire a small number of militants escaped and took refuge in the temple's inner sanctum, the Harminder Sahab. Because this pathway can be easily defended, the militants in the inner sanctum had an advantageous position. Reportedly, no one shot at them as they made their way into the Harminder Sahab, perhaps in hopes of avoiding damage to the temple as had occurred during the 1984 Operation Blue Star and to honor the cease-fire that was offered. In Sarab Jit Singh's account, they were conscious of the ever-present media. It was important that the police both honor its commitments and be seen to do so.[50]

The police conducted a prolonged siege against the temple to oust the militants. Gill recounts some of the methods used:

> We used various tactics to break their morale. . . . Sometimes we enforced total silence followed by ammo and other loud noises. Chances for ceasefire were given during which one chap would go down to the pool to get water from the tank. We wanted to see if they had a container [for storing water]. We timed the water fetching during the ceasefire and assessed that there were some 8 or 9 militants in there as they were drinking from the bucket.

This information allowed the police to ascertain the length of time the militants could stay there without food and water and could calibrate the siege accordingly. This strategy culminated in their defeat.[51]

However, unlike the situation that prevailed in Operation Blue Star, the militants who made their way to the Harmander Sahab had inadequate provisions and very little ammunition. This fact made it very unlikely that they had intended this showdown. When the militants, dehydrated and hungry, finally surrendered with full media coverage, Sarab Jit Singh noted that their behavior was both cowardly and disrespectful. Some laughed as they surrendered. The behavior of the surrendered militants along with the televising of the operation and revelations of militants' miscreant conduct secured public support for the operation, which was widely seen as restoring the sanctity of the temple after the militants defiled it. Restoring the sanctity of the temple required co-optation of local religious leaders, who oversaw the ritual cleansing of the inner sanctum, reinstallation of the sacred text, resumption of recitation of the text, and all the other religious activities associated with the temple. It also involved in great measure restoring the funds and other costly donations to the temple which were looted by the militants.

The successful efforts to restore the temple and its functions following Operation Black Thunder stands in stark contrast to similarly motivated efforts in the wake of Operation Blue Star. In 1984 the central government tried to restore the sanctity of the temple following Operation Blue Star by using central government funds to inter alia rebuild the Akal Takht, clean the bloodied reservoir, and repair the Harmander Sahab. However, many Sikhs were unwilling to accept these repairs from the central government, which had visited such havoc upon the sacred complex. Temple administrators and Sikh devotees destroyed the government-sponsored reparations and various Sikh organizations raised funds from within the Sikh community to make the needed repairs. In contrast, the government's efforts after Black Thunder were not repudiated and indeed largely seen as legitimate, perhaps because the efforts were understood to be local and the central government did not appear to be involved directly in the effort.[52]

As a police action, Operation Black Thunder was relatively minor and resulted in the capture of only a few militants. Shootouts in Amritsar still continued and violence actually escalated. For much of the insurgency's duration (1987–1992), the Punjab was under the control of the central government, known as President's Rule in the

Indian parlance. In the years following Operation Black Thunder, the militancy actually threatened to overwhelm the security forces and brutally sidelined moderates in the Punjab.[53] The militants began planting explosives in scooters, bicycles, and other vehicles, intending to kill randomly and to encourage people to leave the city. This situation persisted for three to four years after the conclusion of Operation Black Thunder.[54]

When one views Operation Black Thunder in the context of continued terrorist activity, it may be tempting to dismiss it as a failure of sorts; however, Operation Black Thunder contributed to the demise of the militancy. The operation, conducted under the watchful eyes of all media, revealed to the public aspects of the militancy that may not have been observed with such clarity before. Through the visibility of this operation, the Sikh public witnessed the depravity that went on within the walls of the Golden Temple. The Khalistan movement would never recover the veneer of religiosity that it had prior to the operation. The operation had denied the militants use of the Golden Temple and gurdwaras for sanctuaries and operational basing.[55]

The operation was also immediately followed by the promulgation of the Religious Institutions (Prevention of Misuse) Act, which went into law on May 26. This act made it illegal to use religious institutions for a broad array of political purposes or for the conduct of any activity that promotes disharmony, that is subversive, or that challenges India's sovereignty. It also criminalized the use of such institutions as safe havens for accused and convicted offenders alike, and it forbade any kind of fortifications within the structure.[56]

The operation, conducted nearly simultaneously with this law, demonstrated resoundingly that the security forces were willing and capable of executing force and demonstrated that insurgent use of religious institutions would no longer be tolerated. The legislation provided the necessary legal mandate to carry out such operations as needed. Black Thunder, along with this legislation, was an important step in denying the militants access to Punjab's massive infrastructure of gurdwaras. The net effect was to negate some of the advantages of militant utilization of these gurdwaras. The same high walls that once provided security became an easily policed perimeter with controlled exit points that facilitated easy capture of insurgents. For the most part, after 1988, denying insurgents the use of gurdwaras adversely affected their ability to recruit, accumulate, and store munitions, enjoy safe havens for operational planning and recuperative breaks, and have ready command and control centers with complete amenities such as phones, electricity, food, and water. As a consequence, militants and their leadership were dispersed into their villages, where they were more susceptible to detection, arrest, and elimination.[57]

The successes of Operation Black Thunder were facilitated by the ongoing process of police reform and augmentation which gathered momentum in the years following the operation. In 1991 the Congress Party returned to power with Narasimha Rao as prime minster. Rao was convinced that dalliances with political solutions had failed. His reasons are debatable (e.g., Delhi did not honor commitments made to Sikh politicians who in turn were unable to curb the violence). For Rao, pacifying the Punjab was a priority, and he empowered the Punjab state government to discharge its duties without interference. In 1991 K. P. S. Gill was reinstated as chief of police and he oversaw the draconian measures that eventually crushed the insurgency. As was noted, Gill inherited a police structure that lacked an effective chain of command. He created a pyramidal structure in which he was the apex. He purged those who were deemed unreliable or uncommitted and replaced them with loyalists. Their effectiveness was judged by their ability to neutralize terrorists, which included a bounty killing program through which police were compensated and even promoted for killing terrorists.[58]

Gill also delineated the contributions of other agencies, with the police figuring as the primary counterterrorism agency. The army was used in a supplementary role and tended to be confined to urban areas, where they guarded infrastructure and manned check posts. These static activities were previously in the purview of the police, who were now freed for more mobile counterterrorism activities. Paramilitary groups assisted the police more directly in the rural areas as well as areas with a high prevalence of terrorism. The Border Security Force was used to seal the border with Pakistan, where training, sanctuary, and weaponry had been provided to the insurgents.[59] With these changes, Gill was able to create an integrated command structure.

There were also great increases in police end strength, with a large recruitment drive beginning in 1989. As a consequence, that year there were 51,833 authorized police billets compared with 32,855 in 1984.[60] Another expansion occurred in 1993 when there were 65,658 such billets, and in 1994 this number increased again to 70,228.[61] (These figures have since been reduced; in 2005 police end strength was 52,142.[62]) With this expansion in manpower, Gill was able to promulgate a more effective counterterrorism posture by increasing the number of patrols and raids and even assigning specific persons to identify and capture particular terrorists.[63]

Not only were there improvements in the quantity of police, there were also improvements in the quality of their training. To address their lack of sufficient counterterrorism training, during the police transformation in the early 1990s the Indian Army provided police with four to ten weeks of training in specific operational tactics to enhance their counterterrorism capabilities. The NSG also trained the Punjab police in counterterrorism operations in the early 1990s.[64] The police equipment was also substantially improved. Their World War II vintage .303 rifles and bolt action 7.62s were replaced with light machine guns and automatic weapons, which finally allowed the police to engage directly the militants who were routinely armed with AK 47s, resulting in high militant casualties and restrictions in their movement. The police also received modern radio communications and additional vehicles, which allowed more frequent patrols over larger areas of coverage and diminished the police response time. In all, these changes transformed the police from a largely unproductive and passive force into a more aggressive and mobile force that was willing and able to engage the militants directly.[65] The net impact of these innovations was a dramatic suppression of violence accompanied by increased apprehension of militants, arms, and explosives.

Over time these innovations—along with the predations of the militant groups—gradually affected a change in public opinion. In the early years militants undoubtedly enjoyed popular support, which was catalyzed by Operations Blue Star and Woodrose and included the provision of logistical, material, financial, and human resources to the militants and their organizations. (Admittedly, sometimes this public assistance was inadvertent or given indirectly to gurdwaras whose management was sympathetic to the militancy.) However, by the early 1990s public opinion had shifted as the militant groups criminalized, targeted Sikh civilians, became enmeshed in local feuds, and engaged in baleful violence as they sought to enrich themselves and eliminate their rivals. By the early 1990s the militants were increasingly vulnerable to the security forces, which had become more effective. At the same time, their public support diminished and increasingly the populace assisted the government's counterterrorism efforts by providing information about the militants and their supporters.[66]

Conclusions: Explaining the Difference

In summary, whereas Operation Blue Star was a bloody mess that spawned a wider insurgency that had widespread support among Punjab's jats and the globally dispersed Sikh diaspora, Operation Black Thunder has been described as a very successful counterterrorism operation that had important long-term impacts upon the militants and their ability to operate in the Punjab. There are several factors that explain the differing outcomes between these two operations, though not all of them can be attributed to the different ways in which the operations were conducted.

Different Policy Environments

Scholars and analysts broadly concur that in the early years of the insurgency the government lacked both a coherent counterterrorism policy and a commitment to bring to fruition either a political solution or an effective security strategy. For much of the insurgency, policy toward the insurgents was shaped by political considerations at the center. Moreover, security agencies were slow to understand the nature of the challenge they were confronting and were poorly resourced by all measures to do so. By the late 1980s and certainly during Prime Minister Rao's tenure, this attitude changed. The government was increasingly convinced that there could be no political solution. In that period there was a transformation of the police and promulgation of new force concepts which enabled the police to work more effectively. While it is not the subject of this paper, the government of India has sustained enduring criticism that it put down the Sikh insurgency at great cost—a view vigorously rejected by the proponents of this policy.[67]

The Standing of the Movement

In the early days of the movement there was considerable ideological coherence that captured and aggregated the accumulating Sikh grievance. The charismatic and religiously pedigreed leader Bhindranwale also contributed to this situation. By 1988 the assorted groups criminalized and engaged in various violent acts that over time increasingly targeted Punjab's civilians. By the late 1980s and early 1990s the tide of public support was turning, with the public increasingly willing to disclose information about the militants. Thus when Blue

Star was launched, security forces faced a very different population terrain than when Black Thunder was launched.

Adversaries' Commitment and Preparations

The Indian Army confronted different adversaries in Operation Blue Star than did the police in Black Thunder. Under Bhindranwale, the insurgents were committed and prepared to hold their position for as long as possible. In contrast, accounts of Black Thunder reveal that the militants were not well prepared for the siege of the Harmander Sahab, lacking adequate food, water, and ammunition. The sustained siege of the temple coupled with periodic cease-fires secured the exodus of most of the militants who had seized the temple, a fact suggesting that they were less committed than the militants ensconced in the temple in 1984.

Different Appraisal of the Sacred Battle Space

Planners of Operation Blue Star made few efforts to treat the Golden Temple differently from other battle spaces on which they would operate. This approach is in clear contrast to that of Black Thunder, where planners were cognizant of the degrees of sacredness embodied in different parts of the temple complex. Moreover, Black Thunder was devised to calibrate a minimum use of force, which could be more intense in some parts of the temple complex than in others. Black Thunder had the benefit of hindsight of Operation Blue Star, which everyone wanted to avoid reproducing. Black Thunder's appraisal of the sacred space can be lauded after the fact because it was successful. Had it failed, then this approach could have been criticized for being "soft on the insurgents." However, in Black Thunder it was kept in mind that in fighting this kind of enemy, the views of the population matter. This was a hard lesson learned from Operation Blue Star.

The Media Utilization

Black Thunder also succeeded in part because everything was televised in real time. Doing so provided the police with ample incentives to honor their commitments, to treat those who surrendered humanely and in accordance with law, and to communicate their actions and their rationale to multiple audiences at home and abroad. Most important, it allowed viewers to contrast the comportment of the police with that of the militants. The media attention continued throughout the cleanup of the temple and the restoration of religious service, which had been suspended. Arguably, the adept use of the media in this operation contributed to further erosion of public support for the militants—such as it was.

Different Views of the Police and the Army

In Operation Blue Star the army led the operation. This decision was undertaken because the police, who are local, were seen to have been co-opted by the militants. They were seen either as being ideological supporters of the insurgents or as having been coerced into inaction against them. Thus the army believed that the police had become part of the problem and not part of the solution. For reasons elaborated earlier, by the late 1980s many steps were taken to augment the capacities of the police to wage more effective counterinsurgency operations. Thus by the time Operation Black Thunder took place, the police were increasingly being seen as a viable force with which to conduct operations.

In conclusion, the success or failure of these two missions has been judged through the lens of more than two decades. Blue Star brought about a disastrous loss of life and massive destruction of the temple and precipitated a further crisis in the Punjab and beyond. In contrast, Black Thunder wrought little bloodshed, resulted in minimal damage to the temple, and, despite continued spikes of violence, contributed to the eventual demise of the insurgency. However, at this point it is far from clear that the outcomes of these two operations hinged decisively on the conduct of the operations and the composition of the force employed or upon the appraisal of the sacredness of the space upon which the counterinsurgent forces operated. While all of these factors were important, the varied outcomes of the two operations were greatly conditioned by the larger contexts in which they were conducted, including the political environment in which they were embedded, the different nature of the insurgents, and the changing public opinion of the militants.

Notes

This chapter was drafted while I was a senior research associate at the United States Institute of Peace (USIP). I am currently a senior political scientist with RAND. This chapter reflects the personal views of the author and not those of USIP or RAND. I am thankful to Sumit Ganguly and Praveen Swami for their corrective guidance and feedback on this chapter. The chapter draws in some part from fieldwork done in India in 2003. For this I thank Ajai Sahni and K. P. S. Gill at the Institute for Conflict Management in New Delhi. Special thanks also to Praveen Swami, who reviewed an earlier draft of this essay.

1. K .P .S. Gill, "Endgame in Punjab: 1988–1993," *Faultlines* 1 (1993). www.satp.org/satporgtp/publication/faultlines/volume1/Fault1-kpstext.htm. Gill suggests that 21,469 died before the insurgency was decisively defeated in 1993. Human Rights Watch suggests a much higher figure of 40,000 due in part to the brutality of the security forces. Human Rights Watch, *Protecting the Killers: A Policy of Impunity in Punjab, India* (Oct. 2007). hrw.org/reports/2007/india1007/india1007web.pdf.

2. The story of Sikh nationalism must be seen in the context of the concurrent Hindu nationalist project, which attempted to absorb Sikhs into the fold of Hinduism. Sikh nationalists rejected the Hindu nationalist claim that Sikhs are Hindus and sought to establish clear boundaries of identity through, inter alia, the development of new Sikh rituals (e.g., for birth, marriage, death, etc.) and the mobilization of the legal system to attain legitimacy for these new rituals (e.g., the Sikh Marriage Act). A thorough discussion of this phenomenon is well beyond the scope of this work. The salient point is that as a result of myriad religio-political identity movements in the subcontinent, a number of Sikh political entrepreneurs began formalizing the demand for Sikh sovereignty well before the 1980s. For comprehensive accounts of this complex and highly contested process, the reader should consult Rajiv Kapur, *Sikh Separatism: The Politics of Faith* (London: Allen and Unwin, 1986); Harjot S. Oberoi, *Construction of Religious Boundaries: Culture, Identity, and Diversity in the Sikh Tradition* (Delhi: Oxford University Press, 1994); N. Gerald Barrier, "Sikh Politics in British Punjab Prior to the Gurdwarda Reform Movement," in Joseph T. O'Connell, ed., *Sikh History and Religion in the Twentieth Century* (Toronto: University of Toronto Press, 1988); Attar Singh, "The Shiromani Gurdwara Prbandhak Committee and the Politicization of the Sikhs," in O'Connell, ed., *Sikh History and Religion in the Twentieth Century*; Cynthia Keppley Mahmood, *Fighting for Faith and Nation: Dialogues with Sikh Militants* (Philadelphia: University of Pennsylvania Press,1996).

3. Mark Tully and Satish Jacobsh, *Amritsar: Mrs. Gandhi's Last Battle* (Calcutta: Rupa and Co;, 1991); Hamish Telford, "The Political Economy of Punjab: Creating Space for Sikh Militancy," *Asian Survey* 32, no. 11 (1992), 969–87; Kapur, *Sikh Separatism*; Joyce Pettigrew, *The Sikhs of the Punjab: Unheard Voices of State and Guerilla Violence* (London: Zed Books, 1995); Yogendra K. Malik, "The Akali Party and Sikh Militancy: Move for Greater Autonomy or Secessionism in Punjab?"*Asian Survey* 26, no. 3 (1986), 345–62.

4. Harjot Oberoi questions these actual connections, noting that before the early 1970s few Sikhs knew of the Damdami Taksal and no major volume on Sikh society, history, or religion mentions the institution. The obscurity of the Damdami Taksal likely aided the insurgents in developing their geneology. Oberoi suggests that while the claims to the tenth guru are plausible, there is no real firm evidence to support it either. Harjot S. Oberoi, "Sikh Fundamentalism: Translating History into Theory," in Martin E. Marty and R. Scott Appleby, eds., *Fundamentalism and the State* (Chicago: University of Chicago Press, 1993), p. 266.

5. See Mahmood, *Fighting for Faith and Nation*; Tully and Jacobsh, *Amritsar*; Pettigrew, *The Sikhs of Punjab*.

6. In particular, many analysts within India and without contend that Giani Zail Singh (who eventually became president of India in 1982) developed Bhindranwale as a foil to the Akali government in order to diminish the ability of the Akalis to challenge the electoral authority of the Congress party in Punjab. See Kuldip Nayar and Khushwant Singh, *Tragedy of Punjab* (New Delhi: Vision Books, 1984). For a more detailed account of this miscalculated strategy of Indira Gandhi's Congress Party, see Tully and Jacobsh, *Amritsar*; Telford, "The Political Economy of Punjab"; Kapur, *Sikh Separatism*; Pettigrew, *The Sikhs of Punjab*; and Malik, "The Akali Party and Sikh Militancy."

7. For a comprehensive account of Operation Blue Star, see Lt. General K. S. Brar, *Operation Blue Star: the True Story* (New Delhi: UBSPD, 1993).

8. D. P. Sharma, *The Punjab Story: Decade of Turmoil* (New Delhi: Aph Publishing, 1996); and Giorgio Shani, "Beyond Khalistan? The Sikh Diaspora and the International Order," paper presented at the International Studies Association Annual Convention, March 27, 2002, New Orleans, isanet.ccit.arizona.edu/noarchive/shani.html.

9. See Apurba Kundu, *Militarism in India: The Army and Civil Society in Consensus* (London: Taurus Academic Studies, 1998).

10. K. P. S. Gill, Punjab: The Knights of Falsehood (New Delhi: Har-Anand Publications, 1997), pp. 95–97.

11. Ibid.

12. Pettigrew, *The Sikhs of the Punjab*; Gill, *Knights of Falsehood*.

13. Ranjit K. Pachnanda, *Terrorism and Response to Terrorist Threat* (New Delhi: UBS Publishers, 2002), pp. 98–99. Also see *Jane's World Insurgency and Terrorism* 17, "Sikh Separatists," March 7, 2003. www.janes.com.

14. Pettigrew, *The Sikhs of Punjab*, pp. 71–75.

15. One crore equals 10 million. This calculation uses the approximate exchange rate of Rs. 33 to 1 U.S. dollar for 1987.

16. Pachnanda, *Terrorism and Response to Terrorist Threat*, pp. 100–103; *Jane's World Insurgency and Terrorism* 17, "Sikh Separatists"; Pettigrew, *The Sikhs of the Punjab*.

17. Pachnanda, *Terrorism and Response to Terrorist Threat*, pp. 103–19; Jane's *World Insurgency and Terrorism* 17, "Sikh Separatists"; Pettigrew, *The Sikhs of the Punjab*.

18. J. S. Grewal, *The Sikhs of the Punjab* (Cambridge: Cambridge University Press, 1990), p. 64.

19. See Sarab Jit Singh, *Operation Black Thunder: An Eye Witness Account of Terrorism in Punjab* (New Delhi: Sage Publications, 2002); Gill, *Knights of Falsehood*;. Tully and Jacobsh, *Amritsar*; Telford, "The Political Economy of Punjab"; Kapur, *Sikh Separatism*; Pettigrew, *The Sikhs of the Punjab*; and Malik, "The Akali Party and Sikh Militancy."

20. For an authoritative discussion of the Golden Temple and the environs, see the official webpage maintained by the Shiromani Gurdwara Prabandhik Committee at www.sgpc.net/golden-temple/around.asp.

21. Singh, *Operation Black Thunder*; Gill, *Knights of Falsehood*.

22. Singh, *Operation Black Thunder*.

23. Singh, *Operation Black Thunder*; Gill, *Knights of Falsehood*.

24. There is not necessarily a religious basis for their use of these terms, which are frequently used in Islamist militant struggles. Rather, Punjabi (the language spoke by the insurgents) draws heavily from the Perso-Arabic vocabulary elements that also occur in Urdu and other northern South Asian languages.

25. For an account of these methods, see Louis E. Fenech, *Martyrdom in the Sikh Tradition: Playing the 'Game of Love'* (Oxford: Oxford University Press, 2001); Pettigrew, *The Sikhs of the Punjab*.

26. Brar, *Operation Blue Star*, pp. 30–31.

27. Ibid., p. 6.

28. Gill, "Endgame in Punjab."

29. Punjab Government, "Statistical Abstract," Section XXXI "Police, Crime and Sudharghar." www.punjab.gov.in.

30. Gill, "Endgame in Punjab."

31. Brar, *Operation Blue Star*, pp. 28, 36, 41–42.

32. Ibid., pp. 41–42, 59.

33. Ibid., pp. 3, 28, 33, 39.

34. Ibid., pp. 49–58.

35. Ibid., pp. 43, 63. For tactical details see pp. 45–73 and 73–128. Note that this claim does not accord well with the account of the operation given by Dar (see note 41).

36. Brar, *Operation Blue Star*, pp. 77–80.

37. Ibid., pp. 77–80

38. Ibid., p. 82

39. Ibid., pp. 83–103.

40. Major General E. H Dar (Retired), "Battle for the Akal Takht: A Military Analysis," *Pakistan Army Journal* 25, no. 3 (Sept. 1984), 18–19.

41. Dar, "Battle for the Akal Takht," p. 19.

42. Brar, *Operation Blue Star*, p. 85.

43. See Gill, "Endgame in Punjab," pp. 14–16. While some of Gill's personal insights cannot be confirmed or disconfirmed in the secondary literature, there is a wide array of other accounts that are more general in nature. For more information about the impacts of Operation Blue Star,

see Man Singh Deora, ed., *Aftermath of Operation Blue Star* (New Delhi: Anmol Publications, 1992); Tully and Jacobsh, *Amritsar*. For more general accounts of the insurgency and police actions there, see Ram Narayan Kumar, *A Complex Denial : Disappearances, Secret Cremations, and the Issue of Truth & Justice in Punjab* (Kathmandu: South Asia Forum for Human Rights, 2001); Julio Ribeiro, *Bullet for Bullet: My Life as a Police Officer* (New Delhi: Viking, 1998); B. S. Danewalia, *Police and Politics in Twentieth Century Punjab* (New Delhi: Ajanta, 1997); and Singh, *Operation Black Thunder*.

44. This information draws both from my June 2003 interview with Mr. Gill and from his article, "Endgame in Punjab: 1988–1993," pp. 14–16. Other accounts of SGPC complicity include inter alia Brar, *Operation Blue Star*; Mahmood, *Fighting for Faith and Nation*; and Tully and Jacobsh, *Amritsar*.

45. This information draws both from my June 2003 interview with Mr. Gill and from his article, "Endgame in Punjab: 1988–1993," pp. 14–16. Other accounts of SGPC complicity include inter alia Brar, *Operation Blue Star*; Mahmood, *Fighting for Faith and Nation*; and Tully and Jacobsh, *Amritsar*.

46. Singh, *Operation Black Thunder*; Gill, *The Knights of Falsehood*.

47. See Gurharpal Singh, "Punjab Since 1984: Disorder, Order and Legitimacy," *Asian Survey* 36, no. 4 (1996), 413–14; Gill, "Endgame in Punjab"; Sharma, *The Punjab Story*; Pettigrew, *The Sikhs of the Punjab*, pp. 55–81, 103–34.

48. This information draws both from my June 2003 interview with Mr. Gill and from his article, "Endgame in Punjab: 1988–1993," pp. 14–16. See also Brar, *Operation Blue Star*; Mahmood, *Fighting for Faith and Nation*; Tully and Jacobsh, *Amritsar*.

49. Interview with K.P.S. Gill in June 2003.

50. Singh, *Operation Black Thunder*; Gill, *The Knights of Falsehood*; interview with K. P. S. Gill in June 2003.

51. Gill's account is generally corroborated here by that of S. J. Singh.

52. S. J. Singh insinuates the possibility that someone from the central government (e.g., the Home Ministry) sought to undermine their efforts to resume religious ceremony (*maryada*) within the Golden Temple in an effort to "claim credit." According to him, they arranged for the chief priest of the Harmander Sahib (Bhai Mohan Singh) to be released from jail such that he could restore the *maryada* with the blessing of the SRSG. Singh strongly suggests that someone, perhaps the Home Minister, coerced the SRSG to withdraw support. In the end, Singh and K. P. S. Gill were able to persuade the SRSG to oversee the restoration of the *maryada*, and the restoration otherwise went largely according to plan. See Singh, *Operation Black Thunder*, pp. 158–62.

53. G. Singh, "Punjab Since 1984," pp. 411–12; Gill, "Endgame in Punjab."

54. Interview with K. P. S. Gill in June 2003.

55. This information draws both from my June 2003 interview with Mr. Gill and from his article, "Endgame in Punjab," pp. 16–17. See Brar, *Operation Blue Star*; Mahmood, *Fighting for Faith and Nation*; Tully and Jacobsh, *Amritsar*; C. Christine Fair, "Military Operations in Urban Areas: The Indian Experience," *India Review* 2, no. 1 (2003).

56. Gazette of India, "The Religious Institutions (Prevention of Misuse) Act, 1988, September 1, 1988. www.mha.nic.in. Does not apply to J & K.

57. Gill, "Endgame in Punjab"; Charanjit Singh Kang, "Counter-terrorism: Punjab a Case Study," Spring 2005. ir.lib.sfu.ca/retrieve/726/etd1604.pdf.

58. Human Rights Watch, *Dead Silence: The Legacy of Human Rights Abuses in Punjab* (New York: Human Rights Watch, 1994), pp. 24–25; Gill, "Endgame in Punjab"; Pettigrew, *The Sikhs of the Punjab.*

59. Pettigrew, *The Sikhs of the Punjab*; Gill, "Endgame in the Punjab"; G. Singh, "Punjab Since 1984."

60. Economics and Statistical Organization. *Statistical Abstract of Punjab* (Chandigarh: Government of Punjab, 1984); Economics and Statistical Organization. *Statistical Abstract of Punjab* (Chandigarh: Government of Punjab, 1990). Both of these are cited in Kang, "Counterterrorism."

61. Figures from the Economics and Statistical Organization. *Statistical Abstract of Punjab* cited in Kang, "Counterterrorism," p. 106.

62. Punjab Government, "Statistical Abstract," Section XXXI "Police, Crime and Sudharghar." www.punjab.gov.in.

63. Gill, "Endgame in Punjab"; Kang, "Counterterrorism."

64. Manoj Joshi, "Combating Terrorism in Punjab," Strategic Digest 23, no. 8 (August 1993), 1261–66; Bharat Rakshak, "National Security Guards." www.bharat-rakshak.com.

65. Gill, "Endgame in the Punjab"; Sharma, *The Punjab Story*; Joshi, "Combating Terrorism in Punjab"; Kang, "Counterterrorism."

66. C. Christine Fair, *Urban Battle Fields of South Asia: Lessons Learned from Sri Lanka, India, and Pakistan* (Santa Monica, Cal.: RAND, 2004), pp. 69–101; Sharma, *The Punjab Story*; Shinder S. Thandi, "Counter-insurgency and Political Violence in Punjab 1980–1994," in Gurharpal Singh and Ian Talbot, eds., *Punjabi Identity: Continuity and Change*, (New Delhi: Manohar, 1995).

67. For a critical view, see Human Rights Watch, *Protecting the Killers*. For a view defending the policy, see Gill, "Endgame in Punjab."

3

A Mosque, a Shrine, and Two Sieges

Sumit Ganguly

Explaining Contrary Outcomes

Police, paramilitary forces, and the military are now increasingly being called upon to flush out religious militants who routinely enter sacred sites and then use them to dramatize their cause and rally their followers. Examples of such actions abound, and several such cases are discussed in other chapters in this volume. These episodes are unlikely to abate in the foreseeable future. Instead they will probably proliferate as religiously inspired militancy continues to rise across the world, especially among recent immigrant populations in Western Europe and elsewhere.

While there is a burgeoning corpus of literature on counterinsurgency, it has important limitations in terms of both theory and policy. Only a small fraction of this literature has an explicit theoretical orientation and is effectively couched in the broader strands of social science research.[1] Other components of this literature focus more on case studies, strategies, and tactics.[2] Despite the growth of this genre, very little of it deals explicitly with the extremely vital question of carrying out counterinsurgency operations in sacred spaces.[3]

This chapter represents an attempt to examine two important cases within the context of the ongoing insurgency in the Indian-controlled portion of the disputed state of Jammu and Kashmir.[4]

In both cases the Indian security forces sought to avoid violence; yet one of these cases was resolved peacefully whereas the other resulted in a bloody battle. Why did the two crises end so differently? Answering this question can help us better to understand the specific trajectory of Indian efforts to pacify Kashmir, improve our theoretical understanding of counterinsurgency operations generally, and suggest policy prescriptions for operations in places like Iraq, where insurgents regularly make use of sacred spaces.[5]

The Indian military (as well as its paramilitary forces, such as the Border Security Force and the Central Reserve Police Force) has had to deal with a range of ethno-religious, civil, and secessionist conflicts in a variety of terrains, both urban and rural. In the 1950s and 1960s Indian security forces had to quell the Mizo and Naga rebels in India's northeast. In the 1970s they had to suppress the neophyte Maoist urban terrorists, the Naxalites, in West Bengal; the Sikh insurgents in the Punjab in the 1980s, and the Kashmiri insurgents since the early 1990s.

Many of these operations have placed the army and the paramilitary forces in extremely fraught situations, especially when having to restore order in communal conflicts.[6] When local police and paramilitary forces have been deemed to be too unreliable or partisan, the army has been called in to end the violence. In virtually all cases, the army has managed to maintain its *esprit de corps* and has not acted as a blatantly partisan force.[7] Only in the aftermath of Operation Blue Star, the siege of the Golden Temple in Amritsar in 1984, did a number of Sikh officers and men desert from the army. In the aftermath of this episode, the Indian Army has sought to minimize the use of force when it is confronted with the possibility of having to conduct military operations on areas that are deemed to be sacred. For both normative as well as instrumental reasons, the army can ill afford to ignore the profound sensitivities of any religious community in India's multireligious society. Normatively, the officers and men of the Indian Army are taught to be sensitive to matters of faith, given the area's diverse religious composition.[8] Failure to take into account such concerns could sow discord within the army and reduce its military effectiveness. [9]

Pertinent to the subject of this volume, the Indian armed forces have fought several important counterinsurgency campaigns within the confines of sacred places. This chapter examines two important cases, both of which occurred within the context of a violent, sanguinary, ethno-religious insurgency that has wracked the Indian-controlled portion of the disputed state of Jammu and Kashmir since

1989. The origins of this insurgency have been discussed at length elsewhere,[10] but it is important to summarize here the origins, evolution, and current state of the insurgency. Various and competing explanations have been proffered for the origins of this insurgency.[11] Most dispassionate observers, however, would argue that it can be traced to two critical sources: first, the political chicanery of various national governments in India in attempts to install pliant regimes in India's only Muslim majority state; and second, Pakistan's successful attempt to exploit the concomitant discontent with Indian rule among significant segments of the Muslim populace.[12]

The Jammu and Kashmir Liberation Front (JKLF), a notionally secular and pro-independence insurgent group, spearheaded the insurgency in December 1989. Ironically, the JKLF faced the full brunt not only of India's security forces and intelligence services but also of Pakistan's Inter-Services Intelligence Directorate (ISI-D).[13] The ISI-D then moved swiftly to try to marginalize the JKLF and turned its attention to more religiously oriented insurgent groups, such as the Hizb-ul-Mujahideen (HUM). Over time the insurgency steadily metamorphosed from its pristine origins. What had started as a spontaneous local rebellion stemming from regional grievances against an overbearing, insensitive, deceitful, and callous Indian state became a highly organized, religiously inspired, and externall directed extortion racket. By the late 1990s the Indian state, through an amalgam of harsh military repression and the promise of political concessions, had managed to contain, if not entirely suppress the insurgency. Nevertheless, it had not succeeded in draining the reservoir of political discontent that still seethed through much of the state.[14]

In both cases analyzed in this chapter, insurgents managed to enter and seize sacred places. The first episode took place at the Hazratbal Mosque in Srinagar, the capital of Jammu and Kashmir, in October 1993. The second took place between February and May 1995 at Charar-e-Sharief, a fifteenth-century wooden shrine. The "sacredness" of these two entities is beyond question. As will be discussed later, the Hazratbal mosque has long been fraught with both religious and political significance. Similarly, the shrine of Sheikh Nooruddin Noorani was of extraordinary importance to both Hindus and Muslim Kashmiris, who had a shared regard for the Sufi tradition of Islam. The outcomes of these cases were dramatically different: the Hazratbal crisis was resolved peacefully, and the Charar-e-Sharief episode resulted in a sanguinary gun battle and the destruction of the shrine.

The failure of the Indian Army to avoid a bloody conflagration at Charar-e-Sharief, the contextual and other differences notwithstanding, remains a puzzle. The military had witnessed the successful (and peaceful) resolution of the Hazratbal crisis. They also had had the sharply contrasting example of the disaster that had befallen their compatriots when they had stormed the Golden Temple in Amritsar in the state of Punjab to flush out Sikh militants who had turned the shrine into a virtual arsenal.[15] This episode proved to be an unmitigated disaster for the Indian security forces and contributed dramatically to the escalation of the Sikh insurgency in the Punjab, prior to its eventual suppression in the early 1990s.

The differing outcomes of civil-military interaction and military choices in these two contexts require explanation. The answer, as will be argued in this chapter, lies in the locations of the two entities, the surrounding geography, and the identities of the insurgents involved in the two crises.[16]

In the first case, the Hazratbal mosque is located in the heart of the city of Srinagar, the capital of the Indian-controlled portion of the disputed state of Jammu and Kashmir. Consequently, the Indian civil and military authorities could ill afford to risk a major confrontation and a possible conflagration as a consequence of the precipitate use of force.[17] The shrine at Charar-e-Sharief, by contrast, was in a more remote part of Kashmir. Despite its location, the military had little leeway in exercising its writ without the consent of civilian authority.[18] By the time the army was deployed (albeit with important constraints), the insurgents had managed to ensconce themselves in the shrine. Finally, in a related vein, the local, national, and international media scrutiny of the Hazratbal mosque episode was intense. In the Charar-e-Sharief case, on the other hand, both the weather (Kashmir at that time of year is blanketed in snow) and the remoteness of the shrine kept media attention at bay. Furthermore, the Indian Army limited access to the shrine in order to prevent the insurgents from manipulating the local, national, and international media.[19] In the wake of its destruction, however, the army made few if any efforts to limit reportage.

The differing identities of the insurgents in the two cases also played a vital role in shaping the outcomes. In the first instance the authorities were dealing primarily with native Kashmiris disaffected with Indian rule. In the second case the insurgents were all of foreign origin. The Indian military historically has had far less tolerance for foreign insurgents but is prepared to grant somewhat greater leeway to domestic insurgents.[20] Moreover, in the Hazratbal case the military and especially the civilian leadership were under intense pressure to reach a swift resolution because a number of local worshippers were trapped in the mosque, virtual hostages to the insurgents. In the second case the only occupants of the shrine were foreign insurgents, and so similar compunctions were not implicated. More to the point, the foreign insurgents had little or no regard for the local religious traditions, customs, and sensitivities of Kashmiris, Hindus, and Muslims, and therefore they were prepared to wreak havoc and engage in mayhem at the shrine.

After first providing a broad historical backdrop of the Indian military's experiences with counterinsurgent operations in and around sacred places, this chapter will present the two contrasting case studies and discuss the markedly different outcomes of each operation. Finally, it will sketch out some preliminary conclusions for both theory and policy.

The Historical Context of Insurgencies

Neither the Indian Army nor the various Indian paramilitary forces have had a dearth of experience in fighting insurgencies. The Indian Army, in particular, had dealt with Naga and Mizo rebels in India's remote northeast as early as the 1950s.[21] India's paramilitary forces had also effectively dealt with neophyte Maoist guerillas, the so-called Naxalites, in the state of West Bengal in the 1970s.[22] However, neither the army nor the paramilitary forces had had extensive experience in fighting with insurgents on sacred ground. Their first significant (and tragic) experience came with Operation Blue Star in 1984 at the principal Sikh shrine, the Golden Temple in the city of Amritsar in the Punjab, a western Indian state. This operation had been designed to flush out a group of Sikh militants who were under the command of a charismatic and violent Sikh leader, Sant Jarnail Singh Bhindranwale, and who had turned the temple into a virtual arsenal and were using it as a sanctuary. For reasons that have been discussed at length elsewhere, the entire operation proved to be a calamitous event involving loss of many innocent lives, the destruction of a substantial portion of the Golden Temple, and the concomitant alienation of vast segments of the Sikh community from the Indian state. The subsequent Operation Black Thunder four years later, also directed at another group of Sikh militants in the Golden Temple, took cognizance of all the errors of the first operation and avoided a similar debacle.[23] In the aftermath of the Golden Temple tragedy, the Indian Army has adopted the principle of the "use of minimum force" as part of its rules of engagement in all counterinsurgency operations in sacred spaces.[24]

A Troubled State

The Hazratbal crisis erupted in October 1993 in the capital of the disputed Muslim-majority state of Jammu and Kashmir. The dispute over the state had already precipitated two Indo-Pakistani conflicts, in 1947–1948 and 1965.[25] The third Indo-Pakistani war in 1971 was not fought over Kashmir, but the Indian military had witnessed some action along the disputed border.[26] In the aftermath of the 1971 war the two sides had signed the Shimla Agreement, by which they had agreed to return to the status quo ante. They had also reaffirmed their intention to abjure from the use of force to resolve the Kashmir dispute.[27] Among other matters, the Shimla Agreement had converted the previous Cease Fire Line (CFL) that had separated the warring forces into the Line of Control (LoC) reflecting the troop deployments at the end of the conflict. In the aftermath of the Shimla Agreement, apart from minor skirmishes along the LoC and some ritualistic Pakistani references to the Kashmir dispute at the United Nations General Assembly, the subject of the dispute had remained mostly dormant. Overwhelming Indian conventional superiority had, for the most part, curbed Pakistani adventurism.[28]

The long, albeit cold, peace that had characterized Indo-Pakistani relations since 1972 came to an abrupt close in early December 1989, when a significant indigenous ethno-religious insurgency erupted in Jammu and Kashmir. Suffice to say that its origins could be traced to the collision of the forces of political mobilization and political decay. In an attempt to win the loyalties of the Kashmiris, the Indian government had flooded the state with development funds and thereby helped create a new generation that was politically sophisticated. On the other hand, fearing that secessionists might come to power through the ballot box, it also tolerated widespread political chicanery, thereby corroding the political institutions of the state. The conjunction of these two forces proved to be highly combustible.[29]

Accordingly, it is important to underscore that the rebellion originally started in 1989 as a mostly spontaneous, indigenous uprising of young Kashmiri men who felt alienated from the Indian state as a consequence of widespread political chicanery. Despite the state's considerable experience in handling insurgencies, its initial response to the uprising had been harsh and ham-handed. The crude response of the Indian security forces had actually exacerbated conditions and generated more popular support for the insurgents. Simultaneously, sensing a critical opportunity to exploit India's vulnerability in Kashmir, Pakistan's Inter-Services Intelligence Directorate (ISI-D) sought to organize, aid, and support some of the insurgents while undermining others. Specifically, they had bolstered pro-Pakistani secessionist entities such as the Hizb-ul-Mujahideen and the Harkat-ul-Ansar and had sought to marginalize the notionally secular and pro-independence Jammu and Kashmir Liberation Front (JKLF).[30] As a consequence of Pakistani material support and, most important, the provision of sanctuaries, the insurgency had become considerably better organized, more violent, and deadlier. The Indian authorities could take only limited solace in the fact that the insurgents not only were at odds with the Indian security forces but also were engaged in brutal internecine warfare.[31]

The Indian state, after having taken initial, fitful steps to curb the insurgents, was now also in the process of calibrating its own counterinsurgency operations. The central goal of the Indian state was to restore a minimum of public order in the state to enable the conduct of reasonably free and fair elections with the hope of restoring a democratically elected government. The siege at the Hazratbal shrine must be placed against this politico-military backdrop.

The Hazratbal Affair

The Hazratbal mosque in Srinagar, which harks back to the seventeenth century, is of considerable religious and political significance in the state. Devout Muslims of the Kashmir Valley believe that the shrine is the repository of a hair of the Prophet Mohammed and therefore they attach considerable importance to the mosque. The mosque has also served as a vital political platform for the state. Sheikh Mohammed Abdullah, the so-called "lion of Kashmir," the founder of the Jammu and Kashmir National Conference and one of the principal political opponents of the last maharaja of Kashmir, Hari Singh, had launched his initial agitation against monarchical rule from the mosque in the 1930s. Subsequently, after India's independence, Abdullah, as the first prime minister of the state, had done much to improve the physical structure of the mosque.[32] Furthermore, an earlier theft of the sacred relic from the mosque in 1963 had lead to substantial political upheaval and violence in the state. Fortunately, the relic was recovered, duly authenticated by religious authorities, and returned to its sanctuary.[33]

Given the religious and political significance of the mosque, a military crisis that threatened its sanctity in the eyes of believers could have had explosive consequences for the already turbulent conditions prevailing. Consequently, when on October 15, 1993, the first intelligence report about Kashmiri militants entering the mosque reached Lieutenant-General Zaki, the security adviser to the governor of Jammu and Kashmir, he acted with considerable alacrity. By the late evening of October 15 he had already deployed two battalions of the Indian Army to seal access to the shrine. Despite his swift actions, a fire broke out in the environs of the shrine on October 16, giving rise to rumors that the military (or other paramilitary forces in the vicinity) had set the fire in an attempt to discredit the militants who had holed up in the shrine.

Probably with an eye to lowering tensions, the army contingent was replaced the next day with members of a paramilitary organization, the Border Security Force (BSF).[34] To avoid a tragedy on the order of the Golden Temple episode of 1984, both the army units and the paramilitary forces were issued orders not to storm the shrine.[35] Instead a crisis management team of sorts was cobbled together to try to negotiate an end to the crisis at the shrine.

On October 17 the insurgents who were in the shrine sent word that they were willing to negotiate only if they could choose their interlocutor. They indicated that they would talk either to Divisional Commissioner Wajahat Habibullah or to Chief Secretary Sheikh Ghulam Rasool, both senior administrative officers in the state. Habibullah promptly expressed his willingness to negotiate and was even prepared to enter the shrine of his own accord to discuss terms.[36] However, the police authorities were loath to let him enter the shrine for fear that he would be taken hostage.[37] Nevertheless, the negotiations started and the insurgents came up with their opening gambit. Their demands were threefold. First, the army and the paramilitary forces would have to be removed from the area. Second, the local *ulema* would have to come in and authenticate the relic. Finally, they would have to be granted free passage.

General Zaki quickly turned down these demands, especially the demand of safe passage. Nevertheless, he refused to allow the use of force to dislodge the insurgents. In the meanwhile Habibullah continued with his negotiations. Following further conversations, he informed the prime minister's office and senior home ministry officials in New Delhi that he was convinced that he could bring an end to the crisis if the government conceded the demand of safe passage. At this point General Zaki and his circle of advisers were prepared only to accept the surrender of the militants and offer them a fair trial. With a limited negotiating brief, Habibullah sought the assistance of two local Muslim notables, Abdul Majid Wani and Maulvi Abbas Ansari. The militants accepted the two new negotiators but insisted that the curfew that had been imposed on the area be lifted and that they be provided food. General Zaki initially agreed to provide food but then backtracked on his offer.[38]

As word of the siege spread across Kashmir, tensions mounted. Tragically, on October 22 in the nearby town of Bijbehara in Anantnag District, which had also been under curfew, some local residents had held a large public demonstration to protest the siege.[39] The local BSF contingent, faced with this large and defiant crowd, panicked and opened fire on them, killing 28 people. Fortunately, the civilian authorities in Kashmir, including Habibullah himself, acted swiftly. They visited the town, reassured the residents that an inquiry would be conducted into the circumstances of the BSF's actions, and also brought charges against the errant BSF personnel. News of the Bijbehara incident and the state's quick reaction to it reached the insurgents in the shrine. According to Habibullah's account, the state's apparent concern for the victims seemed to have a salutary effect on their outlook. Habibullah, in conjunction with a senior officer from Military Intelligence, Major-General Shankar Prashad, conducted protracted negotiations throughout the last week of October. On November 2 they finally reached an accord, under which the militants would surrender their weapons, be taken into military custody, be debriefed, and then be released. The accord would have been implemented promptly, but a tragic car accident almost killed Habibullah and seriously injured General Zaki. Because the insurgents suspected that foul play had led to this apparent accident, the final negotiations dragged on until November 16. After the siege had been lifted, the military found a small cache of weaponry on the premises of the mosque, including 15 AK-56 rifles, a Dragunov sniper rifle, a Universal machine gun, and a rocket-propelled grenade with one cartridge.[40]

The Tragedy at Charar-e-Sharief

Unlike the Hazratbal crisis, which was resolved peacefully, the crisis at Charar-e-Sharief resulted in the destruction of the shrine.[41] First, several differences between the two entities and their locales need to be looked at. Unlike the Hazratbal mosque, Charar-e-Sharief was a shrine to Sheikh Nooruddin Noorani (known as Nand Rishi to the Hindus of Kashmir), a fifteenth-century Sufi saint. Also it was located in a largely rural area near a small town, unlike the Hazratbal mosque, which is in a crowded area of Srinagar. Another critical difference between the two cases was the composition of the insurgents. Whereas virtually all of them at Hazratbal were Kashmiris, those at Charar-e-Sharief were primarily of foreign origin, mostly Afghans or Pakistanis. Finally, since the shrine at Charar-e-Sharief was a wooden structure, it was far more susceptible to fire.

By 1995 the insurgency in Kashmir had undergone a qualitative transformation, evolving from a pristine, indigenous ethno-religious uprising into a well-orchestrated, heavily armed, and vicious extortion racket. The principal indigenous insurgent organization, the notionally secular and pro-independence Jammu and Kashmir Liberation Front (JKLF), had for all practical purposes been marginalized. They had lost their central role because of the steady infiltration of various Pakistan-supported and -abetted insurgent (and terrorist) organizations into the fray.[42] Furthermore, in the aftermath of the fall of the Najibullah regime in Afghanistan in 1992, a substantial number of *mujahideen* chose to direct their ire and energies toward a new *jihad* in Kashmir. Various Pakistani regimes did little to restrain these individuals and groups from entering Kashmir. Instead, as is now well known, Pakistan's Inter-Services Intelligence Directorate (ISI-D) played an active role in arming, training and providing sanctuaries to them.[43] The episode at Charar-e-Sharief must be placed against this dramatically changed backdrop.

The origins of the crisis can be traced to February 1995, when Indian intelligence agencies received information that the self-styled "Major" Mast Gul, an Afghan involved in the insurgency, along with some 60 to 100 of his followers had holed up near the shrine of Sheikh Noorani.[44] On the basis of these reports the security forces moved with dispatch and sought to cordon off access to the town of Charar-e-Sharief, which lies some 20 miles southwest of Srinagar. The shrine itself was located in a bowl-like city center amidst the village.[45] At the time of the infiltration of these insurgents, the military did not have a presence in the village but were stationed two or three miles away.

Two factors inhibited the military from undertaking any drastic military action against the insurgents who were ensconced in the shrine. First, they knew that they could not readily count on the support of the local population, among whom were a substantial number of insurgent sympathizers. Second, given the local significance of the shrine, the governor of Jammu and Kashmir and his security adviser, Lieutenant-General Zaki, ordered the army to stay away from the immediate vicinity of the shrine. Instead their task was to quarantine the area, a task that would have been difficult under the best of circumstances, considering the mountainous terrain and surrounding forest cover nearby.[46] Accordingly, the strategy of the army in conjunction with the BSF (units of which were also deployed around the shrine) was to isolate and coerce the insurgents to surrender over time. To this end members of the 8 Mountain Division from the 56 Mountain Brigade were deployed in this area.[47]

This strategy was fraught with important limitations. Since the military and the BSF were deployed on the outskirts of the town, access to the shrine was not effectively denied. The insurgents and their sympathizers actively exploited these gaps in the security cordon to their fullest advantage, supplying those inside the shrine with tactical information, food, and other supplies.

As the siege of the town of Charar-e-Sharief dragged on through February and March, the military (on the orders of the civil administration) offered the insurgents safe passage to bring an end to the siege. The insurgents promptly spurned this offer, not trusting the bona fides of the military. Throughout this period senior officials in the Ministry of Home Affairs in New Delhi kept a close watch on the evolving situation. However, they did not challenge the military's strategy of simply wearing down the insurgents through a process of isolation. In keeping with this strategy and with the military keen on avoiding the use of force, a final offer of safe passage was renewed to the insurgents toward the end of April. This too was summarily rejected.[48] The endgame to the crisis came swiftly thereafter.

The precise sequence of events is the subject of endless dispute.[49] What is known, however, is that a fire started near the shrine on or about May 8. Indian authorities, without exception, contend that insurgents in the shrine set fire to it as a diversionary tactic. Almost immediately the army called in firefighters. When they arrived, they were greeted with withering gunfire from within the shrine. In desperation, on May 9 the military sought permission from the prime minister's office to enter the town. They received permission on May 11 and promptly surrounded the shrine. Taking advantage of the disturbed conditions, the bulk of the insurgents, including "Major" Mast Gul, made good their escape. In a subsequent cordon and search operation in the area, the military did manage to apprehend some of them, including Abu Jindal (the leader of the Harkat-ul-Ansar, a prominent terrorist organization).[50]

It should be mentioned that the insurgents and their sympathizers in Kashmir and elsewhere argue that it was the military assault on the shrine that ignited the fire.[51] Eyewitness accounts of the events, however, tend to support the version of the authorities.[52] The veracity of these claims, though important, is not critical. It is the destructive outcome of the siege that matters, for questions of both theory and policy. From a theoretical and analytic standpoint, despite the military's emphasis on the "minimum use of force" and its willingness to maintain a long siege in a most adverse terrain amid inhospitable local conditions, the eventual outcome was disastrous. Also, from a policy standpoint this episode revealed the limits of armed restraint and negotiation. In the aftermath of this crisis, the political climate in Kashmir, quite predictably, worsened considerably as the insurgents managed to exploit the tragedy to their fullest advantage by placing the onus of it squarely on the security forces.[53]

Explaining Divergent Outcomes

In neither case did the Indian military fundamentally violate its standard operating procedures regarding action in sacred spaces. In the first case they did not storm the mosque at all but allowed civilian authorities to pursue a strategy based upon dialogue and negotiation. In the second case they resorted to force only in their attempt to prevent the insurgents from escaping. In sum, despite rising tensions and the need to seek swift resolutions to both crises, the military acted with restraint, the claims of motivated propaganda notwithstanding. However, in the first case the location favored the military and paramilitary forces; they could successfully quarantine the area and limit the ability of the insurgents to flee the mosque at will. In the second case the physical location of the shrine in a mountainous area on the outskirts of a small town conferred significant advantages on the insurgents. Apart from these advantages, other, idiosyncratic factors also hobbled the military until the final stages of the conflict, when they were given a free hand. Civilian authorities did not share local intelligence with the military and thereby undermined their ability to calibrate their operations suitably.[54] Finally, in the second case, the bulk of the insurgents were not of local origin, so they had no blood-soil relationship to the region or to the shrine. The destruction of a shrine that represented the syncretic religious heritage of Kashmir meant very little to them. Ironically, despite their foreign origins and their contempt for Kashmir's unique religious traditions, they did have some sympathizers in the region who were of assistance to them throughout the siege.

One of the most important propositions that can be gleaned from these two case studies deals with the identity of insurgent groups. Military authorities may not always be able to prevent foreign insurgents from entering a shrine. However, when the identity of the insurgents is known, military planners should formulate appropriate strategies for dealing with them. Clearly, indigenous insurgents are more amenable to negotiation and compromise. Foreign insurgents, who care little about local religious customs and practices, may force military authorities to adopt harsher tactics.

A few questions persist regarding how the second crisis was handled. Could the civilian and military authorities have generated more support for their decision to pursue a long siege through a careful attempt to win the "hearts and minds" of the local population and through the cultivation of the sentiments of religious authorities in Kashmir? This strategy, though desirable, was very possibly beyond the pale. By 1995 the vicious behavior of the insurgent groups and the harshness of the counterinsurgency strategies of the Indian state had left little room for this form of dialogue. Most important, any religious leaders or local residents who stepped forward to help mediate this crisis could be placing their lives at risk. The foreign insurgents would have had few if any compunctions about ruthlessly assassinating anyone they deemed to be a Quisling. On the other hand, the military and the civilian authorities in Kashmir could have ill afforded to guarantee the insurgents safe passage as a condition for ending the siege. Such a gesture would simply embolden the insurgents, most of whom were of foreign origin and implacable in their hostility toward the Indian state.

Despite these plausible explanations for the markedly divergent outcomes, some questions still remain. Given the significance of the shrine, why was there limited civilian-military coordination to bring the crisis to a less violent end? Does the answer lie in the fraying of institutional procedures as the insurgency had dragged on for over five years but was showing signs of flagging? Or did the authorities in Srinagar (and New Delhi) simply not attach sufficient significance to this shrine located in a rural area and not in the heart of the state's capital?

Finally, how has the Indian military dealt with subsequent operations in or around other shrines and mosques as the insurgency has continued?[55] Have the contrasting experiences of the Hazratbal and Charar-e-Sharief sufficiently informed the military about what strategies may best be adopted and be avoided in future operations?

These questions are important not merely for the Indian Army, paramilitary forces, and police, but for the armed forces of a host of other states. They assume particular significance for democratic states because of their commitment to openness, transparency, and above all some adherence to the expectations of the rule of law. Operations of this order are likely to become more prevalent as armed forces are called upon to cope with religious militants who are deft at exploiting religious sites and sacred spaces. Consequently, this subject should become an important focus of scholars and analysts who are interested in questions of counterinsurgency operations.

Appendix: Insurgent Groups in Jammu and Kashmir

Table 3.1 Insurgent Groups in Jammu and Kashmir

Name	*Formation*	*Strength*	*Stated Objective(s)*
Al Barq (ABQ)	1990	350 (including 20 foreigners)	Liberation of Kashmir through armed struggle and establishment of Islamic Rule; in recent public utterances has opposed acts of random terrorism and frequent strikes (*hartals*); favored a dialogue.
Al Fateh Force (AFF)	1994	35	Merger of J&K with Pakistan
Al Jihad Force (AJF)/ Al Jihad	1991	125 (including 25 foreign mercenaries)	Liberation of Kashmir through armed struggle
Al Mujahid Force (AMF)	1992	125	Secession of Kashmir through armed struggle and merger with Pakistan
Al Umar Mujahideen (AUM)/Al Umar	1989	700	Liberation of Kashmir through armed struggle and merger with Pakistan
Awami Action Committee (AAC)	1964	12,000; 100,000 sympathizers (claimed)	Self-determination for Kashmiris

(*Continued*)

Table 3.1 Continued

Name	*Formation*	*Strength*	*Stated Objective(s)*
Dukhtaran-e-Millat (DEM)	1987	1,000	Merger with Pakistan; Islamic tenets for Muslim women; support to Nizam-e-Mustafa
Harkat-ul-Ansar (HUA)	1993	800 Pakistan/ Afghan trained militants (including 300 to 350 foreigners); 10,000 followers	Establishment of the supremacy of Islam in the world; liberation of Muslims who do not follow *Shariat*; protection of minority Muslims in non-Muslim areas
Hizbul Mujahideen (HUM)	1989	1,400 (Pak-trained)	Secession of J&K through armed struggle and merger with Pakistan
Ikhwan-ul-Musalmeen (IUM)	1989	225 (including Pakistani elements)	Liberation of Kashmir through armed struggle; self-determination to decide Kashmir's future
J&K Democratic Freeedom Party (JKDFP)	1998	N/A	Solution of J&K through peaceful means
Jammu & Kashmir Islamic Front (JKIF)	1995	50	Liberation of Kashmir through armed struggle; right of 'self-determination'
J&K Jamaat-e-Islami (JKJEI)	1942	2,000,000 (including Pakistani elements)	Establishment of an Islamic State (Nizam-e-Mustafa) and merger of J&K with Pakistan
Jammu & Kashmir Liberation Front (JKLF)	1964	150	Liberation and re-unification, through armed struggle, or an independent J&K with POK, Gilgit, Baltistan, Hunza and Aksai Chin areas

Name	*Formation*	*Strength*	*Stated Objective(s)*
J&K People's Conference	1975	60,000 (including foreign elements)	'Autonomy' for J&K
J&K People's League, Rehmani Faction (JKPL-R)	1974	850 (including foreign members)	Liberation of J&K through armed struggle and its accession to Pakistan
J&K People's Political Front (JKPPF)	1993	N/A	Solution of the J&K issue through tripartite talks involving India, Pakistan and the people of J&K
J&K United People's League (JKUPL)	1989	4,000 (including Pakistani elements)	Liberate Kashmir through armed struggle
Jaish-e-Mohammed (JEM)/Tehrik-al-Furqan (TAF)/Al Dawa	2000	600–700	Secession of J&K and merger with Pakistan
Jamaat-ul-Mujahideen (JUM)	December 1990/ April 1991	30 (including foreign elements)	Merger of J&K with Pakistan
Jamaat-ul-Mujahideen Almi (JUMA)	1990	130 (including foreign elements)	Establishment of Islamic supremacy in the world and liberation of Muslim minority areas through armed struggle
Kul Jamaat Hurriyat Conference (KJHC)	1993	N/A	'New' political thrust (from 1993) to ride on terrorist acts for the liberation of J&K along with the (old) concept of tripartite talks involving Pakistan, India and the **KJHC** as the representative

(Continued)

Table 3.1 Continued

Name	*Formation*	*Strength*	*Stated Objective(s)*
			of the Kashmiri people; protection of Islamic identity and the Muslim majority character of J&K
Lashkar-e-Toiba (LET)	1980	500 (including Pakistan/ Afghan trained militants)	Establishment of Nizam-e-Mustafa in the world; merger of J&K with Pakistan; establish the rule of Allah throughout the world
Mahaz-e-Azadi (MEA)	1977	150	'Self-determination' for Kashmiris; mobilisation of opinion against the Indian government; terrorise non-Muslims
Muslim Conference (MC)	1989	10,000	Independent J&K with pre-1947 status
Muslim Janbaaz Force (MJF)/Janbaaz Force	1989	100	Secession of J&K through armed struggle
Muslim Mujahideen (MM)	1993	250	Secession of J&K from India and merger with Pakistan
Pasban-e-Islam (PEI)/ Hizbul Momineen (HMM)	1990 (**PEI**); 1992 (**HMM**)	50–100	Liberation of Kashmir through armed struggle, merger with Pakistan
Shora-e-Jihad (SEJ)	1996	5,000	Liberation of Kashmir through armed struggle and merger with Pakistan

Name	*Formation*	*Strength*	*Stated Objective(s)*
Tehrik-e-Jihad (TEJ)	1997	550–600 (foreign mercenaries, Pak ex-servicemen)	Liberation of Kashmir through armed struggle and secession to Pakistan
Tehrik-ul-Mujahideen (TUM)	1990	65 (including 35 foreign militants)	Merger with Pakistan; promotion of Pan-Islamism

Source: Santhanam, K. Sreedhar, Saxena, Sudhir, Manish. *Jihadis in Jammu and Kashmir: A Portrait Galley* (New Delhi: Sage Publications, 2003).

Notes

I am grateful to Stephen P. Cohen, Christine Fair, Devin Hagerty, Paul Kapur, Ved Prakash Malik, Michael McGinnis, Vinayak Patankar, Brian Rathbun, Praveen Swami, and Harrison Wagner for comments on earlier versions of this chapter. All errors of fact and interpretation are obviously mine.

1. One of the best examples thereof is Michael D. Schafer, *Deadly Paradigms: The Failure of U.S. Counterinsurgency Policy* (Princeton, N.J.: Princeton University Press, 1988).

2. See, for example, Bard E. O'Neill, *Insurgency and Terrorism: Inside Modern Revolutionary Warfare* (Dulles, Va.: Brassey's, 1990); John A Nagl, *Counterinsurgency Lessons from Malaya and Vietnam: Learning to Eat Soup with a Knife* (Westport, Conn.: Praeger, 2002); Anthony James Joes, *Resisting Rebellion: The History and Politics of Counterinsurgency* (Lexington: University of Kentucky, 2004); and Richard H. Schultz and Andrea J. Dew, *Insurgents, Terrorists and Militias* (New York: Columbia University Press, 2006). For an analysis of the putatively paradigmatic case, the British success against the Communist insurgents in colonial Malaya, see Brian Stewart, *Smashing Terrorism in the Malayan Emergency: The Vital Contribution of the Police* (Selangor Darul Eshan: Pelanduk Publications, 2004).

3. An important exception is Ron E. Hassner, "Fighting Insurgency on Sacred Ground," *The Washington Quarterly* 29:2 (2006), 149–66, and Ron E. Hassner, "To Halve and to Hold: Conflicts Over Sacred Space and the Problem of Indivisibility," *Security Studies* 12:4 (Summer 2003), 1–33.

4. On the origins of the Kashmir dispute, see Sumit Ganguly, *Conflict Unending: India–Pakistan Tensions Since 1947* (New York: Columbia University Press, 2001).

5. For a sound discussion of the insurgency in Iraq, see Ahmed S. Hashim, *Insurgency and Counter-Insurgency in Iraq* (Ithaca, N.Y.: Cornell University Press, 2006).

6. The term "communal" in the Indian political context refers to most forms of ethno-religious tensions.

7. For a discussion about the nonpartisan features of the Indian Army and their exemplary conduct when dealing with communal/religious violence in India, see Shekhar Gupta, "Kitne Musalman hain?" ("How Many Muslims Are There?"), *Indian Express*, February 18, 2006. Among other matters, Gupta reports that a recent chief of staff of the army had issued an order banning the display of any overt religious symbols on the part of officers and men. The only exception was the bangle ("karra") that Sikh officers and men wear. He made this exception because members of other religious communities wear similar wrist ornaments.

8. On this subject see the Indian Army's statement on sub-conventional operations. Headquarters Army Training Command, *Doctrine for Sub-Conventional Operations* (Shimla: Headquarters Army Training Command, 2006).

9. For a particularly problematic argument that suggests that the Indian Army has been unable to develop unit cohesion thanks to the institution of caste, see Stephen Peter Rosen, *India and Its Armies* (Ithaca, N.Y.: Cornell University Press, 1996).

10. See, for example, Sumit Ganguly, *The Crisis in Kashmir: Portents of War, Hopes of Peace* (New York: Cambridge University Press, 1997).

11. For a quasi-official Pakistani account which stresses Indian "perfidy," see Shireen Akhtar, *Uprising in Indian-Held Kashmir* (Islamabad: Institute of Regional Studies). For a dispassionate, if journalistic, account of the origins of the insurgency, see Ajit Bhattacharjea, *Kashmir: The Wounded Valley* (New Delhi: UBSPD, 1994). For an account that stresses the long-term Pakistani involvement in Kashmir, see Praveen Swami, *India, Pakistan, and the Secret Jihad: The Covert War in Kashmir, 1947–2004* (London: Routledge, 2007).

12. For a detailed discussion of the specific timing of the insurgency, see Sumit Ganguly, "Explaining the Kashmir Insurgency: Political Mobilization and Institutional Decay," *International Security* 21:2 (Autumn 1996), 76–107.

13. On this subject see Swami, *India, Pakistan, and the Secret Jihad.*

14. For a discussion see Sumit Ganguly, "Will Kashmir Stop India's Rise?" *Foreign Affairs* 85:4 (July/August 2006), 45–57.

15. For a complete discussion of the episode and its political context, see Mark Tully and Satish Jacob, *Amritsar: Mrs. Gandhi's Last Battle* (London: Jonathan Cape, 1985); also see Lieutenant-General K. S. Brar, *Operation Blue Star: The True Story* (New Delhi: UBSPD, 1993).

16. It should be noted that in both cases the military exercised restraint. In the first case the Indian authorities in the state, after much deliberation, chose not to deny the insurgents access to food or water, eschewed the use

of force, and granted safe passage. In the latter case, they offered safe passage and also avoided the use of force during a long siege. However, when faced with the imminent destruction of the shrine, they felt compelled to use force.

17. A prior episode at the mosque in December 1963, which had involved a theft of the sacred relic, had led to widespread rioting across the Kashmir Valley and had misled Pakistan's leaders into believing that the anti-Indian sentiments necessarily translated into support for Pakistan. For a detailed discussion, see Sumit Ganguly, "Deterrence Failure Revisited: The Indo-Pakistani Conflict of 1965," *Journal of Strategic Studies* 13:4 (December 1990), 77–93.

18. In India, thanks to the structure of civil–military relations, significant legal constraints exist on the deployment and use of the army in internal security operations. On this subject see Sumit Ganguly, "From the Defense of the Nation to Aid to the Civil: The Army in Contemporary India," *Journal of Asian and African Affairs* 26 (1991), 1–12.

19. Ironically, this decision, which had been made in haste after the self-styled Major Mast Gul made a series of highly provocative speeches, proved to have adverse consequences for the Indian military and the state. For a discussion, see Major-General Arjun Ray, *Kashmir Diary: Psychology of Militancy* (New Delhi: Manas Publications, 1997).

20. As a senior Indian military officer told the author, "We have little or no patience with foreign insurgents; we give them no quarter." Author's interview with a senior Indian army officer, New Delhi, December 2005.

21. For an early discussion of this subject, see Onkar Marwah, "New Delhi Confronts the Insurgents," *Orbis* 21:1 (1977), 353–73.

22. Ranjit Kumar Gupta, *The Crimson Agenda: Maoist Protest and Terror* (New Delhi: Wordsmiths, 2004).

23. Sarab Jit Singh, *Operation Black Thunder: An Eyewitness Account of Terrorism in Punjab* (New Delhi: Sage, 2002). According to another senior military source, Operation Black Thunder, which was carried out by the elite National Security Guards, proved to be a far superior operation because it was conducted in a transparent fashion with great attention toward minimizing civilian casualties. Author's personal correspondence with a former chief of staff of the Indian Army, February 2007.

24. Author's personal correspondence with a former chief of staff of the Indian Army, December 2006. Of course, how this principle is translated into operational doctrine on the ground during counterinsurgency operations depends in large measure on the officers involved.

25. A subsequent war took place in April–July 1999 near Kargil along the northern reaches of the state. The Indian literature on the Kargil war is substantial. See, for example, Praveen Swami, *The Kargil War* (New Delhi: Leftword Books, 1999); Major-General Ashok Krishna (Ret.) and P. R Chari, eds., *Kargil: The Tables Turned* (New Delhi: Manohar, 2001); Kanti Bajpai, Major-General Afsir Karim (Ret.), and Amitabh Mattoo, eds., *Kargil and After: Challenges for India's Policy* (New Delhi: Manohar, 2001). For the

version of the then chief of staff of the Indian Army, see General Ved Prakash Malik, *Kargil: From Surprise to Victory* (New Delhi: HarperCollins, 2006). For a complete discussion and analysis of the Indo-Pakistani wars including the Kargil war, see Ganguly, *Conflict Unending.*

26. On the 1971 war, see Robert Jackson, *South Asian Crisis: India, Pakistan and Bangladesh* (New York; Praeger, 1975); and Leo Rose and Richard Sisson, *War and Secession: Pakistan, India and the Creation of Bangladesh* (Berkeley: University of California Press, 1990).

27. Contrary to popular belief, India and Pakistan had originally agreed to abjure from the use of force to settle the Kashmir dispute in the 1966 Tashkent Agreement in the wake of the 1965 war. On this subject see Russell Brines, *The Indo-Pakistani Conflict* (New York: Pall Mall, 1968).

28. On this subject see S. Paul Kapur, *Dangerous Deterrent: Nuclear Weapons Proliferation and Conflict in South Asia* (Stanford, Cal.: Stanford University Press, 2007).

29. Ganguly, *The Crisis in Kashmir*; also see Victoria Schofield, *Kashmir in the Crossfire* (London: I. B. Tauris, 1996); Vernon Hewitt, *Kashmir: Reclaiming the Past? The Search for Political and Cultural Unity in Contemporary Jammu and Kashmir* (London: Portland Books, 1995); and Manoj Joshi, *The Lost Rebellion: Kashmir in the Nineties* (New Delhi: Penguin Books, 1999).

30. On this extremely fraught subject of Pakistani involvement in the Kashmir insurgency, see the detailed exposition in Swami, *India, Pakistan, and the Secret Jihad*; also see Daniel Byman, *Deadly Connections: States that Sponsor Terrorism* (Cambridge: Cambridge University, 2005).

31. For details of the differences among the various insurgent groups, see Manoj Joshi, *The Lost Rebellion.*

32. For a more detailed discussion of the significance of the mosque, see Sheikh Mohammed Abdullah, *The Flames of Chinar* (New Delhi: Viking, 1993).

33. For a discussion of the first Hazratbal crisis, see Ganguly, *Conflict Unending.*

34. Though originally designed precisely to secure India's borders in peacetime conditions, the BSF has been routinely used in counterinsurgency operations, especially in Kashmir. Since they were not trained for counter-insurgency operations, their performance in Kashmir and other counterin-surgency theaters has been uneven at best.

35. Arun Joshi, *Eyewitness Kashmir: Teetering on Nuclear War* (Singapore: Marshall Cavendish Academic, 2004).

36. For Habibullah's graphic first-person account of his attempts to negotiate an end to the crisis, see Wajahat Habibullah, "Siege: Hazratbal, Kashmir, 1993," *India Review* 1:3 (July 2002), 73–92.

37. Joshi, *The Lost Rebellion*, p. 259.

38. In Habibullah's judgment, this change in position hurt the negotiations. Subsequently, the Home Minister, S. B. Chavan, rescinded General Zaki's offer. See Habibullah, "Siege," p. 83.

39. Ved Marwah, *Uncivil Wars: Pathology of Terrorism in India* (New Delhi: HarperCollins, 1995).

40. Habibullah, "Siege," p. 90.

41. It should be noted at the outset that there is an asymmetry about the existing state of knowledge about what transpired at the Hazratbal mosque and the Charar-e-Sharief shrine. In the first case, thanks to its location, there is an enormous corpus of primary and secondary literature. This is not the case with the Charar episode. A handful of references to the Charar episode can be found in Marwah, *Uncivil Wars,* and Ray, *Kashmir Diary.*

42. Perhaps the best account of this transformation can be found in Swami, *India, Pakistan, and the Secret Jihad.*

43. On the ISI-D's complicity, see R. A. Davis, "Kashmir in the Balance," *International Defense Review* 4 (1991), 301–4.

44. Some accounts suggest that Gul was of Pakistani origin. His precise national origins are less important than the fact that he was definitely of non-Kashmiri stock. Joshi, *The Lost Rebellion,* suggests that he was from Pakistan.

45. Personal correspondence with a former chief of staff of the Indian Army, December 2006.

46. Personal correspondence with Lieutenant-General Vinayak Patankar, February 2007.

47. Personal correspondence on July 6, 2007, with Major-General Dipankar Banerjee.

48. Joshi, *The Lost Rebellion,* pp. 358–59.

49. The militants even alleged (and some newspapers reported) that Indian Army helicopters had sprayed the entire town and the shrine with some inflammatory substance before setting the shrine on fire. On this allegation see Ray, *Kashmir Diary,* p. 85.

50. Ganguly, *The Crisis in Kashmir,* p.126.

51. Scott Neuman, "India Shocked at Kashmir Battle," United Press International, May 11, 1995.

52. Personal correspondence with Major-General Dipankar Banerjee, December 2006.

53. Shiraz Sidhva, "Burning of Shrine Fuels Kashmir Turmoil," *The Financial Times,* May 12, 1995.

54. This problem of bureaucratic politics and the consequent problems of intelligence sharing is endemic in India. The civilian Intelligence Bureau (IB) is accountable to the Ministry of Home Affairs (MHA). The tensions between the IB and the Indian military are of long standing.

55. For an especially thoughtful account of the politicization of shrines in Kashmir and the attempts of the insurgents to attack them in order to inflame passions, see Praveen Swami, "The Shrine Wars," *Frontline,* 15:02, January 24–February 6, 1998.

4

The Battle for the Soul of Pakistan at Islamabad's Red Mosque

Manjeet S. Pardesi

From July 3 to July 11, 2007, the Pakistani security forces conducted a nine-day-long military operation against armed students, Islamists,[1] and *jihadi* groups who had taken control of Islamabad's Red Mosque (Lal Masjid) and its two madrassas, the Jamia Fareedia for men and the Jamia Hafsa for women. Codenamed "Operation Silence" and later renamed "Operation Sunrise," this military operation included elements of a siege as well as the offensive use of force against the armed insurgents inside the mosque complex.[2] The insurgents' stated aim was to destabilize President General Pervez Musharraf's government, which was seen as hostile to Islam and pro-American. They were calling for an Islamic revolution in Pakistan and the full establishment of Sharia law.[3] In the face of this "creeping Talibanization"[4] at the heart of Pakistan, national and international media called the military operation at the Red Mosque "the battle for the soul of Pakistan."[5] At the end of the military operation, the Pakistani security forces gained control of the mosque complex. According to official reports, close to 100 people were killed during the storming of the mosque by the Pakistani security forces.[6]

However, the Pakistani media claimed that Operation Sunrise had left "several hundred" people dead.[7]

In evaluating the Pakistani military action at the Red Mosque, this chapter will attempt to answer the following questions: Why had the insurgents occupied the Red Mosque? Were nonmilitary means used to defuse the situation? What role, if any, was played by the religious authorities to defuse the tension? When and how was the decision to deploy the military taken? What security forces were engaged in the campaign? How was the military campaign against the militants in the mosque conducted? How did the Pakistani government run its public relations campaign and manage the media during this operation? What groups were most sensitive to the military operations at the mosque? How did Pakistan manage these groups? And finally, what were the political consequences of this military action?

The next section briefly describes the role of Islam in contemporary Pakistan. This discussion is not intended to be exhaustive; rather, it will focus upon the rise of Islamist militant groups, especially those affiliated with the Deobandi school of thought and the nexus between the Establishment[8] and the Islamists in Pakistan. President and General Pervez Musharraf's support for Islamist groups will be an important feature of this section. The subsequent section discusses the growing Islamization of the Pakistani state and society, within which the occupation of the Red Mosque by armed insurgents took place. The conduct of Operation Sunrise and the recapture of the mosque complex by Pakistani security forces comprise the subject of the next section. In conclusion, this chapter argues that while Operation Sunrise was a success in military terms, its political consequences have contributed to Pakistan's ever-deepening instability and to Islamist militancy in the tribal belt and beyond. For reasons discussed herein, prospects are slim that Islamabad has the will or capability to address the structural context within which the events at the Red Mosque transpired.

Islam and Pakistan

Pakistan, the first modern state to be created as a homeland for Muslims (of South Asia), was founded at the end of British colonial rule in the Indian subcontinent in 1947 after the partition of British India.[9] The position of Islam there has been "sacrosanct though ambiguous" ever since the founding of the Pakistani state.[10] Every government of Pakistan has long instrumentalized Islam for a wide array of purposes as a politically expedient tool to enhance its power domestically and in the pursuit of its geopolitical goals abroad (especially in Afghanistan and Kashmir).[11] But no Pakistani government has shown any interest in establishing a theocratic state.

The Pakistani state has promoted Islam as a unifying ideology in the face of considerable ethnic, linguistic, and cultural diversity. Under the leadership of Mohammed Ali Jinnah, Pakistan's nationalist and secular elite began using Islam as a means for strengthening the country's national identity.[12] Islam was also viewed as being useful in promoting a distinct Pakistani identity vis-à-vis India. A perceived threat from India further deepened this ideological commitment to Islam. "Between them, the army, the Muslim League, regional and ethnic parties, the intelligence services, and Pakistan's scholars forged an Establishment view of the link between the state and Islam."[13] Islam became an acceptable ideology for nation-building in Pakistan.

After the loss of East Pakistan, which became Bangladesh in 1971, the emphasis on Islam for the unity of (West) Pakistan further increased, because it was believed that Islam was the only common ideology that could unify Pakistan's diverse ethnic, linguistic, and cultural communities.[14] Zulfiqar Ali Bhutto, who led Pakistan during the 1970s as president and then prime minister, advanced the idea of "Islamic socialism" and began to restructure Pakistan's political economy and society along Islamic lines.[15] While Bhutto began the process of Islamizing Pakistan by banning alcohol and declaring Ahmediyas to be non-Muslim, General Zia ul-Haq (1977–1988) aggressively accelerated this transformation. Not only did Zia enact a number of Islamic ordinances, he also introduced Islamic practices into the military.[16]

Given the centrality of Islam in Pakistan, every government has had to negotiate and compromise with Pakistan's Islamist political parties, theologians, and militant and other Islamist leaders. These negotiations and compromises arose out of the need to interpret and implement Shari'a law as it is variously construed (e.g., the Hudood Ordinance), to use Islamic concepts to organize Pakistan's political economy, and to instrumentalize Islam in the service of Pakistan's domestic and foreign policies. Pakistan has long relied upon Islamist and even militant groups to maintain its influence in the northern areas and along the Afghan border to dampen fissiparous ethnic aspirations (e.g., Baluch, Pashtun) and to promote its foreign policy goals in Afghanistan and Kashmir.[17] Pakistan has long hoped that the broader idea of Pakistan as a Muslim state in the subcontinent would provide sufficient common ground to overcome and subsume the subnational aspirations of Pakistan's numerous ethnic groups.[18]

However, Pakistan's dalliance with Islam and Islamists in the pursuit of its domestic and foreign policy agendas has come at a significant—albeit underestimated—cost. The Pakistani state now faces a typical principal-agent problem: the interests of the principal (the Pakistani state) and those of the Islamist groups that it has thus far supported (the agent) are not fully aligned.[19] This difference in some measure explains why Pakistan is now embattled by some of the very groups that the intelligence agencies and military groomed in the service of securing the state's interests in the past.

Islamists and Pakistan

As is well known, Pakistan is home to many militant organizations that operate—or have operated in the past—with relative impunity. This is true despite the state's various efforts to ban key groups since 2001 and the growing recognition that Islamist militancy is a critical threat to Pakistan's internal security. It is useful to differentiate these militants according to their political and religious objectives and their sectarian affiliation. Groups that have traditionally focused upon Kashmir include the Deobandi organizations Jaish-e-Mohammad (JeM), Harkat-ul-Ansar/Harkat-ul-Mujahideen (HuA/HuM), the Ahl-e-Hadith outfit Lashkar-e-Taiba (LeT), and several groups under the influence of the Jamaat-e-Islami (JI), including Al Badr and Hizbul Mujahideen. Several groups have traditionally been sectarian in nature, including the anti-Shi'a Lashkar-e-Jhangvi (LeJ) and Sipah-e-Sahaba Pakistan (SSP), both of which are under the sway of the Deobandi political party Jamiat-ul-Ulama-i-Islam (JUI). and are funded by wealthy Arab and Pakistani individuals and organizations. In the past there were also Shi'a sectarian groups which targeted Sunni Muslims and obtained funding from Iran. These groups have largely disappeared.[20] It is important to note, of course, that many of these Deobandi militant organizations have strong connections to the JUI.[21] Increasingly, Pakistani Islamist militants are self-referring as Taliban not only in Pakistan's tribal areas but also in the settled areas. The self-proclaimed Taliban supporters in Islamabad's Lal Masjid attest to the fact that Pakistan's self-acclaimed Taliban are not confined to the distant Pashtun belt.[22]

Pakistan is overwhelmingly Muslim (97 percent), and Sikhs, Hindus, and Christians comprise the remaining population. While there are no official or reliable data on the percentage of Pakistanis who ascribe to particular interpretative traditions of Islam, the majority are Sunni, with as many as 20 to 25 percent being Shi'a.[23] It is generally believed that Pakistanis are overwhelmingly Barelvi, a syncretic Sufi tradition. Deobandis (Hanafi adherents) are believed to be a minority in Pakistan; however, they control the majority of Pakistan's *madaris* (pl. of madrassah, or religious schools).[24] The Deobandis have gained widespread notoriety because this movement's madaris produced the Taliban and its leadership.

The key institution of the Deobandi movement was and remains the madrassa.[25] As a colonial revivalist movement, it advocated the purification of Islam from all alien influences and promoted a synthesis of orthodox Islam and classical Persian culture.[26] Initially the Deobandis did not seek an Islamic revolution nor were they serious contenders for political power.[27] However, they created the JUI in the 1920s and began supporting the Muslim League in their demand for a separate Muslim state on the subcontinent.[28] The JUI is a political party led by the *ulama,* who continue to remain actively engaged with Deobandi madrassas. In contemporary Pakistan there are two main factions of the JUI, one led by Maulana Fazlur Rehman and one by Samiul Haq.

As was noted above, there are several militant groups in Pakistan that espouse a wide and varied domestic and international agenda and that are under the sway of Deobandi madaris and the JUI (LeJ, SSP, JeM, and HuA/HuM).[29] However, distinction between these groups has become less clear in recent years as many of them have had "overlapping membership."[30] Although many of these organizations were cultivated by the Pakistani state, including the Inter-Services Intelligence (ISI), a number of them have splintered and some have developed their own sources of funding to pursue agendas with "total disregard" for Pakistan's national interests.[31]

Overview of the Establishment's Support for Islamist Organizations

The Pakistani Establishment began supporting Islamists in the early 1970s. In 1970–1971 the Pakistani army recruited militant Islamists to terrorize and murder Bengali intellectuals and politicians who were supporting the Bangladesh movement in East Pakistan.[32] At the same time, Islamabad also began recruiting militant Islamists to counter Pashtun nationalism in the regions along the Pakistan-Afghanistan border. Kabul had always contested the sanctity of the

Durand Line, which was negotiated by the British in 1893 and constitutes the border between Pakistan and Afghanistan.[33] (Notably Kabul's interpretation enjoys little support among legal scholars, who view the Durand line as the legal border.) The Pakistani state used the influence of Islamists to co-opt and displace ethnic Pashtun nationalism along its border regions with Afghanistan.[34]

Later, under General Zia, Islam was promoted in every aspect of Pakistani society and state. Islamism received a significant boost as a result of Zia's close partnership with Jamaat-e-Islami (JI), an Islamist party that was founded before independence in 1941, with independent chapters now in Pakistan, India, Kashmir, and Bangladesh. Under Zia, thousands of JI members were employed in the Pakistani judiciary, civil service, and other state institutions.[35] Despite its receptivity to electoral politics, the Pakistani JI's stated goals include an Islamic revolution in Pakistan and the imposition of Shari'a law, albeit from the grass roots up and through the processes of democracy. It further advocates the creation of a common Muslim defense arrangement to liberate all "occupied" lands such as Kashmir and Palestine.[36] JI has historically had close links with the Islamist officers of the military and intelligence services and remains one of the most important political and religious parties in Pakistan in terms of its organizational strength and its ability to wield street power in Pakistani towns and cities.[37]

General Zia's attempt to Islamize Pakistan as an explicitly Sunni state led to intense Shi'a resistance.[38] After 1979, with the onset of the Iranian Revolution and the Soviet occupation of Afghanistan, sectarian conflict and increasing Sunni militancy began to unfold in Pakistan.[39] In response to the Soviet invasion of Afghanistan in 1979, the United States along with Saudi Arabia and other international partners financed the *mujahideen* ("Soldiers of God") through Pakistan's ISI to combat the Soviets. Pakistan's ISI trained approximately 83,000 Afghan *mujahideen* between 1983 and 1997.[40]

After the Soviet withdrawal from Afghanistan in 1989, Pakistan redeployed battle-hardened *mujahideen* to Kashmir to exacerbate the indigenous uprising against New Delhi that began to unfold in 1980. Subsequently the infrastructure in Afghanistan to train *mujahideen* was exploited by Pakistan's intelligence services to train militants to fight in Indian-administered Kashmir.[41] Of notable importance for this analysis is the fact that General Zia had enjoyed a close relationship with Maulana Abdullah, the first *imam* of the Red Mosque, as a consequence of Abdullah's support for the *mujahideen* in Afghanistan in the 1980s as well as his anti-Shi'a agenda.[42]

Musharraf's Support for the Islamists

When General Musharraf assumed power as president of Pakistan in a military coup in 1999, he successfully portrayed himself as a moderate Muslim leader who was trying to break away from the legacy of Zia and who sought to bring to Pakistan and the Muslim world a philosophy of "enlightened moderation." However, the veteran Pakistani journalist Zahid Hussain has cogently argued that Musharraf's positions on a number of issues is contradictory.[43] Musharraf was a supporter of the militants operating in Kashmir, and he was the mastermind behind the 1999 Kargil War against India, which rent the concurrent Indo-Pakistan peace process under Prime Ministers Nawaz Sharif and Atal Bihari Vajpayee.[44] He also openly supported the *jihad* culture before the 9/11 terrorist attacks on the United States.[45] During a 1999 interview with Husain Haqqani, Musharraf reportedly explained his support for the Taliban.[46] While Musharraf joined America's "war on terror" against Al Qaeda and the Taliban regime in Afghanistan after the 9/11 attacks, he did so reluctantly and without an intention to fight militant Islam domestically.[47]

Under Musharraf, the historical relationship between the government, the military, religious political parties, madrassas, and the Islamists in Pakistan persisted despite his commitments to the war on terror. Musharraf's aversion to mainstream political parties that were led by former Prime Ministers Benazir Bhutto and Nawaz Sharif paved the way for the emergence of the Muttahida Majlis-e-Amal (MMA) in the 2002 general elections.[48] The MMA is an alliance of six major religious parties, including the JUI. It won power in two provinces in 2002, forming the government in NWFP and sharing power with the pro-military Pakistan Muslim League Quaid-i-Azam (PML-Q) in Baluchistan.[49] A small but important number of madaris run by the local and national leaders of the MMA provide a fertile ground for the recruitment of some kinds of Islamist militants—notably sectarian militants and suicide attackers.[50] The military has sustained an "alliance of expediency" with the Islamist leaders and their constituents to sustain support for the military's policy toward India.[51] Finally, support of the MMA had been essential in order for Musharraf to continue as both the army chief and the president of Pakistan, a situation that violates constitutional principles as well as the oath that all military officers take affirming their commitment to avoid any and all involvement in politics. The pro-Taliban JUI has also helped the center to mitigate the political power of Baluch nationalist parties, which espouse a separatist agenda.[52] As a consequence of this enduring complex set of relationships between the military, the "mullahcracy," and militant organizations, Islamization has affected many of Pakistan's governing institutions.[53]

In recent years the interests of the Pakistani state and some Islamists and militants have come into ever-sharpening conflict.[54] Some of Pakistan's militants and even Islamists want to transform the Pakistani state and society and impose a truly Islamic order.[55] But Pakistan's largely secular elite (including Musharraf) and the country's ordinary people do not wish to establish a theocracy even as they want Islam to play a role in public life.[56] The blowback from Pakistan's support for militant Islamists has begun to show its pernicious effects, including assassination attempts against Musharraf and other high-value civilian and military leaders.[57] There is now a widespread domestic gun culture in Pakistan with nearly five million small arms in circulation.[58] Recent years have witnessed a rise in domestic terrorism and religious violence in Pakistan, and Islamist groups are now active in all of Pakistan's provinces.

Pakistan's Creeping Talibanization

The Taliban and other insurgent and terrorist groups such as Al Qaeda and Hezb-i-Islami Gulbuddin (HIG) have strong support bases along Pakistan's border regions with Afghanistan.[59] Some elements of these groups moved into Pakistan's tribal belt when the United States began military operations in Afghanistan after the 9/11 terrorist attacks.[60] These groups use Pakistan as a base for recruitment and support. Controversially, some analysts have alleged that the ISI has been complicit in directly assisting them through either active or retired agents, although the open-source evidentiary basis for these aggressive claims is weak.[61]

Unfortunately, Musharraf's political requirement to rely upon the MMA, which enjoys political influence in parts of Baluchistan, the tribal belt, and NWFP, made it impossible for him to adopt a consistent policy against these militants and their sanctuaries. And in many cases the militants' ties to the area were historical and their political linkages to Pakistan's Islamist political parties long-standing. It is widely known that the Taliban emerged from the madaris run by the JUI, one of the principle members of the MMA.[62] Quetta in Baluchistan and Peshawar in NWFP host Taliban command and control centers despite the Pakistani military's dominance in these urban centers, a fact that has raised many questions about Pakistani intent and capability to target high-value Taliban assets.[63]

President Musharraf's close association with Washington and his inability to convince his people that this war is "their" war have generated considerable antipathy not only toward the United States, which is seen as co-opting Pakistan's sovereign leadership, but also toward Musharraf and his efforts to target militants in the tribal belt. The tribal leaders in North Waziristan challenged the Pakistani state by setting up a parallel administration there, implementing their own version of Shari'a law and collecting taxes from the local population.[64] In September 2006 the government of Pakistan entered into an agreement with the tribal leaders of North Waziristan,[65] ratifying Pakistan's military defeat and ceding numerous advantages to the "local Taliban" who were among the signatories of the deal. The Pakistani government agreed to discontinue its military operations in that region and promised to release roughly 165 militants incarcerated for attacks on the Pakistani military.[66] In return, the tribal leaders promised that the porous Pakistan-Afghanistan border would not be crossed for purposes of militancy. The agreement also prohibited the parallel administration set up by the tribal leaders. The tribal leaders further promised that members of Pakistan's security forces would not be targeted in Waziristan. The local Taliban broke this agreement almost as soon as it was put into force. Similar developments have spread throughout the tribal belt.[67]

Pakistani ineptitude in executing its military operations in the tribal belt have resulted in civilian casualties and diminished troop morale. Pakistan now confronts a Pashtun militant movement that self-identifies as Taliban and is spreading across the frontier area and adjacent settled areas. As a consequence:

> The new generation of militants are all Pakistanis: they emerged after the US invasion of Afghanistan and represent a revolt against the government's support for the US.... Their jihad is aimed not just at the "infidels occupying Afghanistan," but also the "infidels" who are ruling and running Pakistan and maintaining the secular values of the Pakistani society.[68]

Unfortunately Pakistan's "policy of appeasement" of militants and their political patrons has done little to stem Pakistan's creeping Talibanization.[69] Islamabad's strategy revolves around *containing* the militant Islamists as opposed to defeating them, perhaps because Islamabad still believes that these groups can be manipulated in the future in the pursuit of domestic and foreign policy goals.[70] Thus, as

Lisa Curtis has written, "The Red Mosque siege was a symptom of a larger problem of militancy, which is rooted in the Tribal Areas."[71]

The Road to the Red Mosque Crisis

The foundation stone for the Red Mosque was laid by Maulana Abdullah in 1965.[72] The Red Mosque complex is "state-run and state-funded."[73] President Ayub Khan had appointed Abdullah as the *imam* of the mosque.[74] Zia had rewarded Abdullah for his support for the *mujahideen* in Afghanistan in the 1980s by allotting him a prime sector of Islamabad to establish Jamia Fareedia.[75] In 1992, under the patronage of the ISI, Abdullah established the Jamia Hafsa adjacent to the mosque.[76] Jamia Hafsa is the largest religious school for women in the Muslim world, accommodating up to 9,000 students.[77]

Despite the apparent recency of the crisis, in fact the Red Mosque has a long-standing association with militancy. Abdullah, the Red Mosque's first leader, had met Osama bin Laden in 1998 and promised him to "continue his work inside Pakistan."[78] The Red Mosque's two madrassas have always attracted a large number of deeply conservative Islamic students from NWFP and the tribal areas, many of whom were sympathetic to *jihadi* and sectarian activism. Support for Al Qaeda and the Taliban has always been strong among the students at these madrassas.[79] Abdullah's sons and the leaders of the Red Mosque during the 2007 crisis, Maulana Abdul Aziz (the *khateeb*[80]) and his younger brother Abdul Rashid Ghazi, wanted to create a Taliban-style Islamic regime in Pakistan. They were extremely unhappy with what they regarded as western cultural influences in Pakistan and Musharraf's pro-America policies. According to Ghazi:

> After 9/11, Musharraf made an abrupt change in our policy that was not supported by the people of Pakistan. The attack on Afghanistan caused a lot of resentment, and in the name of war on terror many innocent people were killed. In the name of "enlightened moderation" vulgarity has been promoted—women running marathons, brothels, pornography in CD shops.... The system is the root of all the problems.... God willing, Islamic revolution will be the destiny of this nation.[81]

Ideologically, the Red Mosque and associated madaris are Deobandi institutions. After the Islamic revolution in Iran and during the Iran–Iraq War (1980–1988), Abdullah began promoting Sunni militancy against Shi'a groups in Pakistan. After the Soviet invasion of

Afghanistan, the Red Mosque also became a major "transit camp" for the *jihadis* and the *mujahideen* on their way to Afghanistan (and later into Indian Kashmir).[82] Abdullah was assassinated by Shi'a militants in October 1998 as a consequence of his support for Sunni militants against Pakistan's Shi'a minority.[83] After his death Abdul Aziz and Ghazi took control of the mosque and the religious schools. Initially Ghazi had shown no interest in religious affairs. Refusing to enroll at the Jamia Fareedia, he had obtained a Master's degree in International Relations from the secular Quaid-i-Azam University in Islamabad. He also worked for a while with the ministry of education in Islamabad and the United Nations Educational, Scientific, and Cultural Organization. He decided to join his brother as his deputy at the Red Mosque only after their father's assassination.[84]

In recent times, the first signs of militancy sponsored by the Red Mosque appeared in 2003 after the killing of Azam Tariq, the leader of the now banned SSP.[85] (The SSP was founded in 1985 with the goal of declaring the Shi'a as non-Muslims.[86]) The Red Mosque leadership organized riots in Islamabad after Tariq's death and ransacked cinemas, restaurants, and gas stations.[87] The two brothers also called Musharraf a "traitor" for cooperating with the United States after the 9/11 terrorist attacks.[88] After Pakistan's security forces began conducting military operations in the Federally Administered Tribal Areas (FATA) in 2002 in order to pursue members of Al Qaeda in that region, the Red Mosque issued an edict in 2004 that Pakistani military personnel who were slain fighting in FATA were not martyrs.[89]

However, Musharraf's government did not take any serious action against the Red Mosque clerics, although Abdul Aziz's status as the *khateeb* of the mosque was ended. A warrant against him was also issued, but it was never served. The brothers were allowed to carry on with their activities.[90] The Red Mosque also had close links with violent terrorist outfits in Pakistan, notably the JeM and the sectarian groups LeJ and SSP. After Musharraf had agreed to support the U.S. war on terror, Maulana Masood Azhar, the chief of JeM, called for Musharraf's assassination from the Red Mosque.[91] In 2004 Abdul Aziz and Ghazi were arrested on charges of plotting terrorist attacks after machine guns and explosives were found in Ghazi's car. However, after the intervention of the Pakistani minister for religious affairs, Ijaz-ul-Haq, General Zia's son, the brothers were pardoned.[92]

In part, the government's non-action was due to the Red Mosque's long-standing status as an ISI asset.[93] The Red Mosque had also enjoyed a close association with the MMA. As was described earlier,

Musharraf's government needed the support of the MMA for reasons related to domestic politics. The Red Mosque enjoyed close relations with JUI, the most important Deobandi party in Pakistan and a leading member of the MMA.[94] According to the head of the JUI, Fazl-ur Rehman, "We want to create an atmosphere where every Muslim abides by Islamic laws, enabling us to establish a true Islamic welfare state first within the frontier and then gradually in the whole country."[95] In 2007 Islamization spread out of the frontier regions and hit the Pakistani capital, Islamabad, under the leadership of the Red Mosque clerics.

In sum, the Red Mosque complex was associated with the Deobandi school of thought and had historically enjoyed close links with JUI, the main Deobandi political party. As a result of the role played by the Red Mosque leadership in the anti-Shi'a violence within Pakistan and its support for the Afghan and Kashmiri *mujahideen*, it has had robust ties with Deobandi militant groups such as LeJ, SSP, and JeM. While these Deobandi militant groups were once allies of the Pakistani state, they have now splintered to form new groups that have begun targeting the Pakistani state itself. The Red Mosque crisis and the Deobandi rebels afford an important instance of the reordering of alignment between the state and its erstwhile clients who have risen up against the Musharraf regime in recent years.

Islamization of Islamabad

In January 2007 the Red Mosque leadership demanded an immediate imposition of Shari'a law in Pakistan, after which Islamabad came under "mullah terror."[96] The mosque complex set up self-styled Taliban-vigilante groups to roam the streets and bazaars of Islamabad in order to impose their version of Islamic morality. These activities from the mosque complex that is barely a few kilometers from the ISI headquarters were allowed to continue in full view of the Islamabad police. The male students from Jamia Fareedia terrorized video shop owners after accusing them of spreading pornography.[97] Books, CDs, and DVDs were publicly burned on the streets of Islamabad. The women students from Jamia Hafsa attacked the city's massage parlors, accusing them of doubling as brothels. In a now famous incident, baton-wielding, burqa-clad women from the madrassa abducted three women in March 2007, including "Aunty Shamin," after accusing her of running a brothel.[98]

The Red Mosque leadership was threatened by the government's decision to demolish several mosques that were illegally built on government land.[99] In response, the Jamia Hafsa students illegally occupied a state-run children's library in Pakistan in January 2007.[100] In April 2007 Abdul Aziz announced that he was setting up a Shari'a court inside the Red Mosque. He also warned the Pakistani government that he would retaliate with suicide bombers if attacked by the Pakistani security forces.[101] He further added: "We will never permit dance and music in Pakistan. All those interested in such activities should shift to India. We are tired of waiting. It is Shari'a or martyrdom."[102] The Red Mosque clerics also issued a fatwa against Tourism Minister Nilofar Bakhtiyar after she was photographed hugging her skydiving instructor.[103] The students from the mosque complex then began abducting policemen.[104]

On July 3, 2007, the Red Mosque siege formally began when the paramilitary Rangers began to lay barbed wire around the mosque.[105] However, given the evolving litany of criminal behaviors that began long before July 2007, what was the triggering catalytic event? Why had the Pakistani state not responded sooner to the crisis in the Red Mosque that had been brewing for at least a few years? Why did the government react in early July 2007 by deploying the paramilitary Rangers followed by the army commandos? Why was a police action not contemplated sooner even as members of Islamabad's police forces were for several months being attacked and harassed by the Red Mosque brigade? These questions remain unanswered, though intelligent attempts to answer them can be made based on the available evidence.

In June 2007 the madrassa students raided a clinic and kidnapped nine people, including six Chinese women and one Chinese man.[106] The Pakistani government was under intense pressure from the Chinese government to protect its citizens living and working in Pakistan,[107] and after the abduction of the Chinese citizens, the government of Pakistan deployed the paramilitary Rangers around the mosque complex. After three Chinese men were killed and another injured when gunmen fired on them in Peshawar on July 8, 2007,[108] President Musharraf issued a "last warning" to the Red Mosque militants.[109] Because China is a close military and strategic ally of Pakistan, the Pakistani government was under tremendous pressure to act.[110] In Musharraf's address to the nation after the end of the military operations, he referred to China as Pakistan's "best friend" and said that the abduction of Chinese citizens was "a very shameful act."[111] In August 2007, immediately after the operation in the Red Mosque, the governments of Pakistan and China signed a pact to protect Chinese citizens from "extremists' attacks" in Pakistan.[112]

Thus the timing of the military action against the Red Mosque is closely linked to Chinese pressure.

It is perhaps more difficult to explain why a police action against the Red Mosque was not taken sooner. In part, the Red Mosque's close association with the ISI provides the answer. Furthermore, in a purely operational sense, the Pakistani police is "inadequately linked" with the ISI, the principal federal intelligence collection asset in the country. According to one report, "[T]he ISI frequently fails to disseminate operational intelligence to local officials but always expects free access to law enforcement information."[113] In the absence of adequate intelligence about the militants and their weapons and tactics, the Islamabad police would not have been able to carry out a successful offensive action against the Red Mosque. In fact, some reports indicate that Musharraf had kept the ISI away from the operation at the Red Mosque. The main intelligence support for this operation was provided by Military Intelligence, an organization separate from the ISI that specializes in counterinsurgency operations.[114]

Operation Sunrise

There is a lacuna in the security studies literature on military operations in sacred spaces. Hassner's study on counterinsurgency operations near sacred sites is a notable exception.[115] According to him, "[P]reventive and postaction measures taken by military commanders can have greater impact on the success of an operation than any attempts to constrain the actual use of force at a sacred site."[116] Hassner analyzed India's and Israel's counterinsurgency operations near sacred sites as well as America's experiences in Iraq and drew several guidelines for successfully conducting such operations:

1. A siege should always be the preferred option over offensive use of force. It is preferable to cut off electricity, food, and water supplies to starve out the militants. Negotiations should be an integral part of siege operations. Psychological warfare should also be built into military strategy. If the decision to use offensive military action against the sacred site is taken, it should be quick and decisive in order to cause as little damage to the site as possible.
2. Modern reconnaissance technology must be used to expose what the insurgents are doing inside the shrine (or any sacred space), especially if there is a huge cache of weapons or civilian hostages inside.

3. Public relations campaigns are important to the success of these operations. Involve religious leaders from the very beginning.

Judging by these guidelines, the Pakistani security forces implemented a successful military operation at the Red Mosque complex. As early as April, Musharraf had proposed an air strike on the mosque complex. However, Pakistani commanders were not in favor of such a strategy because of the mosque's proximity to populated areas, and so this proposal was rejected.[117] By the time the siege began on July 3, 2007, there were as many as 4,000 female students (many of them as young as five years old) who were being used as "human shields" to deter the government from using military force.[118] However, by this time some reports claimed that the army had already conducted an aerial surveillance of the mosque complex through unmanned aircraft equipped with GPS (global positioning system) technology.[119] (Despite these common reports, Pakistani army officials later denied such surveillance took place, claiming that Pakistan does not possess the assets described in the media accounts.[120])

There were 1,500 Rangers and 500 police commandos surrounding the mosque complex on July 3, 2007.[121] However, violence began unexpectedly that day when over a hundred students from the mosque complex stormed into a nearby government office and snatched a number of assault rifles and walkie-talkies from the policemen posted there. Ten people were killed in the clashes that followed, including a Ranger, a photojournalist, four students from the mosque complex, and four passers-by. A curfew was imposed late that evening in the areas surrounding the mosque complex.[122] After a meeting of the federal cabinet, power was cut off in the area and army troops from the Rawalpindi-based 111 Brigade were deployed around the mosque.[123] Commandos from Pakistan's elite Special Services Group (SSG) were also deployed.[124] The Red Mosque militants were believed to be equipped with Kalashnikovs, hand grenades, petrol bombs, tear-gas shells, other light weapons, special masks (to be used in the event of a gas attack), and wireless systems. In a TV interview from inside the mosque complex, Ghazi claimed to have enough weapons "to fight for 25 or 30 days."[125]

Beginning on the night of July 3, 2007, when members of the National Assembly from the religious groups attempted to talk the Red Mosque clerics into backing down, negotiations continued with different groups until late in the night on July 9, 2007, without any breakthrough. Several members of the Council of Islamic Ideology and *Wafakul Madaris* (the main grouping of religious seminaries), and even the *Imam-e-Kaaba*[126] talked in vain to the clerics and militants inside the mosque.[127] Throughout this period the Pakistani government kept up the psychological pressure on the militants by continually extending the deadline for negotiations while simultaneously continuing low-level firing against the mosque complex.[128] Ordinary citizens of Islamabad were appalled by the clerics' taking law and order into their own hands and imposing a Taliban-style situation in the heart of the capital city. The government thus secured support from the Pakistani media, which welcomed the armed security operation to put pressure on the militants.[129] Pakistan's Information Minister Muhammad Ali Durrani also called on political leaders, religious leaders, leaders of nongovernmental organizations, intellectuals, and the general public to put pressure on the militants to surrender.

The government deployed massive firepower around the mosque complex—machine- gun–mounted armored personnel carriers, trucks fitted with machine guns, and army gunship helicopters—to put pressure on the militants to surrender unconditionally.[130] This strategy worked to some degree as 1,100 men and women from inside the mosque complex surrendered unconditionally on July 4, 2007.[131] And in a particularly embarrassing moment for the militants, the *khateeb* of the mosque, Abdul Aziz, was caught trying to escape wearing a woman's burqa.[132] After the arrest of Abdul Aziz, his brother Ghazi took over as the leader of the mosque.[133]

Intense firing continued at the mosque complex over the next few days. On July 5, 2007, many members of the banned Jamaat-ud-Dawa (formerly known as Lashkar-i-Tayyaba) were captured among 60 fleeing students.[134] President Musharraf also announced a "general amnesty" for all except those guilty of criminal acts.[135] The security forces had created a 14-foot breach through controlled explosions in the outer wall of the mosque complex to enable willing students to escape.[136] Ghazi demanded a safe passage for himself and the militants (including several foreign militants from Central Asia) who remained in the mosque complex. However, the government demanded an "absolute, total, and unconditional" surrender.[137] On July 6, 2007, the Islamabad police took control of the Jamia Fareedia madrassa (located 5 kilometers away from the Red Mosque) and further cut off the gas supply to the mosque complex in order to mount pressure on the militants.[138] Over the next several days militants affiliated with Harkat-i-Jihad-i-Islami and JeM were captured in addition to those affiliated with Jamaat-ud-Dawa.[139]

On July 9, 2007, a day after three Chinese citizens were killed in Peshawar, President Musharraf presided over a high-level meeting in Islamabad. The attendees included Prime Minister Shaukat Aziz, former Prime Minister and politician Chaudhry Shujaat Hussain, Information Minister Durrani, Interior Minister Aftab Ahmad Khan Sherpao, Vice Chief of the Army Staff General Ahsan Saleem Hayat, Minister of State for Information Tariq Azim, Minister of State for Interior Zafar Iqbal Warraich, and officials from relevant security and intelligence agencies. All possible solutions to the Red Mosque standoff were considered. Musharraf wanted a quick and decisive operation with minimum casualties in the event of an assault on the mosque complex.[140] The assault on the mosque finally began in the early hours of July 10, 2007, after a failed attempt by Shujaat Hussain to negotiate a breakthrough with the militants the previous night.[141]

The objective of the operation was to clear the mosque complex of the militants. There were three major operational difficulties faced by the troops: (1) the issue of ensuring security for women and children, many of whom seemed to be held in the complex against their will; (2) the threat posed by well-armed militants who had put up a serious resistance; and (3) the difficulty of moving around the haphazardly built multistoreyed mosque complex. Security forces deployed in three layers[142]—the army (including the commandos from the SSG) at the forefront, the Rangers at the second line, and the police forces at the third—and stormed the mosque complex in a high-intensity, high-tempo operation that lasted about 36 hours and killed Ghazi.[143] There were at least two instances of suicide bombing by the militants inside the mosque complex in response to the assault by the security forces.[144] It was discovered that the militants also had ten Russian-made rocket-propelled grenades, antitank and antipersonnel mines, and two unexploded suicide vests in addition to the weapons they were believed to have possessed.[145]

The Pakistani media praised the government for showing "utmost restraint" in its use of force.[146] Musharraf claimed that the government had been able to save 3,300 people as a result of the restraint it showed.[147] At the end of the operation all the militants had been killed. The Jamia Hafsa was badly damaged, but the Red Mosque was in a comparatively better condition. The government decided to demolish the building of Jamia Hafsa and all illegal structures in the mosque complex.[148] The international community, led by the United States, supported the assault on the Red Mosque.[149] However, the Pakistani media complained that the government had withheld information on the civilian casualty toll.[150]

Conclusion

Judged from a purely military standpoint, Operation Sunrise was a success as the Pakistani military followed the guidelines spelled out by Hassner for the successful conduct of military operations in sacred spaces. The Pakistani government offered ample opportunity to the militants for a negotiated settlement while psychologically pressuring them through limited but continuous use of firepower. It involved religious as well as political leaders in its negotiations with the militants. The media was also well managed by the government and made constant appeals to the public at large to pressure the militants to surrender. The government employed the army (including its elite commandos from the SSG), the paramilitary Rangers, and the police forces to conduct the operations against the Red Mosque militants. The security forces began with a siege by cutting off the power supply and gas supply. From that point on, the government's response was calibrated. The security forces first captured Jamia Fareedia a few days before storming the Red Mosque and Jamia Hafsa. Abdul Aziz was arrested, and Ghazi was killed during the military operations. After the military action, the mosque complex was finally rid of the militants. And an important factor was that the central edifice of the Red Mosque stood relatively undamaged after the assault.

However, the structural conditions in the Pakistani polity that gave rise to the crisis at Red Mosque in the first place—the links between the Establishment and the Islamists—have not yet been severed. Pakistan has not yet begun to seriously debate the role of Islam in its society and politics. Soon after the end of the assault on the Red Mosque, Musharraf renewed military operations in FATA. However, Islamist militants have responded by taking several hundred Pakistani troops as prisoners and also retaliated with suicide bombing.[151]

The Red Mosque was temporarily reopened on July 27, 2007. Maulana Ashfaq, a government-appointed cleric, was put in charge of leading the prayers. However, angry protestors tried to reoccupy the mosque. A large number of them were in fact students from the seminaries. They barred the government-appointed cleric from leading the prayers and began calling for *jihad* and an Islamic revolution in Pakistan. They demanded that Abdul Aziz, the cleric who was caught trying to flee in a burqa, be brought back. The protestors also tried to repaint the mosque red; it had been painted beige by the authorities after the end of Operation Sunrise. In order to prevent the mosque from reoccupation, the police arrested dozens of students and also fired tear gas on the crowd of protestors. As the protestors clashed with the police, a suicide bomber killed at least thirteen people including seven police officers. Fortunately, the authorities were successful in preventing the occupation, and the mosque was closed on the same evening.[152]

Once the mosque was retaken by the authorities, they again repainted it beige.[153] In September 2007 hundreds of people staged a protest rally in Islamabad and demanded the reopening of the Red Mosque and the release of Abdul Aziz.[154] The Red Mosque was finally reopened on October 3, 2007, under orders from the Supreme Court.[155] Furthermore, it was handed back to its former management.[156] Given the unrest when the mosque was temporarily opened on July 27, 2007, it is not entirely clear why the Supreme Court issued these orders. It is entirely plausible that the judiciary was colluding with the leadership of the Red Mosque to defy Musharraf's authority. Musharraf's suspension of Pakistan's Chief Justice Iftikhar Chaudhry in March 2007 had created serious tensions between the country's judiciary and the army-led political leadership.[157] However, Chaudhry was reinstated in July 2007.[158] Significantly, the Supreme Court had made its decision after consultations with the Red Mosque leadership. Umme Hasan, the wife of Adul Aziz, had promised that the mosque would not be used for political activity.[159]

Maulana Ghaffar, a religious teacher at the Jamia Fareedia, was appointed the new *imam*, and Amir Siddique, a close relative of Umme Hasan, was made Ghaffar's deputy.[160] The Supreme Court further ordered that the mosque be repainted red and that the demolished women's seminary, Jamia Hafsa, be constructed within a year.[161] Unlike the July 27 reopening, the October 3 reopening was peaceful,[162] primarily because, unlike in July, the mosque was reopened under the leadership of its former management. In spite of its peaceful reopening, however, the bellicosity of the mosque's leadership and attendees remained unchanged. Their prayers called for an Islamic revolution in Pakistan, and the worshippers spoke about overthrowing the Musharraf government and replacing it with a Taliban-style government.[163] And more ominously, the crowd that turned out for prayers was significantly larger than the relatively modest size of the congregation before the siege.[164] Operation Sunrise seems to be providing a fertile ground for militant recruitment in Pakistan.

The Operation at the Red Mosque was also the precipitant for the suicide bombing at a military installation, Tarbela Ghazi, which killed more than a dozen SSG commandos, some of whom had been involved in the assault on the mosque.[165] Throughout FATA and adjacent Pashtun areas, mosques are being renamed "Lal Masjid" and madaris "Jamia Hafsa."[166] Finally, the frontier agencies have unilaterally withdrawn from the peace agreements that they had struck with the government in Islamabad.[167] The Talibanization of Pakistan is continuing, as is evidenced by its spread outside the tribal regions into the Swat Valley.[168] Al Qaeda's second in command, Ayman al-Zawahiri, has called for attacks on Pakistan in revenge for the assault on the Red Mosque.[169] Osama bin Laden has allegedly vowed to retaliate against the "infidel" Musharraf.[170]

While the Pakistani state achieved its military objective of ridding the Red Mosque of Islamist militants, it is clearly losing the war against militancy. Pakistan is losing the war arguably because the state has not decisively learned that militancy cannot be instrumentalized. This is the principal-agent problem facing the Pakistani state. Notably, while Musharraf was rounding up politicians, lawyers, and human rights activists under his newly declared state of emergency,[171] his government released two dozen militant Islamists out of jail. Among the militants released was Mullah Obaidullah Akhund, the highest-ranking Taliban official ever captured by Pakistan.[172] Even as the Pakistani military successfully conducted the operations at the Red Mosque, Islamabad seems to be ignoring Hassner's advice on taking post-action measures to prevent such incidents from occurring in the first place. No attempts have yet been made to break the links between the Establishment and the Islamists even as Talibanization is beginning to spread out of the frontier regions of Pakistan.

Notes

1. "Islamist" refers to groups that advocate Islamism. "Islamism... is a form of instrumentalization of Islam by individuals, groups, and organizations that pursue political objectives. It provides political responses to today's societal challenges by imagining a future, the foundations for which rest on reappropriated, reinvented concepts borrowed from the Islamic tradition." See Guilain Denoeux, "The Forgotten Swamp: Navigating Political Islam," *Middle East Policy* 9, no. 2 (June 2002) 61.

2. The military action was initially named "Operation Silence." However, at least partly because of embarrassing editorials claiming that the operation was intended to silence former ISI operatives, it was renamed "Operation Sunrise." Press reports "officially confirmed" that the operation conducted by the Special Services Group was codenamed

'Operation Sunrise.' See Qudssia Akhlaque, "It's 'Operation Sunrise' not 'Silence,'" *Dawn*, July 12, 2007. This study will use the purported official moniker "Operation Sunrise" to refer to the military action conducted by all the Pakistani security forces involved (including the Special Services Group).

3. William Dalrymple, "Days of Rage: Challenges for the Nation's Future," *The New Yorker*, July 23, 2007.

4. President Musharraf had referred to the Islamization of parts of Pakistan along the Afghan border as "creeping Talibanization." See Carlotta Gall and Ismail Khan, "A Taliban Ministate Arises in Pakistan," *International Herald Tribune*, December 11, 2006.

5. Zahid Hussain, "The Battle for the Soul of Pakistan," *Newsline*, July 2007; and Rageh Omaar, "Battle for Pakistan's Soul," *New Statesman*, July 12, 2007.

6. The military spokesman and the police spokesman gave conflicting casualty figures. According to the Inter-Services Public Relations chief, 11 army soldiers and 75 militants were killed, but the senior superintendent of police of Islamabad said that 11 soldiers and 91 militants were killed. See Syed Irfan Raza, "Charred Remains Speak of Fierce Battles," *Dawn*, July 13, 2007.

7. "Blow By Blow," *Newsline*, July 2007, p. 32.

8. The "Establishment" refers to the oligarchy comprising Pakistan's ruling elite. Its members include the senior ranks of the civilian and military state apparatus, key members of the judiciary, and other elites. See Stephen Philip Cohen, *The Idea of Pakistan* (New Delhi: Oxford University Press, 2005), pp. 68–73.

9. See Sugata Bose and Ayesha Jalal, *Modern South Asia: History, Culture, Political Economy*, 2nd ed. (London: Routledge, 2004), pp. 135–156.

10. Mandavi Mehta and Teresita C. Schaffer, "Islam in Pakistan: Unity and Contradictions" (A Report from the CSIS Project 'Pakistan's Future and U.S. Policy Options), October 7, 2002. www.csis.org.

11. Vali Nasr, "Islamic Extremism and Regional Conflict in South Asia," in Rafiq Dossani and Henry S.. Rowen, eds., *Prospects for Peace in South Asia* (Stanford, Cal.: Stanford University Press, 2005), pp. 19–36.

12. Husain Haqqani, "The Role of Islam in Pakistan's Future," *The Washington Quarterly* 28, no. 1 (Winter 2004–5), 89.

13. Cohen, *The Idea of Pakistan*, p. 167.

14. Bangladesh was created after India's military intervention in a civil war in East Pakistan. See Richard Sisson and Leo E. Rose, *War and Secession: Pakistan, India, and the Creation of Bangladesh* (Berkeley: University of California Press, 1990).

15. Anwar H. Syed, "Z. A. Bhutto's Self-Characterizations and Pakistani Political Culture," *Asian Survey* 18, no. 12 (Dec. 1978), 1250–66.

16. Charles H. Kennedy, "Islamization and Legal Reform in Pakistan, 1979–1989," *Pacific Affairs* 63, no. 1 (Spring 1990), 62–77.

17. Julian Schofield and Michael Zekulin, "Appraising the Threat of Islamist Take-Over in Pakistan" (Centre d'Études des politiques étrangères et de sécurité, Université du Québec à Montréal), March 2007. www.er.uqam.ca.

18. Schofield and Zekulin, "Appraising the Threat of Islamist Take-Over in Pakistan," p. 4.

19. Jessica Stern, "Pakistan's Jihad Culture," *Foreign Affairs* 79, no. 6 (Nov./Dec. 2000).

20. Since the onset of sanguinary sectarian violence in Iraq and Iran's 2006 victory in Lebanon, it has been suspected that Iran may once again be involved in inciting anti-Sunni violence in Pakistan. Indeed throughout 2007 Pakistan has seen a sharp increase in sectarian violence over that in 2006 or previous years. However, the overwhelming preponderance of those attacks have been perpetrated by anti-Shi'a militias. Thus the allegations of Iran's involvement are not supported empirically at this point.

21. Mariam Abou Zahab and Olivier Roy, *Islamist Networks: The Afghan-Pakistan Connection* (London: C. Hurst & Co., 2004), p 3.

22. See C. Christine Fair, "Militant Recruitment in Pakistan: Implications for Al-Qa'ida and Other Organizations," *Studies in Conflict and Terrorism* 27, no. 6 (2004), 489–504; C. Christine Fair, "The Educated Militants of Pakistan: Implications for Pakistan's Domestic Security," *Contemporary South Asia* 17, no. 1 (forthcoming Winter 2008).

23. The Pakistani census excludes the northern areas where many Shi'a live. Thus there are no exact numbers of Shi'a in Pakistan. The U.S. Central Intelligence Agency estimates that some 77 percent of Pakistanis are Sunni and 20 percent are Shi'a. See U.S. Central Intelligence Agency, *The World Factbook-Pakistan*, November 15, 2007. www.cia.gov.

24. For a number of reasons, it is difficult to know the precise counts of madaris in Pakistan. According to Tariq Rahman, in 2002 Deobandis accounted for some 7,000 out of 9,880 known madaris. See Tariq Rahman, "Madrassas: Religion, Poverty and the Potential for Violence in Pakistan," *IPRI Journal* 5, no. 1 (Winter 2005). ipripak.org/journal/winter2005/madrassas.shtml#_ftn14. Other estimates are much lower. The Institute of Policy Studies reports that in 2002, Deobandis controlled 1,947 of 6,761 known madaris, only slightly more than the 1,363 controlled by Barelvis. Institute of Policy Studies, *Religious Education in Pakistan* (Islamabad: IPS, 2002), p. 32. The Deobandi school of thought emerged in colonial India, in the town of Deoband to the northeast of Delhi, as a revivalist movement in reaction to British imperialism. Barbara D. Metcalf, *Islamic Revival in British India: Deoband 1860–1900* (Princeton, N.J.: Princeton University Press, 1982).

25. Barbara D. Metcalf, "Traditionalist' Islamic Activism: Deoband, Tablighis, and Talibs" (International. Institute for the Study of Islam in the Modern World, Leiden), 2002. www.isim.nl.

26. Oliver Roy, "Islamic Radicalism in Afghanistan and Pakistan" (UNHCR Emergency and Security Service, WriteNet Paper No. 06/2001), January 2002. ww.unhcr.org/publ/RSDCOI/3c6a3f7d2.pdf.

27. Hussain Haqqani, *Pakistan: Between the Mosque and the Military* (Washington, D.C.: Carnegie Endowment for International Peace, 2005), p. 151.

28. Initially the JUI was against the creation of Pakistan and threw their lot with the Indian National Congress. See Metcalf, "Traditionalist' Islamic Activism," p. 12.

29. For an account of the groups mentioned in this section, see "Terrorist and Extremist Groups of Pakistan" (South Asia Terrorism Portal, n.d.) www.satp.org.

30. Fair, "Militant Recruitment in Pakistan," p. 491.

31. C. Christine Fair and Peter Chalk, "Domestic Disputes: Pakistani Internal Security," *Georgetown Journal of International Affairs* 5, no. 2 (Summer/Fall 2004), 43.

32. Stephen P. Cohen, "The Jihadist Threat to Pakistan," *The Washington Quarterly* 26, no. 3 (Summer 2003), p. 15. However, it must be noted that much of the killing in East Pakistan was done by the Pakistani military itself.

33. The Durand Line divided the Pashtuns between Pakistan and Afghanistan. The NWFP and northern Baluchistan in Pakistan are dominated by the Pashtuns. On the Durand Line, see Tariq Mahmood, "The Durand Line: South Asia's Next Trouble Spot" (Monterey, Cal.: Master's Thesis, Naval Postgraduate School, 2005). www.ccc.nps.navy.mil.

34. Schofield and Zekulin, "Appraising the Threat of Islamist Take-Over in Pakistan," p. 4.

35. Owen Bennett Jones, *Pakistan: Eye of the Storm*, 2nd ed. (New Haven, Conn.: Yale Nota Bene, 2003), p. 17.

36. Jones, *Pakistan*, p. 6.

37. Cohen, *The Idea of Pakistan*, pp. 175–76. The Jamaat currently counts Lieutenant General Hamid Gul (former head of the Inter-Services Intelligence) and A. Q. Khan (a prominent scientist in Pakistan's nuclear program) as its members.

38. Metcalf, " 'Traditionalist' Islamic Activism," p. 13.

39. S V. R. Nasr, "The Rise of Sunni Militancy in Pakistan: The Changing Role of Islamism and the Ulama in Pakistani Politics," *Modern Asian Studies* 34, no. 1 (Feb. 2000), 139–80.

40. Sean P. Winchell, "Pakistan's ISI: The Invisible Government," *International Journal of Intelligence and Counterintelligence* 16, no. 3 (2003) 378.

41. On Pakistan's support for militants in Kashmir, see Daniel Byman, *Deadly Connections: States that Sponsor Terrorism* (New York: Cambridge University Press, 2005), pp. 155–85. On the insurgency in Kashmir, see Sumit Ganguly, *The Crisis in Kashmir: Portents of War, Hopes of Peace* (Cambridge: Cambridge University Press, 1997).

42. Hassan Abbas, "The Road to Lal Masjid and Its Aftermath," *Terrorism Monitor* 5, no. 14 (July 19, 2007) 5.

43. Zahid Hussain, *Frontline Pakistan: The Struggle with Militant Islam* (New York: Palgrave Macmillan, 2007).

44. On the Kargil War, see Shaukat Qadir, "An Analysis of the Kargil Conflict 1999," *RUSI Journal* 147, no. 2 (April 2002).

45. "Interview with Zahid Hussain" (Asia Source), March 20, 2007. www.asiasource.org.

46. Husain Haqqani,. Remarks at the Heritage Foundation, November 27, 2007.

47. "Interview with Zahid Hussain."

48. *Pakistan: The Mullahs and the Military* (Islamabad/Brussels: International Crisis Group, Asia Report No. 49, March 20, 2003, p. i.

49. The PML-Q strongly supports Musharraf at the center.

50. On the links between madrasas and militants, see C. Christine Fair, "Militant Recruitment in Pakistan: A New Look at the Militancy-Madrasah Connection," *Asia Policy* no. 4 (July 2007), pp. 107–34. On the links between the Taliban and MMA, see Magnus Norell, "The Taliban and the Muttahida Majlis-e-Amal (MMA)," *China and Eurasia Forum Quarterly* 5, no. 3 (2007), 70–1.

51. *Pakistan: The Mullahs and the Military*, p. ii.

52. *Elections, Democracy and Stability in Pakistan* (Brussels: International Crisis Group, Asia Report No. 137, July 31, 2007), p. i.

53. Cappelli argues that Pakistan suffers from abiding "structural pathologies." See Vanni Cappelli, "Containing Pakistan: Engaging the *Raja-Mandala* in South-Central Asia," *Orbis* 51, no. 1 (Winter 2007), 55–70.

54. Stern, "Pakistan's Jihad Culture."

55. "Factors Underlying Religious Extremism in Pakistan" (United States Institute of Peace, Special Report 89), July 2002. www.usip.org.

56. Cohen, *The Idea of Pakistan*, p. 168.

57. For details, see Schofield and Zekulin, "Appraising the Threat of Islamist Take-Over in Pakistan," p. 5.

58. Schofield and Zekulin, "Appraising the Threat of Islamist Take-Over in Pakistan," p. 5.

59. On Pakistan's support for the Taliban, Al Qaeda, and the HIG, and on the role played by the ISI, see Seth G. Jones, "Pakistan's Dangerous Game," *Survival* 49, no. 1 (Spring 2007), 15–32.

60. On America's military operations in Afghanistan, see Michael E. O'Hanlon, "A Flawed Masterpiece," *Foreign Affairs* 81, no. 3 (May–June 2002).

61. Jones, "Pakistan's Dangerous Game."

62. Metcalf, "Traditionalist' Islamic Activism."

63. Samina Ahmed, "Extremist Madrasas, Ghost Schools, and US Aid to Pakistan: Are We Making the Grade of 9/11 Commission Report Card?" (Testimony to the House of Representatives Subcommittee on National Security and Foreign Affairs, Committee on Oversight and Government Reform Hearing), May 9, 2007. Accessible via http://nationalsecurity.oversight.house.gov/documents/20070509164247.pdf (accessed: Oct. 22, 2007), p. 5.

64. Eric Sayers, "The Islamic Emirate of Waziristan and the Bajaur Tribal Region: The Strategic Threat of Terrorist Sanctuaries" (Center for Security Policy), February 2007. www.centerforsecuritypolicy.org.

65. For the details of this agreement, see Jan Cartwright, "Musharraf's Waziristan Deal: Shrewd Strategy or Tacit Surrender?" *South Asia Monitor* Issue 100, November 2006. This deal in Waziristan was the fourth of five similar deals. See C. Christine Fair, Nicholas Howenstein, and J. Alexander Their, "Troubles on the Pakistan-Afghanistan Border" (USIPeace Briefing), December 2006. www.usip.org.

66. There is now awareness in the United States for the need for an explanation behind an insufficient Pakistani military deployment north of the Khyber Pass. This is the region where high-value targets such as Gulbuddin Hekmatyar, Ayman al-Zawahiri, and Osama bin Laden are suspected to be hiding. See David O. Smith, "Facing Up to the Trust Deficit: The Key to an Enhanced US–Pakistan Defense Relationship," *Strategic Insights* 6, no. 4 (June 2007). www.ccc.nps.navy.mil.

67. See Hassan Abbas, "Increasing Talibanization in Pakistan's Seven Tribal Agencies," *Terrorism Monitor* 5, no. 18 (Sept. 27, 2007), 1–5.

68. Ziauddin Sardar, "Pakistan: The Taliban Takeover," *NewStatesman*, April 30, 2007.

69. *Pakistan's Tribal Areas: Appeasing the Militants* (Brussels: International Crisis Group, Asia Report No. 125, Dec. 11, 2006).

70. Sardar, "Pakistan."

71. Lisa A. Curtis, "Bolstering Pakistan in Its Fight Against Extremism" (WebMemo No. 1554, The Heritage Foundation), July 13, 2007. www.heritage.org.

72. Abbas, "The Road to Lal Masjid and Its Aftermath," p. 5.

73. Ahmed, "Extremist Madrasas," p. 2.

74. Abbas, "The Road to Lal Masjid and Its Aftermath," p. 5.

75. Abbas, "The Road to Lal Masjid and Its Aftermath," p. 5. Arab financing was also crucial in setting up this madrasa for men.

76. Abbas, "The Road to Lal Masjid and Its Aftermath," p. 5.

77. André Burstin, "Now that the Red Mosque has been taken, what does the future hold for Pakistan?" (Strategic Asia Online, European Strategic Intelligence & Security Center), July 16, 2007. www.esisc.org.

78. Omaar, "Battle for Pakistan's Soul."

79. Syed Shoaib Hasan, "Profile: Islamabad's Red Mosque" (BBC News), July 27, 2007. news.bbc.co.uk/2/hi/south_asia/6503477.stm.

80. A *khateeb* is a Muslim religious leader who delivers sermons during Friday prayers.

81. Quoted in Dalrymple, "Days of Rage."

82. Tariq Ali, "Pakistan at Sixty," *London Review of Books* 29, no. 19 (Oct. 4, 2007) 14.

83. Ali, "Pakistan at Sixty," p. 14.

84. Abbas, "The Road to Lal Masjid and Its Aftermath," p. 5.

85. Abbas, "The Road to Lal Masjid and Its Aftermath," p. 6.

86. Jones, *Pakistan*, p. 22. In 2002 the SSP was declared a terrorist organization and banned by Musharraf.

87. Abbas, "The Road to Lal Masjid and Its Aftermath," p. 6.

88. Ibid.

89. Ibid.; Curtis, "Bolstering Pakistan in Its Fight Against Extremism," p. 1.

90. Ali, "Pakistan at Sixty," p. 14.

91. Hasan, "Profile: Islamabad's Red Mosque."

92. Ali, "Pakistan at Sixty," p. 14.

93. The ISI was a strong supporter of the Red Mosque leadership and even provided the latter with funds. See Abbas, "The Road to Lal Masjid and Its Aftermath," p. 5. Also see Graham Usher, "Red Mosque: Endgame for Musharraf?" *The Nation*, July 19, 2007. www.thenation.com.

94. Burstin, "Now that the Red Mosque has been taken," p. 3.

95. Owais Tohid, "Pakistan's Frontier Passes Islamic Law, Rankling Islamabad," *The Christian Science Monitor*, June 10, 2003. www.csmonitor.com.

96. Ali, "Pakistan at Sixty," p. 14; Pervez Hoodbhoy, "Pakistan—The Threat from Within" (Pakistan Security Research Unit, Brief Number 13), May 23, 2007.spaces.brad.ac.uk:8080/download/attachments/748/Brief+number+13.pdf.

97. Hoodbhoy, "Pakistan," p.6.

98. The women were later released unharmed, but only after they were forced to admit that they had committed immoral acts. See "Pakistan 'Brothel Woman' Released" (BBC News), March 29, 2007. news.bbc.co.uk/2/hi/south_asia/6507205.stm.

99. Ali, "Pakistan at Sixty," p. 14.

100. Shahzad Malik, "Mosque Demolition: Girl Students Occupy Government Library," *Daily Times*, January 22, 2007.

101. Salman Masood, "Radical Pakistani Cleric Threatens Suicide Attacks in Capital," *The New York Times*, April 7, 2007.

102. Ali, "Pakistan at Sixty," p. 14.

103. Syed Irfan Raza, "Fatwa against Nilofar Issued," *Dawn*, April 9, 2007.

104. Kamran Haider, "Pakistani Religious Students Seize More Police" (Reuters), May 21, 2007. www.reuters.com.

105. Ali, "Pakistan at Sixty," p. 14.

106. "Hardline Pakistani Students Kidnap Chinese Women" (ABC News), June 23, 2007. www.abc.net.au.

107. "Punish Criminals, China Asks Sherpao: Kidnapping in Islamabad," *Dawn*, June 28, 2007.

108. Waseem Ahmad Shah, "3 Chinese Shot Dead in Peshawar," *Dawn*, July 9, 2007.

109. "Last Warning," *Dawn*, July 9, 2007.

110. See Robert G. Wirsing, "The Enemy of My Enemy: Pakistan's China Debate" (Asia-Pacific Center for Security Studies), December 2003. www.apcss.org. Also see Esther Pan, *China and Pakistan: A Deepening Bond* (Council on Foreign Relations), March 8, 2006. http://www.cfr.org.

111. "President Musharraf's address to the nation" (President of Pakistan), July 12, 2007. http://www.presidentofpakistan.gov.pk.

112. Li Xiaokun, "Pact with Pakistan to Protect Chinese," *China Daily*, August 8, 2007. www.chinadaily.com.cn.

113. Fair and Chalk, "Domestic Disputes," p. 44.

114. Roger Faligot, "Pakistan: The Hidden Side of the Attack on the Red Mosque" (Rue89), October 8, 2007. www.rue89.com. Rue89 is a news website set up by some former journalists of the French daily newspaper Libération.

115. Ron E. Hassner, "Fighting Insurgency on Sacred Ground," *The Washington Quarterly* 29, no. 2 (Spring 2006), 149–66.

116. Hassner, "Fighting Insurgency on Sacred Ground," p. 150.

117. Ayesha Siddiqa, "Pakistan: Between Military and Militants," *The World Today* 63, no. 4 (April 2007).

118. Hussain, "The Battle for the Soul of Pakistan."

119. Massoud Ansari, "Fight to the Finish," *Newsline*, July 2007.

120. C. Christine Fair interview with Maj-Gen Waheed Arshad, Director-General, Inter-Services Public Relations (ISPR) in Islamabad in July 2007.

121. Syed Irfan Raza, "Reinforcement around Lal Masjid," *Dawn*, July 3, 2007.

122. Syed Irfan Raza and Munawar Azeem, "Fierce Gunbattles Rock Capital," *Dawn*, July 4, 2007.

123. Ansari, "Fight to the Finish," p. 32.

124. A total of 164 SSG men took part in the operation. See Syed Irfan Raza and Khaleeq Kiani, "Resistance Wiped Out: ISPR," *Dawn*, July 12, 2007.

125. Ansari, "Fight to the Finish," p. 34.

126. The *Imam-e-Kaaba* is the leader of Islam's holiest shrine in Mecca, Saudi Arabia.

127. "President Musharraf's address to the nation," pp. 2–3.

128. Ansari, "Fight to the Finish," p. 34.

129. "Press Backs Tactics at Red Mosque" (BBC News), July 6, 2007. Accessible via http://news.bbc.co.uk/2/hi/south_asia/6276340.stm (accessed: October 22, 2007).

130. Umer Farooq, "Red Siege in Capital," *The Herald* 38, no. 7 (July 2007), 74.

131. Syed Irfan Raza, "1,100 Students Surrender," *Dawn*, July 5, 2007.

132. "Mosque Leader in Burka Escape Bid" (BBC News), July 4, 2007. Accessible via http://news.bbc.co.uk/2/hi/south_asia/6270626.stm (accessed: October 22, 2007).

133. Some analysts believe that while Ghazi may have been the public face of the leadership at the mosque complex after the arrest of his brother,

no single individual ran the show. The militants had probably formed a *shoora* (council) and decisions were being taken through consensus. See Ansari, "Fight to the Finish," p. 34.

134. Mohammad Asghar and Munawer Azeem, "Late-Night Round," *Dawn*, July 6, 2007.

135. "Musharraf Approves Amnesty for Lal Masjid Extremists" (Asia-News), July 6, 2007. http://www.asianews.it

136. This may also have been a preparation for an impending assault. See Syed Irfan Raza, "Besieged Cleric Seeks Passage," *Dawn*, July 6, 2007.

137. Raza, "Besieged Cleric Seeks Passage."

138. Raza, "Ghazi, Militants Vow to Fight till Bitter End."

139. "Who Are These Militants?" *Dawn*, July 9, 2007.

140. Ihtasham ul Haque, "President Asks for Ending Standoff Peacefully," *Dawn*, July 10, 2007.

141. Syed Irfan Raza and Munawer Azeem, "Breakthrough in Sight: Lal Masjid-Jamia Hafsa Standoff," *Dawn*, July 10, 2007.

142. Ansari, "Fight to the Finish," p. 32.

143. For the details of the objective, operational difficulties, and the killing of Ghazi, see Dawn Report, "It's All Over as Ghazi Is Killed," *Dawn*, July 11, 2007.

144. Syed Irfan Raza, "Charred Remains Speak of Fierce Battles," *Dawn*, July 13, 2007.

145. Raza, "Charred Remains Speak of Fierce Battles."

146. "A Gruesome End," *Dawn*, July 11, 2007.

147. "President Musharraf's address to the nation," p. 2.

148. Syed Irfan Raza and Mohammed Asghar, "All Illegal Structures to Be Raised: Lal Masjid," *Dawn*, July 11, 2007.

149. Anwar Iqbal, "Musharraf Gets a Pat from Bush," *Dawn*, July 12, 2007.

150. Syed Irfan Raza and Khaleeq Kiani, "Mystery Shrouds Exact Casualty Figures," *Dawn*, July 12, 2007.

151. "Volatile Pakistan: Future in Balance," *IISS Strategic Comments* 13, Issue 8 (Oct. 2007). Also see Andrew Buncombe, "Suicide Bombers Kill 48 in Red Mosque Backlash," *The Independent*, July 20, 2007.

152. On the events of July 27, 2007, see Salman Masood and David Rhode, "Suicide Attack and Protests over Red Mosque Reopening," *The New York Times*, July 28, 2007, and "Thirteen Dead in Red Mosque Blast" (BBC News), July 27, 2007. Accessible via http://news.bbc.co.uk/2/hi/south_asia/6918558.stm (accessed: December 3, 2007).

153. In fact, the mosque changed colors a number of times. See Syed Irfan Raza, "Lal Masjid to Turn Red after Eid," *Dawn*, October 14, 2007.

154. "Reopening of Lal Masjid Demanded," *Dawn*, September 15, 2007.

155. "Pakistan's Red Mosque Open Again" (BBC News), Oct. 3, 2007. Accessible via http://news.bbc.co.uk/1/hi/world/south_asia/7025477.stm (accessed: December 3, 2007).

156. Syed Irfan Raza and Iftikhar A. Khan, "Lal Masjid Goes Back To Former Clerics," *Dawn*, October 3, 2007.

157. "Pakistan's Top Judge Suspended" (BBC News), March 9, 2007. Accessible via http://news.bbc.co.uk/2/hi/south_asia/6434271.stm (accessed: December 3, 2007), and "Pakistan: Mission of Justice" (BBC News), May 31, 2007. Accessible via http://news.bbc.co.uk/2/hi/south_asia/6707377.stm (accessed: December 3, 2007).

158. "Pakistan's Top Judge Reinstated" (BBC News), July 20, 2007. Accessible via http://news.bbc.co.uk/2/hi/south_asia/6907685.stm (accessed: December 3, 2007).

159. "Pakistan's Red Mosque Open Again."

160. Raza and Khan, "Lal Masjid Goes Back to Former Clerics."

161. Ibid.:and Raza, "Lal Masjid to Turn Red after Eid."

162. Jeremy Page, "Survivors Defiant as Siege Mosque Reopens," *The Times*, October 4, 2007.

163. Griffe Witte, "Pakistan's Embattled Mosque Reopens with Fresh Momentum," *The Washington Post*, October 14, 2007.

164. Witte, "Pakistan's Embattled Mosque Reopens with Fresh Momentum."

165. Salman Masood and Ismail Khan, "Bomb in Pakistan Kills at Least 15 from Elite Unit," *The New York Times*, September 14, 2007.

166. For an example, see Rahimullah Yusufzai, "Accord and Discord," *Newsline*, August 2007.

167. On these developments in Pakistan after the assault on the Red Mosque, see Daniel Markey, "The Summer of Pakistan's Discontent" (Foreign Affairs Web Exclusive), September 20, 2007. www.foreignaffairs.org.

168. Yassin Musharbash, "The Talibanization of Pakistan: Islamists Destroy Buddha Statue" (Spiegel Online International), November 8, 2007. www.spiegel.de.

169. "Al Qaeda Issues Pakistan Threat" (BBC News), July 11, 2007. news.bbc.co.uk. Some reports indicate that Zawahiri was secretly directing the Islamic militants in the Red Mosque. See Dean Nelson and Ghulam Hasnain, "Bin Laden's Deputy Behind the Red Mosque Bloodbath," *The Sunday Times*, July 15, 2007. www.timesonline.co.uk.

170. "Bin Laden Vows Revenge on 'Infidel' Musharraf" (Reuters), September 20, 2007. www.alertnet.org. However, the authenticity of this message could not be established.

171. Musharraf declared emergency on November 3, 2007, after suspending the constitution and firing the country's chief justice. See Griff Witte, "Musharraf Declares Emergency Rule in Pakistan," *The Washington Post*, November 4, 2007.

172. Sami Yuusafzai and Ron Moreau, "While Pakistan Burns," *Newsweek*, November 9, 2007. www.newsweek.com.

5

Fighting for the Holy Mosque

The 1979 Mecca Insurgency

Pascal Ménoret

Some insurrections end with the defeat of all the parties involved, even if the government and its security forces eventually manage to pacify them. By striking at the core of a political system, some insurgents may successfully reveal the government's weakness or injustice or contradictions, should they be eliminated during the state's counterinsurgency operations. Juhayman al-'Utaybi's famous 1979 occupation of the Mecca Grand Mosque, the most sacred space in Islam, was an insurrection with such ambiguous outcomes. While the Saudi security forces, with the help of Western experts, ousted the insurgents from the shrine, they imperiled the legitimacy of the state's political rule by undermining its religious credentials. Over the longer term, the insurgents clearly opened a path of religious and political rebellion that persists to this date, with many Islamic groups in the Arabian Peninsula still—consciously or unconsciously—holding a part of Juhayman's heritage. Juhayman's deconstruction of the Islamic legitimacy of the state has survived the 1980 repression and become a durable motto of popular Islamist agitation. The Mecca events later provided a subject of mourning for Al Qaeda ideologues and militants: "I still remember the bulldozer's tracks on the paving stone of the Grand Mosque," Osama bin Laden claimed in a December 2004 speech.[1]

This chapter retraces the history of the 1979 Mecca insurgency, focusing on several questions, including: who were the insurgents and why did they occupy the Mecca Grand Mosque? How did the Saudi government and its political leadership react to the insurgency? What strategies were adopted by the security forces, and how did they eventually end the occupation of the Grand Mosque? Finally, what was the outcome of the rebellion, the siege of the Grand Mosque, and the security forces' operation to pacify the mosque?

This chapter explores these queries in five parts. It first examines the history of Juhayman's movement, "The Salafi Group that commands virtue and combats sin," from its creation as a semi-official body in 1965 to the first signs of secession between its political wing, headed by Juhayman, and a pietistic minority. Second, the chapter details the open confrontation of Juhayman's followers with the Saudi authorities and the ensuing crackdown in 1976–1978. These efforts to repress the movement appear to have further radicalized it, since its violent millenarianism can be traced from that point. The third section analyzes the group's strategy and exposes why insurgents sought to occupy the Grand Mosque. The fourth section analyzes the counterinsurgency operations, which spanned two weeks from November 20 to December 4, 1979. Finally, the chapter details the ways in which the insurgency revealed the weaknesses of a government whose military and media strategies decisively failed.

The Salafi Group That Commands Virtue and Combats Sin: 1965–1976

The group that took over the Mecca Grand Mosque under the leadership of Juhayman al-'Utaybi was in fact a part of a more inclusive Islamic group that emerged in 1965 in association with Medina's Islamic educational institutions. The Islamic University of Medina was created in 1961 by Sheikh Muhammad bin Ibrahim Al al-Shaykh, then head of the Saudi official religious institution. It soon attracted professors and students from every corner of the Islamic world. Together with the influx of rural immigrants from within the country, the presence of several activist groups and figures around the newly created Saudi Islamic institutions[2] radically changed the Saudi religious and political landscape over the following decades. The creation of Juhayman's group was hastened by an incident that occurred in 1965. Young Islamic activists, most of whom were students at the Islamic University, regularly preached to their fellow citizens against well-established local practices such as Sufism, the visit of tombs, and other practices that they deemed heterodox innovations. Driven ostensibly by their religious zeal, on several occasions they broke shop windows to remove the mannequins and photos that they saw as forbidden. During one such incident in 1965 some citizens of Medina defended their property against the vigilantes. A larger conflagration ensued and the police arrested several students and deported non-Saudi activists.

In response to this breakdown, six young men, five of them from a Tablighi[3] background and the sixth a Muslim Brother, set up a proselytizing group that would advocate for religious purity with the benediction of the state.[4] Their leader, Juhayman al-'Utaybi, had worked in the Saudi National Guard prior to devoting his life to religious studies. The group was soon officially acknowledged by the sheikh 'Abd al-'Aziz bin Baz[5] (one of the leading Saudi *'ulama*, or religious scholars), who declared the movement to be the "Predication Group that commands virtue and combats sin" (*Jama'a ad-da'wa al-muhtasiba*).[6] Other sources suggest it was bestowed the title "The Salafi Group that commands virtue and combats sin" (*al-Jama'a as-salafiyya al-muhtasiba*).[7] Its members would simply call themselves the "Brethren" (*al-Ikhwan*). The group based itself in and around the holy sanctuaries of Mecca and Medina and in the educational institutions that prepared pupils for the Islamic universities. It attracted mainly Bedouin Saudi youth who had recently arrived at the urban areas as well as young pilgrims who decided to stay in Saudi Arabia. Egyptians, Yemenis, Syrians, Palestinians, and even African-American Muslims joined the group. They forged connections with some of the most radical Islamist movements of the time, such as the Egyptian "Muslims group" (*Jama'at al-Muslimin*) and "Islamic groups" (*al-Jama'at al-Islamiyya*).[8] The group soon founded branches in important Saudi cities, including Riyadh and Jeddah, and may have gathered several hundred followers throughout the 1970s. Although limited in number, Juhayman's followers gained nationwide celebrity status after their first experience in jail in 1978, which will be discussed below.

Juhayman's group was doctrinally Salafist and its members sought to return to the practices of the three first generations of Muslims (the "predecessors" or *as-salaf*) in their beliefs and daily life. It is worth noting here that Salafism is not in itself a political doctrine but rather a moral and juridical methodology. Therefore it may be conservative as well as contentious. In Saudi Arabia the official religious institution may be described as having adopted a conservative and apolitical Salafism, whereas some opposition groups adopted a more or less revolutionary Salafism. What is particularly interesting in this case is that Juhayman's group moved from a politically quietist toward a more rebellious stance, contesting in 1979 the very institutions that had recognized its existence some 14 years earlier.

Before resorting to underground and violent activities, the Brethren adopted ideas and religious practices that became tantamount to Islamic activism during the 1980s, most notably the way they emphasized *Hadith* (sayings of the Prophet; Hadith, along with the *Sira* [biography of the Prophet] and the Koran, form the basis of Shari'a [Islamic law]). While the Koran is a stable set of texts, the Hadith is a highly historicized collection of sayings, hence the Salafis' interest in its critique and edition. The most famous of the Brethren's religious references was the sheikh Muhammad Nasir ad-Din al-Albani,[9] who introduced into the everyday life of the believers the critique of *Hadith* that had once been limited to small coteries of jurists. According to Nasir al-Huzaymi, who was a member of the Brethren in the late 1970s:

> These views were totally new for the public.... You could hardly find a sheikh mastering the edition and critique of the Hadith.... The Brethren had broken the obstacle of respectful fear between the mufti and the believer. They had made the legal science—which was the monopoly of the sheikhs and the students of religion—popular. They instilled in the masses the spirit of religious controversy.[10]

This direct experience of the sacred text is partly responsible for bringing the Brethren to their textual and later political[11] adventurism. Young people could well be fascinated by the "adventure of students of religion...who could leave their town for one *Hadith*'s sake, just one! And who travelled in foreign lands to hear it from the mouth of a narrator."[12] Yet the real adventure was the questioning of religious and political authority through one of its foundations: the *Hadith*. Compared with the juridical sclerosis of the official religious institution, this "critique of well-known *Hadith*'s that were considered to be genuine"[13] was seen as a novelty and a revival of religious norms.

This theoretical straightforwardness soon led the group to radically question the very principles of power in the Saudi kingdom. Juhayman's argument against the ruling family was derived from his familiarity with *Hadith* and the very set of religious texts used by the Saudi dynasty to legitimize its power. According to Juhayman, the main sin of the Al Saud family had been to "take the allegiance of the people, not by the hand and the heart, freely and by choice, but by force and constraint."[14] While the allegiance to the Al Saud family was thought to be the cornerstone of the state–society relationship, it had little religious value because it was imposed upon the Saudi people and not freely chosen by them in a public oath of allegiance. The simplicity and readability of the argument proved highly effective.

The clear-cut Salafi doctrine of Juhayman's supporters appealed to young people, most notably those from genuine Bedouin or recently settled backgrounds. "The group was dominated by the Bedouin element," not only in terms of social composition, but even in its worldview. "Their speech was one of confrontation between the city and the Bedouins."[15] Juhayman's tribe, 'Utayba, is one of the most important Bedouin confederations of Saudi Arabia, and it is characterized by its tumultuous relationship with the sedentary Al Saud elite. 'Utayba became famous through its participation in the first "Ikhwan"[16] movement, created by the Saudi government. This "Ikhwan movement" was essentially a Bedouin army that the founder of the Saudi kingdom, 'Abd al-'Aziz Al Saud ("Ibn Saud"), formed in the 1910s to conquer the Arabian Peninsula. In the 1920s the first Ikhwan rebelled against the many ties between the Saudi princes and the British colonial power.

Juhayman, who was born in the 1930s in the Ikhwan settlement of Sajir, was deeply impressed by the "rebellious environment" in which he was raised.[17] Yet his movement cannot be analyzed as a mere extension of the 1910s and 1920s Ikhwan, which was an army combating for the throne's sake, whereas the Brethren were religious students struggling in the path of God. The tribal and Bedouin nature of Juhayman's movement nevertheless explains some aspects of its radical views of the Saudi state. In a social and economic environment undermined by anarchic modernization and an unfair distribution of newly generated wealth, such a conspicuously Bedouin and religious worldview appealed to many perplexed youth who "entered in rebellion while entering the group."[18]

Scission within the Group and Confrontation with the Government: 1976–1979

The Brethren soon criticized and verbally opposed all other religious groups or interpretative schools, and the Brethren's Mecca branch turned the Grand Mosque into a theoretical and religious battlefield.

Nasir al-Huzaymi recalls how he and his comrades once opposed an aged Iranian sheikh who was reading and criticizing the Bible with his students. In the young Salafis' eyes, the very presence of the Jews' and Christians' holy book was a reason for sedition: "We were mere adolescents. He was an old man whose Arabic was better than ours, he spoke six languages, had several PhDs.... But we made such a noise at the shrine's administration that they banned him from teaching."[19] Yet the policing of the holy shrine was not always in their favor: one of the group's sheikhs was once summoned by the administration because of his rough manners:

> [They] forbade the sheikh to teach us Ibn Hazm's book.[20]...Ibn Hazm was violently attacking the four schools of jurisprudence, most notably the Hanafi School. And next to the sheikh's group of students, in the Great Mosque, there was a group...studying the Hanafi method. Our sheikh was raising his voice in order to be heard by them.... He told us once: "Look at these faggots: they leave our Prophet's *Hadith* for man-made opinions!" Of course, the other students complained to the sheikh Muhammad bin Subayyil, who was in charge of the Religious Affairs in the shrine.... Our sheikh was soon summoned and asked to moderate his language.[21]

Because of its intransigence, the Brethren's religious positions on several points of Islamic jurisprudence are often labeled as resorting to an "extreme social conservatism and...a 'rejectionist' attitude toward many aspects of modernity."[22] Yet these very points either had to do with ahistorical details of ritual practice, such as the prayer call or the legal condition of fasting during Ramadan, or were related to the group's refusal of everything connected with the Saudi government (the group banned ID cards and passports, refused public jobs such as teaching or serving in the military, etc.). Matters of ritual and rejection of the Saudi state do not signal any social conservatism or an antimodern attitude. Juhayman's followers probably never intended to oppose modernity or even thought of doing so; rather, they saw themselves opposing the traditional and well-known ways of practicing one's Islam, and they heavily criticized the Saudi state for having rendered religion into a mere means of regime legitimization. One may even say that the gesture of the Brethren is in itself very "modern" in that it sought to return to the text, to the pure norm, beyond accumulated and historical traditions. Al-Rasheed thus sees in Juhayman's movement a "part and parcel of the material modernization of the 1970s. It was a political awakening drawing on religious rhetoric."[23]

It is because of this political aggressiveness that in 1976 the Brethren entered the most troubled period of its history. Three years before the Mecca event, a schism developed among members of the group: Juhayman wanted to openly oppose the government and the ruling family while others were eager to integrate the group into the official religious institutions.[24] The group's capacity for mobilizing a transnational youth movement and forging networks around a rigorous set of practices and doctrines had already drawn the attention of the religious and academic authorities in Mecca and Medina. Its political activism had already discomfited the civil authorities, who narrowly monitored the group, and they asked the Medinan sheikhs to put an end to their sedition. The Medinan sheikhs called a meeting in the group's house and asked the Brethren to renounce many of their heterodox positions. A majority of Brethren followed Juhayman, whose popularity deepened after he refused to submit to the official scholars and government sheikhs. After the Medina meeting, Juhayman, who was already

> managing the collective action and the ideas of the group,... intensified his speeches against the state and the civil servants: it became ominous to belong to the Brethren and to work for the state. These anti-government views encompassed the studies in public schools.... That is why some adolescents who had run away from home joined the group.[25]

In the immediate aftermath of this rift, some Medinan sheikhs accused Juhayman's group of having weapons. The authorities were eager to end the group's activities and jailed many Brethren, yet they failed to capture Juhayman. The repression failed on three fronts. First, it further politicized the Brethren, who soon adopted the singular goal of openly confronting the state. Second, it conferred to the Brethren a revolutionary aura: "jail had turned them into heroes and had magnetised the Islamic public,"[26] which helped them attract new adherents. Third, the repression forced the Brethren to resort to clandestine activities, driving them to the desert and beyond the state's monitoring capacity.

It is in this heated climate that Juhayman distributed the first of his famous *Letters*, which was printed in Kuwait by a leftist publisher and smuggled into Saudi Arabia through Juhayman's Bedouin networks.[27] The Brethren distributed it during Ramadan in 1978 in several towns, including Mecca. In the holy city it was a rehearsal of the insurrection: the Brethren occupied cells in the basement of the Grand Mosque before the dawn prayer and distributed the letter after the last prostration.[28] During their two years in the desert, the

Brethren had been trained in the use of weapons, which they gathered through their familial and tribal links to many National Guards. The desert, as well as the two holy shrines and the Islamic universities and institutes, had been turned into a resource for contention.

Why Did the Insurgents Choose the Grand Mosque?

The Mecca Grand Mosque (*al-masjid al-haram*) is unanimously recognized in the Islamic world as the most sacred of spaces. Located in a valley near the big port city of Jeddah, it is surrounded by a zone exclusively reserved for Muslims. Non-Muslims traveling by land from Jeddah to Riyadh have to go round it through the so-called "Non-Muslims Road," which does not cross the Haram (forbidden, sacred zone). The sacred nature of the Grand Mosque is a fact of revelation and is embodied in several key rituals: In the middle of the mosque yard, the *Ka'ba* is the direction toward which Muslims pray worldwide, and the pilgrimage to Mecca is one of Islam's Five Pillars. The Grand Mosque has been built, destroyed, and rebuilt many times, most recently in 1955–1973 and 1982, when the Saudi government ordered two huge extensions of the building. Annexed in 1925 to the Saudi realm, Mecca and its province are central to the Saudi modern identity, and the state has imposed upon its subjects a teleological reading of history that places the current dynasty within the sacred history of revelation itself. The so-called Saudi exception (*al-khususiyya as-Sa'ûdiyya*), which is the ideological backbone of the regime, has its discursive origin in the very presence of the two holy shrines on Saudi land. The state's official discourse extends this sacredness to the ruling family as well.

Since 1925, the Grand Mosque has been at the crossroad between the multiform and transnational history of Islam, on the one hand, and the will of power of the newly created Saudi national state, on the other. This situation makes the Grand Mosque a highly symbolic and controversial place, subject to many political and religious demonstrations.[29] Yet the Koran explicitly bans any manifestation of violence in the mosque and prohibits any fight other than defensive: "And fight them not at the Holy Mosque unless they first fight you there, but if they fight you, slay them. Such is the reward of the disbelievers" (Koran, 2:19). Even though Juhayman's followers knew the verse very well, they decided to risk their religious credentials: they could eventually appear as the group that had occupied and therefore desecrated the Grand Mosque. If the shrine could be a formidable tribune for the group's opposition to the royal family, the

Koranic verse could become a trap if the insurgents were the first to open fire, shed blood, or use their weapons in any way. The state propaganda would stress this point in order to criminalize the movement and thus justify a violent repression.

Yet the insurgents' choice of the Grand Mosque was first due to religious considerations. In 1979, during the last months of the fourteenth century of Hegira, the Brethren adopted millenarian ideas that allowed them both to accept the state's corruption ("corruption increases at the end of time"[30]) and to rebel against it (at the end of time comes the Messiah who wins over the tyrants). They eventually recognized one of them, Muhammad bin 'Abd Allah al-Qahtani, as the "awaited Messiah." At the end of time, according to the *Hadith*, the believers will swear allegiance to the awaited Messiah in the Mecca Grand Mosque, "between the *Rukn* and the *Maqam*."[31] This oath will eventually lead to the defeat of the tyrants and their army, the return of Jesus Christ, and the Judgment day. The occupation of the Grand Mosque was a goal imposed by the group's "dream" and religious "enthusiasm" rather than by the "methods of modern armed rebellion movements."[32] They believed the shrine to be a space whose rightful and ritual occupation could accelerate history and bring the world—and therefore the Al Saud rule—to its end.

On the early morning of November 20, 1979, several hundred supporters of Juhayman entered the Mecca Grand Mosque with their wives and children while chanting, "Allahu akbar! Allahu akbar!" (God is the greatest!). They closed the mosque's doors and, at the end of the dawn prayer, one of them, Khalid al-Iami, grabbed the microphone from the hands of the *imam*, the shaykh Muhammad bin Subayyil,[33] and asked for the abolition of the Al Saud monarchy. Al-Iami accused the royal family of compelling the Saudis to make allegiance, thus making their submission religiously invalid. He asked for the abolition of the Saudi monarchy and the severing of the military and diplomatic ties with the United States as well as the expulsion of Western experts. He denounced the moral and financial corruption of the princes. He asked for a strict application of Shari'a. He ended up introducing to the believers and pilgrims the awaited Messiah.[34]

It is difficult to interpret the event from a rationalist and univocal perspective. Every insurgent entered the Mecca sanctuary with his own motivation, be it millenarian, political, tribal, or the allure of Juhayman's charisma. There is no evidence that they functionally analyzed the sacred space as a resource they would mobilize and instrumentalize against the state. Rather, they *knew* that they had to go there, partly because the *Hadith* was urging them to do so and partly because they had lived many years in Mecca and Medina and therefore found it easier to defy the state from what they perceived as being their own space.

Juhayman's followers occupied the Grand Mosque partly because it was a place where they had gained "spatial routines" and that they had transformed through their "spatial agency."[35] Their intimate knowledge of the mosque is one of the main reasons why they thought it natural to oppose the Saudi government in this, and no other, place. As al-Huzaymi put it:

> There were a great number of cells in the basement of the mosque, which the worshippers used to retire, pray or rest. The Brethren knew every single corner of the basement and this knowledge was to prove very useful to Juhayman during the takeover of the Grand Mosque. I was even sleeping there, except when it was forbidden to stay in the mosque because of the flood that broke from the heights of Mecca and concentrated on the lowest point, where the mosque was built. Despite the drains, the water was sometimes flooding the basement of the mosque.[36]

Yet religious enthusiasm and spatial agency do not explain the political dimension of the Grand Mosque occupation. First, the occupation was not an isolated event; rather, it was the final development of an insurrection that began several weeks before. Some sources describe it as an antigovernmental uprising in the Hijaz western province. Vassiliev describes "small armed detachments" that "engage[d] in surprise attacks on the regular troops and seized positions on the roads leading to Medina," while several tribes were protesting against the seizure of their lands by princes, an encroachment legalized by the 1969 law banning tribal property. On November 19, 1979, on the eve of the Mosque's takeover, "several soldiers of the regular army and National Guard joined the rebels."[37] Second, even if the group had been driven by its millenarian faith in the Messiah's return, Khalid al-Iami nevertheless justified the occupation in political terms. Having been lavishly rebuilt by the princes and constantly associated with their image, the mosque was the very symbol of the subservience of religion and the religious to the Al Saud dynasty. The insurgents rendered it a means and site of resistance against the dynasty itself. Thus the rebels proclaimed that Saudi citizens were not mere passive believers and subjects and their faith was not a submissive operation. The insurgents made clear that the sacred could be a site of contention. By the power of contention and their long and pervasive agency, the insurgents turned the Grand Mosque into a political slogan. Years after the rebellion, the Saudi king had to call himself the "Custodian of the two Holy Mosques" to regain his lost legitimacy.

The Mecca Days: November 20–December 4, 1979

On November 20, insurgents went to the mosque's basement, returned with weapons they had previously hidden, and distributed them among their comrades. Several insurgents who had been trained as snipers during their years in the desert or in the National Guard climbed up the mosque's minarets while others closed the doors.[38] Upon hearing news of the event some three hours later, the Saudi princes took a series of unprecedented measures. The regular police and army forces were disarmed in fear of a coup. Several ministries, embassies, and royal palaces received reinforced protection, and a curfew was set in Medina, Mecca, and Ta'if. All telecommunications with the outside world were cut, and the airports and frontiers were closed. Many Asian workers were expelled, and about 9,000 political activists and religious figures were arrested, questioned, and tortured.[39] Coming a few months after the Iranian Islamic revolution in February 1979, the Mecca insurrection was a severe blow to the Saudi government. A complete blackout was imposed upon the Saudi, Arab, and even Western media. Saudi embassies prevented reporters from entering the country. When the *Voice of America* broadcast the news a few hours after the occupation, the Saudi government was forced to admit publicly that an insurrection had taken place in the most sacred of all places.[40]

The security forces, including the Saudi army and the National Guard, attempted to clear the occupation on November 20 after dark, following an order of then Crown Prince Fahd, who was attending an Arab summit in Tunis. The counterinsurgency operations were waged on the two distinct but connected military and religious fronts. It was indeed impossible for the Saudi leadership to launch any operation without taking symbolic measures intended to conform to the Koranic injunction that both protects the mosque ("Fight them not at the Holy Mosque") and allows fighting inside it ("If they fight you, slay them"). Therefore, on the following day the Saudi ministry of interior issued the following communiqué:

> A clique of anti-religious rebels [*khawarij*] has abused the Islamic religion during the dawn prayer...and has infiltrated the Grand Mosque in Mecca with weapons.... They have presented one of them to the believers as being the awaited Messiah and have compelled them to pay

> allegiance to him. . . . The authorities have taken all necessary measures in order to manage the situation and, in accordance with a *fatwa* signed by all the *'ulama*,[41] will protect the lives of the believers who are in the Grand Mosque.[42]

"Antireligious rebels" was the first label put on Juhayman's followers: the main princes would soon refer to them as "religious freaks," "arrogant maniacs," a "deviant group,"[43] and even "deviant homosexuals,"[44] alleging that the Brethren had sexual intercourse inside the mosque, which would have been a serious violation of the shrine's sanctity.[45] From the government's perspective, the rebels had to be expelled from the realm of Islam and morality prior to any operation. It was to be made clear that they were carrying weapons, thus breaching the sanctity of the shrine. Interestingly, the ministry of interior accused the group of the very sin the Saudi state had committed in Juhayman's eyes: imposing a compelled allegiance upon the believers.

It remains controversial even today to identify the person or persons who began using weapons in the sanctuary. The Brethren had infiltrated weapons for the first time before November 20, smuggling guns and ammunitions in three pickup trucks,[46] and a second time on the morning of November 20, hiding them under their clothes. According to the authorities, they had shot down several policemen and taken the worshippers as hostages, clearly breaching the sanctity of the mosque. This view is contested by Juhayman's followers and the Saudi (notably Shi'ite) opposition, who claim that the state's forces had introduced armed policemen first, in order to guard the shrine. They claim that the first bullet was shot by the army and that Juhayman's followers took no hostages and opened the mosque's doors one hour after the end of the dawn's prayer on November 20.

With the passage of time and subsequent research, it seems that the insurgents were the first to shoot; they first shot into the air and later fired upon the police cars that came up around the shrine.[47] The official Saudi media and the main Saudi princes confirm the claims that the insurgents freed the hostages. The minister of interior, Prince Nayif, admitted one month after the insurrection that the insurgents "did not intend to fight but were carrying weapons in order to defend their lives."[48] As for the hostages, Radio Riyadh announced on November 21 that all worshippers had left the mosque, while testimonies of Lebanese and Moroccan pilgrims prove that the insurgents had allowed the pilgrims to leave.[49] In January 1980, more than one month after the end of the insurrection, the minister of defence, Prince Sultan, conceded that there were no hostages in the mosque.[50] The authorities treated the worshippers who had stayed inside as "rebels" and spared no one in their efforts to put down the rebellion.[51]

The government's religious concerns and precautions were not groundless. Many within the army and National Guard initially refused to attack the Grand Mosque and asked to see the promised—but not yet written—*fatwa* of the religious scholars. Prince Sultan, who had come to Mecca to organize the counterinsurgency operations, proposed instead to call in some sheikhs who would exhort them to combat. The military still refused to fight and requested that sheikh 'Abd al-'Aziz bin Baz himself come and justify the need to attack. According to a well-known—but certainly apocryphal—account, Sultan put his own authority on trial, using national pride and xenophobia in order to persuade them to combat: "If you don't defend God's house, who will? Shall I go to Pakistan and bring back troops from there?" The prince threatened to put the recalcitrant elements in jail, and the army finally attacked the mosque, leaving behind hundreds of soldiers and National Guards who refused to fight.[52] The army fired at the minarets, and the intermittent exchange of firing that began on the morning of November 20 continued until noon the next day. When this first tactic failed to produce results, a decision was taken on November 22 to dispatch a battalion of paratroopers inside the shrine. This operation was planned hurriedly and it failed. The insurgents simply killed the paratroopers when they entered the mosque. The security forces then resorted to heavy tactics, using armored personnel carriers (APCs) to break down several doors. In the course of the operation, several walls were destroyed and five of the seven minarets of the mosque, in which snipers were hiding, were destroyed. After the Saudi troops and APCs entered the mosque on November 24, the insurgents took refuge in the basement, under the courtyard. Saudi forces were unable to expel them. (See fig. 5.1.)

The 'Ulama's *fatwa,* published on November 25 and clearly supporting the government's repression, was not helpful: after many attempts at entering the mosque's basement, Prince Sultan had to ask the U.S. Central Intelligence Agency for help on November 27. The CIA's management of a chemical attack proved "a complete fiasco,"[53] and on November 28 the princes turned to the French GIGN (Intervention Group of the National Gendarmerie). Hired as coordinators and consultants, three French gendarmes headed by Captain Paul Barril drew the plans that allowed the Saudi forces eventually to exterminate or expel the last insurgents. They flooded

Figure 5.1. Main sites in the Grand Mosque's courtyard in Mecca (Source: Zeghidour 1989: XII and Bianchi 2004: 10): 1) The *Ka'aba*; 2) The Black Stone (*al-Hajr al-aswad*); 3) Isma'îl's corner (*Rukn Isma'îl*); 4) Ibrahim's station (*Maqam Ibrâhîm*); 5) Entrance of the underground well of Zamzam.

the basement with polluted waters and used combat gas (dichloro-benzylidene-malononitrile) to successfully and significantly weaken the rebels, thereby allowing the Saudi security forces to take over the mosque on December 4.

The repression was extremely violent. One of the insurgents later recalled the hallucinating effects of gas and hunger: "I was alone, in one of the cells, with the wounded. The bizarre thing is that rumours and visions propagated among us in a weird way."[54] After the death of the "Messiah" Muhammad al-Qahtani, the remaining 170 insurgents surrendered upon Juhayman's order. Casualty estimates still vary wildly. While the Saudi government claimed that its repression resulted in 135 deaths, the French GIGN claim that 4,000 died [55] and French journalists alleged that 5,000 died.[56] Somewhere in the middle, Al-Qahtani estimates some 2,600 deaths (among which 450 were rebels) and 4,000 wounded.[57]

An Ambiguous Outcome

The end of the siege marked the clear defeat of Juhayman's group, whose members were either killed during the operations, executed in January 1980, or condemned to long-term prison sentences. Yet the siege also proved to be a severe pitfall for the Saudi government: the disorganization of the military, the lack of well-trained security forces, the weak allegiance of the military to the political authority of the state, the clumsy decision making, and the poor media strategy of the government were the symptoms of a clear failure. In contrast, the insurgents demonstrated their ability to utilize sacred space and mobilize military and civilian support around them.

Generally speaking, the attack laid bare the poor preparation of the Saudi forces and the National Guard's sympathy toward the insurgents. According to one source, 1,000 Guards joined Juhayman's group before the end of the siege,[58] a fact suggesting that one-third of the 3,000 deployed military defected.[59] In addition, many of the National Guards refused to obey direct orders. On the second day of operation Prince Sultan had to severely punish the deserters in order to sustain the military effort, executing 13 soldiers on November 21 because they had refused to aim their guns at the Grand Mosque.[60]

For the Saudi government, a principal outcome of the siege was a clear statement of the poor quality and lack of reliability of the Saudi troops: they had long been divided by the political leadership, which since the Egyptian and Yemeni revolutions feared a military coup. After the end of the siege, the need for a counterinsurgency force led the princes to create, with the help of international experts, the Special Forces (*al-quwat al-khassa*), which was a local equivalent of the U.S. Special Weapons and Tactics Team (SWAT). Over several months the government also doubled the salaries of the army and National Guard. In addition, the government turned a blind eye to the many "businesses" established by several officers. Regular troops were eventually removed from the towns and dispersed along the endless borders of the country. It seems that during the siege the National Guard was closer to the insurgents than was the army. The National Guard, whose members are primarily recruited from the Bedouin tribes that had participated in the Ikhwan movement (such as 'Utayba or Mutayr), was less devoted to the Al Saud rhetoric of power than was the military. The Al Saud leadership was helpless in the face of such a military and political failure. During the first days of the operation Prince Sultan had to replace National Guard officers with army officers to ensure an effective chain of command, a strategy that threw the National Guard into organizational disarray. Military decision making was scarcely better. The operation was ill timed given that both Crown Prince Fahd and the head of Saudi intelligence, Prince Turki al-Faisal, were attending a summit in Tunis.

Moreover, Prince 'Abd Allah, commander in chief of the National Guard, was on vacation in Morocco. To exacerbate the poor timing, a large Shi'ite insurrection took root in the eastern provinces of the country on November 25, further undermining the state's military and political capacity for reaction. Because of the need to repress the Shi'ites, the National Guard had inadequate supplies of nonlethal weapons, requiring the princes to seek provisions (e.g., tear gas) from the U.S. mission in Jeddah.[61]

Because of the low level of trust between the princes and the military leadership, Prince Sultan, the defense minister, came to Mecca to personally lead the counterinsurgency operations, a task for which he himself was ill prepared. Prince Nayif, the interior minister, managed the media coverage of the operation and the communication policy of the ruling family. Under his supervision, the Saudi government first orchestrated a complete media blackout. When the first leaks occurred and news of the operations was broadcast by *The Voice of America*, Nayif allowed a very carefully monitored coverage of the issue by local media. But the Saudi media were soon confronted by a critical communication challenge. They had announced that the rebellion was very limited, in order not to show to the outside world the poor legitimacy of a government praised for its "stability." Numerous premature proclamations of victory were thus issued by various officials. As early as November 21 Radio Riyadh and the main Saudi newspaper proclaimed that the insurrection was nearly over while in fact the insurgents were successfully battling the armed forces, which were enjoying little success. The same erroneous communiqué was published and broadcast every single day of the insurrection, from November 21 to December 4, thus clearly revealing the poor media strategy of the government and fostering doubt about the nature of the operation and its principal actors.

The government's strategy also failed to address the political nature of the insurrection, opting to pursue an exclusively religious effort to discredit the rebels. For example, the official communiqués as well as the Saudi, and often Arab, press reduced Juhayman's group to its doctrine of the Messiah. This depiction allowed the Saudi government to launch a heated theological debate about this controversial issue in Sunni Islam, in order to sideline and even silence the political dimension of the insurrection.[62] The Saudi state's often inconsistent arguments were published and broadcast all through the Middle East. After having dismissed the insurrection as the work of a few individuals, the Saudi media overplayed the miraculous nature of the operations that had eventually led to the death of so many insurgents and military personnel. The *al-Madina* newspaper explained that the rebels had not been killed by any human intervention, but by God Himself:

> During the last hours of the extermination of the deviant group, yesterday December 5, 1979, while the security forces were entering the cells that had been turned into hideouts by the criminals, God's will was with our boys who were defending His sacred house, and the Zamzam waters[63] have been seen overflowing and flooding seven rebels who were hiding near the well of Zamzam. Thus God takes His revenge on the extremists and the rebels![64]

The heavy losses encountered by the security forces also led the Saudi princes to use the *topos* of martyrdom. Nayif, for example, justified the death of numerous soldiers by explaining that he "who dies this noble way is lucky in this world and in the other,"[65] while Crown Prince Fahd declared that every man "hopes to martyr for God's sake and to die while defending His house."[66]

This official strategy of managing the fallout of the operation could not hide the violent nature of the repression nor the fact that the Saudi princes were forced to rely upon American and French "unbelievers" in order to "free" the most important mosque of Islam. The *'ulama*'s heavy dependence upon the political power of the state was obvious enough to arouse disobedience among the armed forces. After the insurrection, the absolute subservience of the government's *'ulama* would become a topic of popular defiance against the state. In the words of the Yemeni sheikh Muqbil al-Wadi'i, one of Juhayman's comrades, "Saudi Arabia is the graveyard of the *'ulama*."[67] The insurgents' arguments, although momentarily smothered by the powerful voice of the Saudi media, were and still are heard by many. Juhayman's followers mastered the geography of the shrine, turning spatial constraints into advantages and using minarets, corridors, cells, and basements in a way that far exceeded the state's capacity to react. They also gained support among the civil population. On November 24 several thousand Saudis[68] demonstrated in Jeddah, showing their solidarity with Juhayman's group before facing a massive crackdown.

Conclusion

Before the Mecca events, the Saudi state seemed able to successfully confront a contentious movement. Its religious legitimacy and its authority over national—and international—Islamic institutions had allowed it to direct Saudi public opinion against previous leftist and nationalist opposition movements of the 1950s and 1960s. Yet after the end of the 1979 insurrection, various Islamic groups seemed to have developed an operation space of their own, and in ensuing decades these groups have sought to undermine the Saudi state and its institutions. This result came about arguably because of the efforts of one of the first Saudi Islamic groups to turn the Grand Mosque into a space of contention for religious actors in confrontation with the Saudi state. In the eyes of Juhayman and his followers, the Grand Mosque had to be freed of the unjust grip of the Al Saud family. It also was a space in which the world order could radically change. In some measure, this vision was shared by the Saudi leadership, which believed that the Grand Mosque had to be cleansed of the insurgents and returned to the worshippers and their calm subservience to the "Custodian of the two Holy Mosques."

The operation proved to be perilous for the state and its legitimacy. For millions of Muslims, the Saudi royal family became the one that bombed the holiest mosque of Islam, that called in the "infidel" French intervention team to repress Muslims in Mecca, and that cracked down on every Islamic group between 1979 and 1980. For the Western allies of the kingdom, the Saudi dynasty had proven its inefficiency and its weakness in contending with a serious internal challenge. The Western powers would continue to intervene in managing the security of the kingdom, thus arguably contributing to a long-term destabilization of the regime and region.

In 2003 and 2004 al Qaeda attacked the very security institutions that had been established in the aftermath of the 1979 Mecca siege. From 1979 through 2003, between the takeover of the Grand Mosque in Mecca and the al Qaeda bombings in Saudi Arabia against "polytheist" (Western) and security targets, the scope of the sacred space was redefined and widened. Whereas once it had been constrained to the Mecca Grand Mosque, the expanse of sacred space now reached the borders of the Arabian Peninsula. While delaying a clear solution to the political issues at stake in 1979, the Saudi dynasty allowed its enemy space to grow and become ever more dangerous and transnational.

The state's failure was manifest in several areas. First, the counterinsurgency operations demonstrated the poor organization and institutionalization of the Saudi state. Two decades of antinationalist and antisocialist repression in the ranks of the military likely resulted in the disunity of the armed forces, weakening the allegiance they should have shown to the tenants of political authority. Poor training and monitoring compelled the military to use heavy and destructive means in order to "clean up" the Grand Mosque. Even these means did not allow them to expel the insurgents, and thus the military resorted to using particularly "dirty" weapons against them and to rely upon a locally infamous foreign intervention.

Second, the religious policy of the regime was also a clear failure. The princes should have conferred a greater role to the *'ulama*, perhaps letting the well-respected sheikh 'Abd al-'Aziz bin Baz come to Mecca and negotiate an honorable surrender for both the royal family and the insurgents. The government instead humiliated the religious establishment—the attack of the security forces was launched four days before the *fatwa* of the official *'ulama*—while paradoxically overplaying its Islamic puritanical nature. After the events, "women's hairdressing salons and women's clubs were closed down and female announcers were dismissed from the TV. . . . New regulations prohibited girls from continuing their education abroad."[69] Cultural centers and movie theaters were closed down, songs were banned from TV, and the so-called "religious police's" activities were extended.[70] Becoming more apparently religious than the religious opposition itself nevertheless did nothing to enhance the Al Saud image at home and abroad.

Third, rough tactics of misinformation and a media blackout had led the princes to lose Muslims' attention worldwide, further undermining their own political position inside Saudi Arabia. A more mature media policy would have relied upon more fidelity to the truth in explaining the events to Saudis and other Muslims, detailing the movement's political demands and the state's constraints. The only available repertoire seemed to be sheer violence, not only toward the insurgents but also toward the military, the civilian worshippers, and even the Grand Mosque itself. Perhaps such a bloody outcome could have been avoided. It is possible—but unknowable—that a more peaceful resolution of the Mecca insurgency might have strengthened the Saudi state. But the very conditions in which the royal family had ruled for over half a century seemed to have prevented any solution of this nature.

Notes

This chapter is dedicated to Khaled.

1. Bruce Lawrence, *Messages to the World: The Statements of Osama Bin Laden* (New York: Verso, 2005), p. 266.

2. Besides the Islamic University of Medina, others include the Muslim World League (created in 1962), the World Assembly of Muslim Youth (1972), and the small-scale "Scientific Institutes" in all the Saudi cities or the Hadith Institute of Mecca and Medina (created in 1932 and 1930), in which a majority of Juhayman's followers were studying.

3. The Tabligh is a predication group that was founded on a Sufi basis in the 1920s by an Indian scholar, Muhammad Iliyas. It penetrated Saudi Arabia during the 1950s and focuses mainly on social and moral issues.

4. Nasir al-Huzaymi, *Ayam ma' Juhayman* (Days with Juhayman) (Riyadh: n. p., 2007), p. 16.

5. 'Abd al-'Aziz bin Baz (1912–1999) became the most prominent Saudi religious scholar during the 1970s, after the death of the sheikh Muhammad bin Ibrahim Al al-Shaykh, grand mufti of the kingdom. Bin Baz became grand mufti in 1993, after the post had been vacant 24 years. See Madawi al-Rasheed, *Contesting the Saudi State: Islamic Voices from a New Generation* (Cambridge: Cambridge University Press, 2007), p. 32.

6. Fahd al-Qahtani, *Zilzal Juhayman fi Makka* (Juhayman's Earthquake in Mecca) (London: Organisation of the Islamic Revolution in the Arabian Peninsula, 1987), p. 15.

7. Al-Huzaymi, *Ayam ma' Juhayman,* p. 1.

8. Ibid., p. 18.

9. Muhammad Nasir ad-Din al-Albani (1914–1999), a Syrian religious scholar, taught at the Islamic University of Medina (1961–1963) but was soon expelled for his disputed positions. He is known for having allowed women to show their face and hands, which in the conservative context of the Arabian Peninsula was controversial. He then came back to Syria and moved to Jordan in 1979. See Thomas Heghammer and Stéphane Lacroix, "Rejectionist Islamism in Saudi Arabia: The Story of Juhayman al-'Utaybi Revisited," *International Journal of Middle East Studies* 39 (2007), 105–6; Al-Huzaymi, *Ayan ma' Juhayman,* pp. 4–5; Quintan Wiktorowicz, *The Management of Islamic Activism: Salafis, the Muslim Brotherhood, and State Power in Jordan* (New York: SUNY, 2001), 120–21. alalbany.net.

10. Al-Huzaymi, *Ayan ma' Juhayman,* p. 21.

11. I mean by "political" what Sidney Tarrow describes as "contentious politics," that is, "public, collective, episodic interactions among makers of claims when (a) at least some of the interaction adopts noninstitutional forms, (b) at least one government is a claimant, an object of claims, or a party to the claims, and (c) the claims would, if realized, affect the interests of at least one of the claimants." See Sidney Tarrow, "Silence and Voice in the Study of Contentious Politics: Introduction," in Ronald R. Aminzade,

Jack A. Goldstone, Doug McAdam, Elizabeth J. Perry, William H. Sewell, Jr., Sydney Tarrow, and Charles Tilley, eds., *Silence and Voice in the Study of Contentious Politics* (Cambridge: Cambridge University Press, 2001), p. 7.

12. Interview with Nasir al-Huzaymi, Riyadh, March 19, 2007.

13. Interview with Nasir al-Huzaymi, Riyadh, March 19, 2007.

14. Raf'at Sayyid Ahmad, *Rasa'il Juhayman al-'Utaybi, Qa'id al-muqtahimin li-l-masjid al-haram bi-Makka* (The Letters of Juhayman al-Utaybi, Leader of the Grand Mosque Insurgents) (Cairo: Madbûli, 2004).

15. Interview with Nasir al-Huzaymi, Riyadh, March 19, 2007.

16. There are two movements called "The Ikhwan" in modern Saudi history. The first one was created by King 'Abd al-'Aziz Al Sa'ûd in the 1910s in order to settle the menacing Bedouin tribes and use them in the conquest of the Arabian Peninsula. This Bedouin army was repressed by the Royal Air Force in 1929 at the battle of Sbilla after it revolted against what it believed was a British colonization of Arabia. The second movement was created by Juhayman al-'Utaybi in 1965. Juhayman's movement is sometimes referred to as the "neo-Ikhwan," or as a revival of King 'Abd al-'Aziz's Bedouin army.

17. Al-Huzaymi, *Ayan ma' Juhayman,* p. 15.

18. Interview with Nasir al-Huzaymi, Riyadh, March 19, 2007.

19. Interview with Nasir al-Huzaymi, Riyadh, April 17, 2007.

20. Ibn Hazm al-Andalusi (384–456 H.) is one of the founders of a theological school known as Thahiriyya (lit. "formalism") because of its very literalist readings of the sacred texts. The Thahiriyya does still exist in Najd; it traditionally opposes the plurality of schools of jurisprudence and calls for the unification of the four Hanafi, Maliki, Shafi'i, and Hanbali Sunnin schools of jurisprudence.

21. Al-Huzaymi, *Ayan ma' Juhayman,* p. 11.

22. Heghammer and Lacroix, "Rejectionist Islamism in Saudi Arabia," p. 108.

23. Al-Rasheed, *Contesting the Saudi State,* p. 146.

24. Al-Qahtani, *Zilzal Juhayman fi Makka,* pp. 53–56.

25. Al-Huzaymi, *Ayan ma' Juhayman,* p. 23.

26. Ibid., pp. 25–26.

27. Before becoming religious, Juhayman had worked in cigarette smuggling between Kuwait and Saudi Arabia. See al-Huzaymi, *Ayan ma' Juhayman,* p. 15. The main letters of Juhayman have been published in Ahmad, *Rasa'il Juhayman al-'Utaybi.*

28. Al-Huzaymi, *Ayan ma' Juhayman,* p. 28.

29. The Mecca Grand Mosque has been the site of many protests throughout the history of Islam, the last of which were the 1979 uprising and the 1987 riots.

30. Interview with Nasir al-Huzaymi, Riyadh, March 10, 2007.

31. Ahmad, *Rasa'il Juhayman al-'Utaybi.* p. 206; see figure 5.1.

32. Ayman Al-Yasini, *Al-Islam wa-l-'arsh. Ad-din wa-d-dawla fi-s-sa'ûdiyya* (Islam and the Throne. Religion and State in Saudi Arabia). (Cairo: Kitab al-Ahaly, 1990), p. 198.

33. Interview with Nasir al-Huzaymi, Riyadh, March 10, 2007. Interestingly enough, all the protagonists of the insurrection (be they pro- or anti-government) knew each other, sometimes for years.

34. Al-Qahtani, *Zilzal Juhayman fi Makka,* p. 125.

35. William H. Sewell, Jr., "Space in Contentious Politics," in Ronald R. Aminzade et al., eds., *Silence and Voice in the Study of Contentious Politics*, pp. 55–64.

36. Al-Huzaymi, *Ayan ma' Juhayman,* p. 7.

37. Alexei Vassiliev, *The History of Saudi Arabia* (London: Saqi, 2000), pp. 395–96.

38. Al-Qahtani, *Zilzal Juhayman fi Makka,* p. 126.

39. Ibid., pp. 155–67.

40. News of the takeover and rumors of American involvement triggered a series of unprecedented riots near U.S. diplomatic representations, namely in Islamabad (on November 21), Izmir (Turkey) and Dacca (Bangladesh) (on November 22), Kuwait (on November 30), and Tripoli (Libya) (on December 2).

41. This fatwa was not published until November 25; the princes moved forward before receiving the green light from the religious establishment.

42. Al-Qahtani, *Zilzal Juhayman fi Makka,* p. 21.

43. The label of deviant group (*fi'at dhala*) is still synonymous with "opposition movement" in the official Saudi phraseology.

44. Al-Qahtani, *Zilzal Juhayman fi Makka,* pp. 28–29.

45. James Buchan, "The Return of the Ikhwan—1979," in David Holden and Richard Johns, eds., *The House of Saud: The Rise and Rule of the Most Powerful Dynasty in the Arab World* (New York: Rinehart and Winston, 1981), p. 512.

46. Yaroslav Trofimov, *The Siege of Mecca: The Forgotten Uprising* (London: Allen Lane, 2007), pp. 66–67.

47. Trofimov, *The Siege of Mecca*, pp. 71–74.

48. *As-Safir*, January 20, 1980; al-Qahtani, *Zilzal Juhayman fi Makka,* p. 175.

49. *As-Safir*, November 29, 1979; *an-Nahar*, November 24 and 25, 1979; al-Qahtani, *Zilzal Juhayman fi Makka,* p. 149.

50. *Al-Hawadith*, January 18, 1980; al-Qahtani, *Zilzal Juhayman fi Makka,* p. 151.

51. A man who was praying in the Grand Mosque on November 20, 1979, and who escaped when the insurgents opened the doors, was questioned at length by the Saudi secret services; although he did not belong to Juhayman's group, he was placed under surveillance for many years (interview with an Islamic activist, Riyadh, May 18, 2006). This treatment has been the best the "hostages" whose lives were to be "protected" could expect from the Saudi government. Others encountered death, torture, or jail.

52. Al-Qahtani, *Zilzal Juhayman fi Makka,* pp. 182–83.

53. Trofimov, *The Siege of Mecca*, p. 173.

54. Al-Huzaymi, *Ayan ma' Juhayman,* p. 33.
55. Cf. www.gign.org/groupe-intervention-gign/missions-zoom.php?id=8.
56. Roger Faligot and Jean Guisnel, eds,. *Histoire secrète de la Ve République* (Paris: La Découverte, 2006).
57. Al-Qahtani, *Zilzal Juhayman fi Makka,* p. 230.
58. Ibid., p. 194.
59. Cf. http://www.gign.org/groupe-intervention-gign/missions-zoom.php?id=8.
60. Al-Qahtani, *Zilzal Juhayman fi Makka,* pp. 182–83.
61. Ibid., p. 191.
62. Ibid., p. 83; al-Rasheed, *Contesting the Saudi State,* pp. 145–46.
63. The holy water of Zamzam is flowing from a well in the courtyard of the Grand Mosque. See figure 5.1.
64. *Al-Madina,* December 6, 1979; al-Qahtani, *Zilzal Juhayman fi Makka,* p. 206.
65. *Ar-Riyadh,* December 4, 1979; al-Qahtani, *Zilzal Juhayman fi Makka* (Earthquake in Mecca), p. 208.
66. *Al-Madina,* December 2, 1979; al-Qahtani, *Zilzal Juhayman fi Makka,* p. 208.
67. François Burgat and Mohammed Sbitli, "Les Salafis au Yemen ou la modernisation malgré tout," Chroniques *Yéménites* 12 (2002), http://cy.revues.org/document137.html.
68. 10,000 according to al-Qahtani. See al-Qahtani, *Zilzal Juhayman fi Makka,* pp. 282–83.
69. Vassiliev, *The History of Saudi Arabia,* p. 397.
70. Al-Huzaymi, *Ayan ma' Juhayman,* p. 5.

6

Insurgency and Counterinsurgency in Iraq's Sacred Spaces

David Siddhartha Patel

In 2004 the U.S. military twice fought armed followers of Moqtada al-Sadr in Najaf, one of the holiest cities in Shi'ite Islam. Compared with counterinsurgency operations elsewhere in Iraq, these battles were particularly perilous for the U.S.-led coalition. Significant damage to or a perceived desecration of the Imam Ali shrine would have alienated Iraqi Shi'ites, who widely supported the overthrow of Saddam Hussein and, until then, had tolerated the foreign military presence. Sadr's rebellions, however, destabilized southern Iraq and threatened to undermine the tenuous transition process. Planners faced the difficult task of suppressing nascent rebellions in Najaf without taking actions that might lead additional Shi'ites to support insurgency.

Yet despite similar risks, U.S. counterinsurgency operations in Najaf differed considerably in these two uprisings. When Sadr's followers occupied the Imam Ali shrine amid a general uprising in April, U.S. Army forces immediately attacked affiliated insurgents elsewhere in Iraq, but they waited four weeks before beginning significant offensive operations against those in Najaf and they did not pursue insurgents in Najaf's old city or the shrine. Interlocutors sought negotiated solutions to the standoff. Relative to their concurrent operations, U.S. forces in April and May also exercised tactical restraint in

Najaf. They unilaterally established exclusion and no-fire zones that kept U.S. ground forces far from the city's most sacred sites. U.S. decision makers were unwilling to raid the Imam Ali shrine.

In contrast, when Sadr's armed followers rose up again in August, U.S. Marines immediately and decisively attacked them throughout Najaf. U.S. forces repeatedly reduced their exclusion zone around the Imam Ali shrine and abandoned no-fire zones. Marine and Army units advanced deep into Najaf's Old City and held positions near the shrine. Aerial forces and tanks repeatedly struck targets adjacent to the shrine. When Grand Ayatollah Ali al-Sistani intervened in late August, an assault on the shrine by Iraqi security forces cooperating with U.S. forces appeared imminent.

Why did U.S. forces aggressively pursue insurgents in Najaf's sacred spaces in August but not in April? Why were they unwilling in the earlier uprising to conduct aggressive offensive operations against insurgents in Najaf but willing to do so elsewhere? This variation in outcomes is puzzling because, as this chapter details, the insurgents, counterinsurgency forces, location, and risks were similar in both cases, and both uprisings occurred at tenuous moments in Iraq's political transition.

I argue that the key difference in these two uprisings was the nature of the Iraqi government at the time of the operations. U.S. planners were willing to assault Najaf's sacred sites when a nominally sovereign Iraqi government existed and unambiguously supported controversial operations in sacred space. Occupying forces were unwilling to risk alienating Shi'ites without this authorization. Iraqi government support mattered, I argue, because of how U.S. decision makers expected Iraqi Shi'ites to react to U.S. military operations in Najaf's sacred spaces.

During the April–June crisis L. Paul Bremer III, administrator of the Coalition Provisional Authority (CPA), exercised all executive, legislative, and judicial authority in Iraq. He had appointed a 25-member Iraqi Governing Council (IGC). While the IGC was relatively powerless, it represented the most prominent Iraqi government authority at the time. IGC members publicly disagreed over offensive counterinsurgency operations in Najaf, with most Shi'ite members opposing U.S. operations. Dissension in the IGC and the prominence of U.S. spokesmen during the operation allowed insurgents to portray counterinsurgency operations as an assault by foreign occupiers on Najaf, Iraq, and Islam itself. Moqtada al-Sadr compared the threat of U.S. operations to previous assaults on Najaf by the Ottomans and the British.

By August, however, the CPA had dissolved and transferred "power" to an appointed Iraqi Interim Government. Authority was concentrated in the hands of Prime Minister Iyad Allawi, whose government vociferously supported decisive action against the insurgents in Najaf. No Iraqi legislature existed at the time to offer a dissenting view from within the government. Allawi publicly linked U.S. operations to efforts to reestablish the Iraqi government's control throughout the country, which polls show Iraqis widely supported at the time. The legitimacy of the Iraqi government appears to have been less important than the fact that it existed and unambiguously endorsed U.S. counterinsurgency operations. Other factors appear less important in explaining the difference in outcomes across these two cases.

These Najaf cases have implications for counterinsurgency operations on sacred space by *foreign* occupiers.. The existence of an indigenous government, even if appointed by foreign occupiers and clearly reliant upon the occupiers' support, reduced risks associated with offensive operations on sacred space by portraying the operations as necessary for the (re)establishment of government authority. Without this indigenous government support, such offensive operations may have been seen as suppression of dissent and desecration of sacred space by foreigners.

The next two sections contextualize Sadr's two uprisings, first discussing the nature of his insurgencies and then identifying Najaf's relevant sacred spaces and their appeal to insurgents. The two sections after that present the two contrasting cases—insurgency and counterinsurgency operations in Najaf from April to June 2004 and in August 2004, respectively. The fourth section proffers a possible explanation for the operational differences between the two cases. The final section offers preliminary conclusions for both theory and policy.

Political and Sacred Context

Iraqi resistance to prolonged foreign occupation began almost immediately after a U.S.-led coalition overthrew Saddam Hussein's regime in April 2003. The burgeoning armed insurgency, however, was limited mostly to Baghdad and the Sunni Arab-majority governates to the north and west of the capital. Shi'ite-majority southern governates remained relatively stable.[1] While dissident Shi'ite militias developed, they rarely targeted coalition forces. Most organized Shi'ite political factions cooperated with the Coalition Provisional

Authority (CPA), or at least grudgingly tolerated a temporary occupation. For example, the Supreme Council for the Islamic Revolution in Iraq (SCIRI), its Badr Corps militia, and most factions of the Islamic Da'wa Party met regularly with coalition officials and accepted seats on the Iraqi Governing Council.

Moqtada al-Sadr, in contrast, claimed to speak for the most prominent Shi'ite dissident social movement openly opposed to occupation. When state provision of public services collapsed in April 2003, followers of the late Grand Ayatollah Mohammad Sadiq al-Sadr (d. 1999) quickly reestablished security and services in some poor, urban Shi'ite areas, most notably in East Baghdad's sprawling projects, which they renamed "Sadr City." From his father, the Grand Ayatollah, and from other relatives, Moqtada inherited a well-known family legacy of "resisting tyranny" and promoting Islamist social and political agendas. Although not a senior cleric, he attempted to position himself as the leader of his father's social movement and as an Iraqi nationalist leader by condemning the U.S. occupation and Western social and political influences in post-Saddam Iraq. This stance differentiated him from more established Shi'ite political leaders and partly explains why, despite few dedicated followers, he remained popular among Iraq's Shi'ite masses.

On July 18, 2003, Sadr announced the formation of the Mahdi Army, which his followers initially claimed was more of a social movement than a standing armed force.[2] In late 2003 he attempted to form a shadow government but abandoned this endeavor when it failed to attract support. A few skirmishes occurred between coalition forces and militiamen affiliated with Sadr, but the April 2004 uprising was the first wide-scale military confrontation. The most notable prior engagement occurred when a U.S. Army task force cleared Sadr-affiliated militia from a mosque and hotel in Karbala in October 2003. Until April 2004, however, Shi'ite resistance to occupation was relatively peaceful. Unlike Baghdad and Sunni Arab-majority governates, no insurgency existed. Operations in Najaf threatened to spread sustained insurgency in the Shi'ite south.

Najaf's Sacred Spaces

The Iraqi cities of Najaf, Karbala, Kadhimiyah, and Samarra hold special positions in the spiritual geography of Twelver Shi'ite Islam. They contain the graves of six of the twelve Imams, the most venerated descendants of the Prophet Muhammad, and the site of the Twelfth Imam's occultation.[3] These shrine cities are centers of pilgrimage, trade, and clerical scholarship. This section describes the principal sacred space of Najaf, Iraq's paramount shrine city, and discusses its appeal to insurgents.

Najaf contains the purported grave of Ali ibn Abi Talib (circa 599–661), the cousin and son-in-law of the Prophet Muhammad. Sunnis acknowledge Ali as the fourth and final "Rightly Guided" Caliph. Shi'ites claim that the Prophet Muhammad designated him as his successor and that the first three Caliphs usurped his legitimate authority. For Shi'ites, he is the first Imam and was infallible. Ali was murdered in Kufa in 661 and buried in an uninhabited area approximately six miles to the southwest. After the location of his grave was publicly revealed almost a century later, pilgrims began to visit the site. Islamic scholars relocated to the area to teach and spread what became Shi'ite traditions.[4] The shrine over Ali's grave and the surrounding town of residences, pilgrims' facilities, hospices, and seminaries grew with the patronage of distant Shi'ite rulers. Damaged and rebuilt over time, a sizable town developed around the increasingly elaborate shrine complex.

Ali's underground tomb is the heart of Najaf's sacred space. Many Shi'ites believe the remains of the Prophets Adam and Noah lie in the same grave. Surrounding the grave is an elaborate shrine complex, known as a *mashhad* (lit. "a place where a martyr died," although Ali actually died in Kufa), currently stretching approximately 400 feet by 400 feet. Like all mashhads, the shrine of Imam Ali in Najaf is first and foremost a tomb, not a mosque. Its sacredness emanates from the presence of human remains, not from being a place of traditional worship.

The mashhad of Ali lies at the center of Najaf's circular "Old City," a dense residential and commercial area just over a half mile in diameter. Najaf's newer districts lie to the immediate southeast of the Old City and continue further east. The Old City contains residences, extensive shopping bazaars, facilities for pilgrims, hospices, mosques, and religious seminaries. Such proximity to Ali's shrine provides a path to paradise. For centuries Najaf has been a place of refuge and shelter, drawing the dying, refugees, and outlaws. The religious schools and seminaries are collectively referred to as the *hawza* (lit. "territory of learning"), though a central campus and formal organization do not exist. Najaf has been a center of scholarship and training for generations, and prominent clerics live and maintain offices near the shrine. Although they will never meet him, most Shi'ites throughout the world nominally claim Najaf's paramount cleric as their religious guide.

The Valley of Peace (*Wadi al-Salam*) Cemetery stretches for more than two miles immediately north of the Old City. Najaf became a major burial site after the large-scale conversions to Shi'ism of Iranians from the sixteenth century and southern Iraqi tribesmen from the late eighteenth century.[5] Families could demonstrate great respect for a dead relative by transporting and burying his or her corpse in one of Iraq's shrine cities, preferably Najaf. A large and lucrative industry developed around the transportation of corpses to Najaf. Most Shi'ites in Iraq and many in Iran can claim family members buried in the cemetery's acres. Some Shi'ites believe the Prophets Hud and Saleh are buried in the cemetery. The Prophet Abraham also supposedly visited the area and prophesized that it would become a sacred resting place centuries later. Tens of thousands of headstones dot the cemetery amid larger mausoleums and shrines. Elaborate tunnels lie underneath the cemetery, and many underground movements flourished in these catacombs. The tombs of numerous religious scholars are located in the southern parts of the cemetery or in the Old City close to the Imam Ali shrine.

Although Najaf's political and theological influence fluctuates, its sacredness for Shi'ites remains constant. Najaf is a major pilgrimage destination, especially on anniversaries commemorating the births and deaths of the Imams. For many Shi'ites, especially poor Iraqis and Iranians, a pilgrimage to Najaf substitutes for the religious obligation to go to Mecca on *hajj* at least once in one's life. Visiting Ali's shrine is believed to absolve pilgrims of their sins and provide a share in the Imams' inevitable victory.

Imam Ali's tomb and Imam Hussein's in Karbala are key components in Shi'ites' shared spiritual imagination. Mass-produced images and posters of Imam Ali's shrine and his grave grace the walls of Shi'ite homes and businesses throughout the world, from India to Lebanon to Nigeria to the United States. The image of the central shrine building and tomb inside is something that a Shi'ite knows almost all other Shi'ites will recognize.

Najaf's sacred space afforded Iraq's Shi'ite insurgents a number of advantages. First, the physical layout of a mashhad offers potential as a redoubt, especially of last resort. Its perimeter wall provides defensible space, and minarets can be used as sniper positions. The primary advantage of operating on Najaf's sacred space, however, is the potential to mobilize supporters and attract clerical support.

Second, by occupying Najaf's shrines or mosques, insurgents may provoke a response from counterinsurgency forces that could radicalize Shi'ite moderates or otherwise garner newfound support by galvanizing the noncommitted or reducing resistance among opponents.[6] The mobilizing potential of such attacks relies in part upon the fact that images of Imam Ali's shrine are ubiquitous in Shi'ite communities. Because most Shi'ites possess a mental image of it, insurgents know Shi'ites can easily imagine damage to it. Even rumors of damage to the shrine's golden dome, the most visible and easiest to visualize part of a mashhad, would likely incite emotion among believers—even those far removed from Najaf.

Third, insurgents can exploit the history of previous desecrations that Iraq's Shi'ites collectively remember. These historical memories allow insurgents to situate the actions of their foes to a long lineage of enemies. Important past assaults include the Wahhabi sack of Karbala in 1801, the Ottoman siege of Karbala in 1843, the British blockades of Najaf in 1918 and of Karbala and Najaf in 1920, and the Baathist assaults on both cities in 1991. Moqtada al-Sadr, for example, repeatedly compared U.S. forces in 2004 to what he claimed were Najaf's previously defeated foreign occupiers, the Ottomans and the British.

Fourth, occupying or fighting on sacred space may permit Shi'ite insurgents to involve recalcitrant senior clerics in their uprising. Najaf's established clerics usually discourage unrest in the city, partly because fighting in the shrine cities disrupts lucrative trade and pilgrimages. Contemporary Shi'ite theology divides the Muslim community into two groups: jurists qualified to interpret Islamic law by deducing God's orders from religious sources (*mujtahids*), and everyone else. Everyone unqualified must choose and follow the guidance of one of the most senior *mujtahids*, called a *marja' al-taqlid* (lit. "source of emulation"). Although religious authority in contemporary Shi'ite Islam is hierarchical, no central mechanism exists for establishing relative authority among senior clerics. A cleric's prominence is a function of his supposed learning and, just as important, his ability to attract lay followers who will emulate his rulings and give him religious alms.

Insurgent occupation of Najaf's sacred sites poses a direct challenge to the city's *mujtahids,* whom Iraq's Shi'ites expect to be the ultimate preservers of the shrine. Fighting in a mashhad, particularly counterinsurgency operations by non-Shi'ites, undermines the authority of Najaf's senior clergy in a very public way. All Shi'ites would know that resident *marja's* were unable or unwilling to stand up to tyranny and injustice, as Imams Ali and Hussein did in their times. In the 2004 uprisings Sadr's apparent deference to the *hawza* challenged Grand Ayatollah Sistani to either become involved or see his authority undermined. If Sistani remained silent as Sadr stood up to perceived tyranny, Sadr could then claim that he was continuing the legacy of his martyred relatives, Grand Ayatollahs Muhammad Muhammad Sadiq al-Sadr and Muhammad Baqir al-Sadr, who were murdered with little reaction from senior clerics. His inaction might also encourage the up-and-coming generation of Shi'ite clerics to increase their independence from Sistani and position themselves to potentially attain prominence after his passing. The generational transfer of religious authority can induce significant competition between scholars for supporters. In 2004, Sadr lacked a supportive senior clerical patron for his social movement. He perhaps sought to draw at least one to his side. Finally, insurgents might use Najaf to immediately mobilize Shi'ites to their cause—pilgrims and relatively sophisticated seminary students locally and Shi'ites elsewhere.

Insurgency and Counterinsurgency in April–June 2004

By early 2004 Moqtada al-Sadr's supporters ran vigilante courts and vice squads in parts of southern Iraq. Among their most egregious actions was the destruction, in March 2004, of the gypsy village of Qawliya, which they claimed was a source of immorality and corruption of Islamic mores.[7] On March 28, 2004, the CPA, in a step to reign in Sadr's followers and send a message to other opposition groups with militias before the upcoming transition to Iraqi sovereignty, closed Sadr's inflammatory newspaper, *al-Hawza* ("The Seminary"), for 60 days. Sadr's aides thought a retaliatory show of force was necessary to deter further crackdowns, and they organized demonstrations outside CPA's "Green Zone" headquarters in Baghdad.[8] Then on April 3, 2004, U.S. forces arrested a close aide of Moqtada in Najaf, Shaykh Mustafa al-Yacoubi, and 12 other Sadr supporters.[9] Throughout that night, buses transported Sadr's followers from Sadr City in Baghdad to the Kufa and Najaf area, where demonstrations were planned for the following day.

On the morning of April 4 Sadr's supporters took over the headquarters of Najaf's traffic police station and other government buildings. Clashes between demonstrators and Honduran and El Salvadoran troops outside the Spanish-led military compound in Najaf killed 22 Iraqis and wounded over 200. Late that afternoon, after this fighting had begun, Moqtada called on his followers to "terrorize your enemy." Throughout Shi'ite areas of Iraq, protestors clashed with coalition forces, setting off the first widespread armed confrontation between Shi'ite dissidents and U.S.-led occupation authorities.

Recognizing that his arrest was imminent, Moqtada declared that he was going into a protected retreat (*itisam*) in Kufa. He soon relocated to the Imam Ali shrine in Najaf after armed followers seized it. His choice of words portrayed his move as a form of sanctuary-seeking in Najaf's most sacred space. Accounts differ on how Sadr's followers entered the shrine despite the presence of its unofficial Badr Corps guardians, but they did so without a fight.[10] Supporters from East Baghdad reinforced local insurgents in Kufa and Najaf. Most of the insurgents were from elsewhere, quickly resulting in tensions with residents of Najaf who resented the disruption of lucrative pilgrim traffic and the threat of destructive counterinsurgency operations.

Sadr's militiamen deployed throughout Najaf's Old City, cemetery, and key government buildings. Although few reliable sources on the insurgents' strategy are available, it appears that the most loyal and best-trained of Sadr's militia deployed around Moqtada, in the Imam Ali shrine, and in Kufa's Grand Mosque. Three- and four-man offensive teams armed with rocket-propelled grenades (RPGs) and mortars moved opportunistically around the Old City and cemetery. Less trained supporters from Baghdad and elsewhere deployed on the outer perimeter of or outside Najaf's sacred spaces. A U.S. commander in Najaf at the time summarized the insurgents' deployment:

> The outer perimeter around Najaf is what I like to call the "true believer." It was the complete fanatic who was willing to do anything—and quite literally these were the types of individuals that would run at a tank with a rifle. So they were pretty easy to find in that manner. As you got closer into either Najaf or closer actually to the mosques, that's where you began finding the trained militiamen.[11]

U.S. troops quickly reinforced Spanish-led coalition forces in Najaf. While U.S. troops assaulted insurgents elsewhere in Iraq, they did not immediately do so in Najaf. U.S. forces immediately launched attrition operations against Sadr-affiliated insurgents everywhere except Najaf, where they waited weeks before commencing an offensive. Planners did not anticipate the uprising and suddenly found themselves confronting two insurgencies. On the same day that Moqtada sought sanctuary in the Imam Ali shrine, approximately 2,000 U.S. Marines encircled and began to assault unaffiliated insurgents entrenched in the Sunni Arab city of Fallujah.

Sadr's uprising coincided with the arrival of hundreds of thousands of pilgrims in Najaf and Karbala in anticipation on April 9 of Arba'een, which commemorates mourning on the fortieth day after the death of Imam Hussein. Although Arba'een centers on Karbala, pilgrims also visit the Imam Ali shrine in Najaf. Moqtada exploited this coincidence by declaring a three-day cease-fire for Arba'een almost immediately after encouraging insurgency. He later extended the cease-fire two days in honor of the anniversary of the Prophet Muhammad's death. By declaring a cease-fire, Moqtada portrayed his followers as pilgrims and baited counterinsurgency forces to respond and thereby violate sacred space during a holy period. If he had induced fighting during Arba'een, pilgrim volunteers might have swelled his ranks.

Sadr's unilateral cease-fire put pressure on other Iraqi Shi'ite leaders to condemn any counterinsurgency operations during the holy days, and coalition planners weighed the implications. Brigadier General Fulgencio Coll, the Spanish commander in Najaf, was initially a key source of local understanding for coalition planners and warned of severe repercussions.[12] U.S. Brigadier General Mark Kimmitt, deputy director for Coalition Operations, publicly worried that pilgrims would be alienated.[13] Bremer concluded that regaining Najaf was "impossible during the week of Arbain."[14] Although it was unmentioned in unclassified documents, planners likely considered the fact that April 8 was the fifth anniversary of the assassination of Sadr's father, Grand Ayatollah Muhammad Muhammad Sadiq al-Sadr, in Najaf. They may have expected Moqtada to exploit the commemoration of his father's martyrdom had coalition forces moved against him at that time. Even after the holy period ended, however, U.S. forces did not begin operations.

As approximately 2,500 U.S. troops surrounded Najaf by mid-April, Lieutenant General Ricardo Sanchez, commander of coalition forces in Iraq, created a two-mile exclusion zone around the Imam Ali shrine until conditions were set for an attack on the insurgents.[15] The exclusion zone limited possible operations and provided insurgents an identifiable safe haven on sacred ground. When asked why counterinsurgency forces did not "take out" Moqtada in early April when they had an opportunity to do so, Major Barry Wiltcher, U.S. military liaison officer in Najaf's CPA office at the time, replied

> Because it was considered an exclusionary zone, and anything inside the exclusionary zone we were not to conduct offensive operations. If he drove up to the front gate [of CPA] and started shooting an AK-47 with the Mahdi Army, we could have killed him then, but he was smart enough to understand the rules of engagement. As long as he was operating within his offices and the Imam Ali Mosque, he was permitted freedom of movement.[16]

Instead of directly retaking Najaf, Bremer says he recommended,

> what I dubbed the "Anaconda Strategy," a term borrowed from the Civil War plan of General Winfield Scott to strangle the Confederacy by pushing in from its periphery. Since we *could not* retake the holy cities by force, I proposed we hit other Moqtada targets—safe houses, training camps, Mahdi Army units, his colleagues—where and whenever we found them, except in Najaf. [emphasis added][17]

Throughout April U.S. commanders repeatedly stated that they had no intention of moving into Najaf's city center. Brigadier General Mark Hartling, an assistant commander of the First Armored Division, for example, told the *New York Times*, "We have not and do not foresee conducting military operations within the holy city."[18]

The slow development of military operations in Najaf differs considerably from concurrent U.S. counterinsurgency operations elsewhere, which were aggressive and resulted in tremendous damage to urban areas. Sadr's followers had driven coalition troops out of al-Kut and seized the local CPA headquarters.[19] A battalion of approximately 1,000 U.S. soldiers quickly moved to and attacked Sadr forces in al-Kut on April 8, using weapons that commanders restricted in Najaf (armored personnel carriers, tanks, mechanized infantry vehicles, attack helicopters, and AC-130 gunships).[20] Facing an unconnected uprising in Fallujah, military planners developed a counterinsurgency plan to aggressively penetrate the insurgent-held city from multiple angles and capture key leaders through a series of raids. On April 1, when Secretary of Defense Donald Rumsfeld and Commander of U.S. Central Command General John Abizaid presented to President George Bush the plan to seize Fallujah with overwhelming force, the president reportedly approved it on the spot.[21] If planners developed a similar operation for Najaf, it never saw the light of day.

Over a month after Sadr's insurgency began, offensive operations against insurgents in Najaf finally unfolded on May 6 when U.S. forces captured the governor's office, approximately two miles from the Imam Ali shrine. U.S. forces had decreased their exclusion and no-fire zones, albeit slightly. When they finally entered Najaf in mid-May, commanders prevented their units from traveling within one mile of the shrine area. This was a smaller, but still stringent, exclusion area that limited possible operations. For the first seven to ten days of offensive action, counterinsurgency forces probed insurgents' defenses in what some officers described as a "penetration exercise" to see "how far we could go in."

Field commanders still found their ability to call in artillery or airstrikes significantly curtailed, especially against targets near the Imam Ali shrine and Kufa's Grand Mosque. A senior artillery fire support officer recalled:

> My guidance from Colonel [Bradley] May [commander, 2nd Armored Cavalry Regiment] was that no indirect fires, fast movers or rotary-wing will have any effects on the Kufa Mosque or the main An Najaf Mosque. The Grand Ayatollah Ali Al-Sistani also lived there, so we had to protect some areas. At times, they [insurgents] would use those as safe havens. They would come out, stay within the buffer zone of maybe 500 meters that we put around them. They would fire mortars at us and then go back into the mosque.[22]

Artillery officers claim that Colonel May and Major General Martin Dempsey, commander of the 1st Armored Division, demanded and reportedly enforced 100 percent positive identification of targets before officers were authorized to use certain weapon systems. Central Command (CENTCOM) maintained a list of restricted sites, and all targets had to be vetted through their system before authority was given to engage.

Elsewhere in Iraq at the time, less stringent requirements or less enforcement of targeting guidelines by senior commanders made it easier for local commanders to engage targets in urban areas with powerful weapons, such as 500-pound bombs dropped from F-16s. The U.S. military showed significant restraint against insurgents in Najaf, despite local commanders' priority of theater assets, including tanks, artillery, helicopter gunships, an AC-130 gunship, F-16 fighter aircraft, armed unmanned aerial vehicles, and a special forces "A-team." Some capabilities of these weapons systems were used with more restraint than elsewhere out of a concern for inadvertent damage to holy sites. For example, one officer's account suggests that units in Najaf ceased using the M1 Abrams tanks' .50-caliber armor piercing incendiary rounds because the round "will pass through four to five buildings without slowing down. The round demolishes concrete structures and sets flammable materials, such as palm and date trees, ablaze."[23]

The safety of Grand Ayatollah Ali al-Sistani in Najaf was an important concern for counterinsurgency planners. One senior U.S. officer claimed: "We also ensured that Al-Sistani, who was an HVT [high-value target] in a different category, was also protected. He was an HVTP, a high-value target protected. Al-Sistani had absolute carte blanche protection from us anywhere, anytime."[24] Sistani is the most widely followed Shi'ite cleric in the world. His death or even rumors of his wounding would have provoked Shi'ites in Iraq and elsewhere to action. Shi'ites throughout Iraq likely would have risen up against coalition forces, or at least ceased cooperation. Sistani's death might have splintered Shi'ite religious authority as well. Many U.S. officials at the time considered Sistani's clerical preeminence a useful check on Sadr's influence.

According to Bremer, U.S. ground counterinsurgency operations in the Old City and near the Imam Ali shrine were never a real possibility, although planners wanted to maintain a strategic ambiguity about whether U.S. forces would fight there. He claims he told National Security Advisor Condoleeza Rice: "The Najaf crowd is scared to death we'll assault the holy cities. *I told her I could not imagine circumstances in which the President would order such an assault,* but added, 'I don't want to make a public commitment not to invade the holy cities because that'd relieve pressure on the Shi'a to deal with Moqtada'" (emphasis added).[25] Bremer's statement implies that in April–May President Bush held final authority to order operations on the most sacred of Najaf's spaces.

Although U.S. forces never approached the Imam Ali shrine during counterinsurgency operations in April and May, operations were conducted on other sacred spaces in the area. In mid-May, U.S. aerial forces attacked insurgents that were firing heavy weapons from the Valley of Peace cemetery. On May 22 counterinsurgency forces also assaulted al-Sahla Mosque in Kufa, one of the area's holiest sites. U.S. soldiers raided the mosque for weapons only after Iraqi counterterrorist troops had supposedly cleared insurgents from the site.[26] At the time, General Dempsey reiterated that U.S. forces had no intention of entering shrines, but he added that Iraqi security forces would enter holy places if doing so became necessary. The entrance to the Sahla complex was damaged, and media accounts described significant fighting.[27] Al-Ahram reported, "According to witnesses, tanks smashed through the gates of the mosque compound as helicopters hovered overhead. Blood, spent shells and tank tracks covered the grounds of the mosque compound, the walls riddled with bullet holes. Pools of blood inside the mosque indicated that the injured were left to bleed to death."[28] The Sahla Mosque is the most sacred site entered by U.S. troops in May. The timing and manner in which it was raided was perhaps meant to demonstrate to insurgents that the United States was willing and able to assault holy sites using Iraqi forces. Until this raid, insurgents in Najaf had little reason to believe that Iraqi security forces deployed alongside U.S. troops could defeat entrenched militiamen.

Officers' accounts consistently show that planners considered political backlash from any damage to the Imam Ali shrine and, in the words of one company commander, "planned around them by using precision fire, nonlethal fire, or bypassing the site."[29] After beginning offensive operations on May 6, counterinsurgency forces advanced more slowly than was tactically necessary. U.S. tanks did not reach the center of Najaf until May 14 and the center of Kufa until May 23.

On May 14 fighting in the cemetery left several small holes in the Imam Ali shrine, about a quarter mile south.[30] This was the first of several occasions in May when fighting slightly damaged the shrine. Referring to the risk of damaging the shrine, Bremer claims that General Sanchez wanted to declare a unilateral cease-fire "to avoid having our forces 'cross any red lines.'"[31] On May 25 the Imam Ali shrine was damaged for the second time. At least three projectiles hit the complex, damaging a gate in the inner courtyard. Ali Allawi, the Iraqi defense minister at the time, recalled:

> The stand-off in Najaf was dangerously accentuated when a stray shell landed on the dome of the shrine. The *maji'iyya* came under pressure from opinion leaders in the worldwide Shi'i community to take a firm position, one way or another, on the occupation of the shrine. These communities were naturally concerned in case the fighting escalated to the point where the shrine itself might become seriously damaged.[32]

After it became clear that the "anaconda strategy" of attrition warfare on his supporters elsewhere would not lead Moqtada to abandon his shrine redoubt, the conflict in Najaf was temporarily resolved through mediation. A group of Shi'ite leaders, acting in the name of the clerical establishment and possibly Najaf's new governor, presented a four-point plan. Unlike the numerous failed mediation attempts undertaken in April, this proposal separated the issue of disarming and dissolving Sadr's militia from abandoning the Imam Ali shrine. When Moqtada accepted its conditions, U.S. forces withdrew to their bases and insurgents temporarily pulled out of the shrine. After the cease-fire, Sadr's followers negotiated with Najaf's governor to establish an "official" exclusion zone for U.S. forces. Then militiamen reoccupied the shrine.

Counterinsurgency in August 2004

The 11th Marine Expeditionary Unit replaced U.S. Army forces outside Najaf on July 31, 2004. Within days of their arrival, a Marine unit came under fire near one of Sadr's houses on August 2. Either they were en route to arrest him, or they strayed into the exclusion zone agreed to by Najaf's governor after June's cease-fire. In retaliation, two days later Sadr militiamen attacked the Najaf police station and governor's office, thereby ending the shaky truce that had existed since early June and leading the governor to request assistance from the Marines, who skirmished with militiamen.

On the morning of August 5 Moqtada called for a national uprising against coalition forces. In contrast to the month's delay before May's offensive operations, U.S. forces in August immediately launched wide-scale counterinsurgency operations in Najaf after Sadr summoned reinforcements from other cities. Marines attacked Mahdi Army units in Najaf from the first day of the uprising, and fighting quickly moved to sacred sites. Counterinsurgency forces decreased or abandoned exclusion zones. U.S. ground forces eventually advanced almost to the gates of the Imam Ali shrine, and tanks and airships repeatedly struck targets adjacent to it.

It is unclear which U.S. officials, military or executive, were involved in the decision(s) to enter Najaf's sacred space, but the operational demands of battle quickly drew unconstrained counterinsurgency forces deep into the cemetery and then the Old City. The initial abandonment of no-fire zones might have been a tactical decision to protect U.S. Marines, not a strategic decision to expand offensive operations to sacred space. Sergeant Jason McManus, part of a Marine weapons company in Najaf at the time, gave a street-level description of the exclusion zone that existed on the morning of August 5: "There were no-fire areas and basically all the old city of Najaf was no-go for us. . . . Intel showed us that there were a lot of Mahdi Army in the area, especially in the old city. That was their sanctuary. That's where the Imam Ali Mosque was and they were using it as their headquarters."[33] The Valley of Peace Cemetery was inside the exclusion zone, and hundreds of insurgents were using its protection to fire and launch mortars at U.S. forces. Insurgents shot down a Huey helicopter near McManus's squad just outside the perimeter of the cemetery. McManus remembered, "The cemetery was huge. It was probably five miles long and it was bordering the old city. We couldn't fire into it because it was the border of our no-fire area."[34] Marine units secured the crash site and began the hours-long process of loading the helicopter chassis onto a seven-ton truck. In the meantime insurgents inside the cemetery directed intense fire on the crash site, wounding several Marines. McManus stated, "We could definitely tell that more crew-serviced type weapons were being used by the Mahdi Army inside the cemetery."[35] Lieutenant Colonel John Mayer, the battalion commander on the scene, might have given the initial order to return fire into the cemetery. McManus recalled, "That's when we noticed that the amphibious assault vehicles [AAVs] [perhaps from a mechanized 'quick reaction force' dispatched to reinforce the site] were returning fire into the cemetery."[36]

At around 3:00 P.M. on August 5, Marine assault vehicles and infantrymen entered the cemetery in a picket line to clear insurgents still firing on the Huey recovery operation. This action appears to have been the first deliberate reduction in the exclusion zone for U.S. ground troops. McManus described the tactical challenges of fighting in Najaf's cemetery:

> The cemetery had a lot of crypts and broken ground. It was very compact and close together. There were a lot of different places the enemy could hide.... There were a lot of gated crypts that went underground but there was fire coming from the front of us, so we just kept pushing and clearing as fast as we could.... [T]he squad next to me lost sight of the squad next to them. They got split up because it was very dense with crypts and tombstones. Not the tombstones that we would be familiar with. These were about a foot by a foot square and sticking up about waist high, some with weird monuments on the top and things of that nature. It was very hard to see.... We started getting a lot of ricochets off the hard mud and concrete in the cemetery.... At that time outside of the cemetery, on the other side, light armored vehicles (LAVs) were heavily engaged with fire coming from buildings inside the old city. We could see the Imam Ali Mosque and the LAVs were heavily engaged. RPGs were coming out every which way.[37]

Although the entry of Marine infantrymen into the cemetery reduced the exclusion zone, artillery units still considered it a limited-fire zone. Marine Lieutenant Lamar Breshears wrote in an after-action report that he requested supportive artillery fire while engaged in the cemetery, "but the mission was denied because it was politically insensitive to fire into the cemetery," a restriction that put "the entire 1st Section [of the 81-mm mortar platoon of the 4th Marine Regiment] in danger of being overrun by a numerically superior enemy."[38] It is unclear when all fire restrictions were lifted in the cemetery, but F-15 fighters and helicopter gunships soon attacked insurgents inside the cemetery and continued for several days. Extremely heavy fighting occurred as the Marines captured much of the cemetery and killed perhaps 300 militiamen in the first three days.

From the beginning of the August operation, therefore, U.S. forces were willing to fight on Najaf's sacred space. After Marines took the cemetery, reinforcing U.S. Army cavalry units established a cordon around the Old City and cemetery to prevent the reinforcement and resupply of the estimated 1,000 remaining insurgents. Before the August uprising, U.S. forces respected a two-mile exclusion zone around this area. The incursion into the cemetery on August 5 signaled its first significant reduction. By August 9 the exclusion zone was reduced, at its closest point, to one mile from the shrine. On August 12 the blockade line was again moved in, with Iraqi police and national guardsmen moving into the Old City itself. By this time armed Sadr supporters had been cleared from most other areas of Najaf. By August 17 Army ground forces were within a half mile of the shrine, and helicopters attacked buildings adjacent to it. Five days later U.S. troops cleared the neighborhood south of the shrine and approached from the north, operating within 250 yards of the shrine. Fighting occurred amidst Najaf's mosques, seminaries, secondary shrines, and religious libraries. On August 24 U.S. forces advanced into and held positions in the inner ring of the Old City for the first time. Until then they had not held positions in the immediate proximity of the shrine.

As U.S. forces moved closer to the Imam Ali shrine in late August, Moqtada and his lieutenants suggested that Mahdi Army fighters would agree to leave the shrine and Old City if requested to do so by Najaf's preeminent clerics. During a Friday sermon on August 20 in Kufa's Grand Mosque, Sheikh Jabbar al-Hafaji said that Moqtada would "hand over the keys" of the Ali shrine to the *marja'iyya*, a euphemism for Sistani and Najaf's three other preeminent Grand Ayatollahs. A central challenge of a cease-fire, however, was how counterinsurgency forces could credibly guarantee that the insurgents would not be attacked as they left their ever-shrinking sanctuary in Najaf. U.S. forces had surrounded Najaf's Old City and used aerial weapons to kill Mahdi Army fighters everywhere they found them, except inside the courtyards of the Imam Ali shrine and Kufa's Grand Mosque. Responding to the suggestion in Hajafi's sermon, Sistani's representative in London, Sayyid Murtadha al-Kashmiri, issued a statement that referred to the Mahdi Army occupants in the Ali shrine as *al-mutassimum*, which implied that they were in the shrine as a form of retreat or seeking sanctuary.[39] This choice of words echoes Sadr's claim at the beginning of the April uprising that his presence on sacred space was a form of protected retreat (*itisam*).

As Sadr's August insurgency began, Sistani left Iraq for medical treatment near London. He returned to Iraq on August 25, arriving in Basra via a convoy from Kuwait. In a written statement, Sistani explained at the time, "I have come for the sake of Najaf, and I will stay in Najaf until the crisis ends."[40] The following day Sistani departed Basra for Najaf, and his clerical representatives throughout Iraq urged his followers to flock to the holy city but not to enter the gates until he arrived. Thousands gathered in Karbala at Hussein's shrine before moving south to Najaf. Despite Sistani's approach, U.S. forces advanced through the Old City, almost to the gates of the shrine. Before Sistani arrived in Najaf, U.S. commanders ordered a 2,000-pound laser-guided bomb to be dropped on an insurgent-held hotel 130 yards southwest of the Ali shrine. This was the most powerful weapon used during either counterinsurgency campaign in Najaf, and numerous accounts of the battle mention it as a sign of U.S. forces' resolve to decisively defeat Sadr's militia, even in the heart of Najaf. Commanders perhaps meant to convey to Sadr the consequences of his failure to reach an agreement with Sistani to end the uprising. U.S. military operations ceased upon Sistani's arrival in Najaf.

After arriving in Najaf on August 26, Sistani met with Moqtada al-Sadr, and they reached an agreement to end the three-week siege. At that time Iraqis widely believed that Sistani told Sadr that he would support an assault on the shrine if Sadr did not remove the insurgents. The central elements of the agreement included a withdrawal of insurgents from Najaf and Kufa, a pullout of U.S. forces from the area, and the introduction of Iraqi government control through a strengthened police presence. Unlike the case with previous offers to Moqtada, the Mahdi Army was allowed to keep its weapons and go free. The Iraqi government would pay compensation for the damage to Najaf. Sistani's and Sadr's agreement contained references to the conducting of a census and general elections. On the side of the agreement, Moqtada wrote a message couching his agreement as submission to the demands of the highest religious authority. Sistani's representatives photocopied this handwritten statement from Moqtada and distributed it to the press.

One issue initially remained unclear. How could U.S. forces credibly commit to avoid targeting armed Mahdi Army militiamen as they redeployed? During a press conference that evening Sistani's aides gave no details about the militiamen's withdrawal from the shrine. Instead they described how pilgrims sent by Sistani's representatives should come to the shrine and leave by 10:00 A.M. the next day, Friday, August 27. The following morning insurgents inside the shrine handed over control, and Moqtada used the shrine's loudspeakers to instruct fighters to join the throng of pilgrims when they left. The *New York Times* reported: "With thousands of civilians having poured into the shrine from all over Iraq, some of them weeping and kissing the walls of the damaged building, the insurgents who had commandeered the holy site for nearly a month joined the departing pilgrims and headed out through its vaulting gates."[41] The nature of Najaf's sacred space allowed interlocutors to portray insurgents as protected pilgrims and guarantee them a secure exit from their redoubt. Without these abilities, it would have been difficult for insurgents to trust a pledge by U.S. forces not to attack them as they departed their sanctuary.

Explaining Counterinsurgency Differences

In April planners waited one month before commencing offensive counterinsurgency operations in Najaf, but they immediately attacked affiliated insurgents elsewhere. Operations in Najaf unfolded slowly, and ground forces avoided altogether or operated temporarily on sacred space, such as the Valley of Peace Cemetery and al-Sahla Mosque in Kufa. Counterinsurgency forces were unwilling to assault the Imam Ali shrine. In contrast, in August counterinsurgency operations in Najaf developed quickly and decisively. U.S. ground forces abandoned exclusion and no-fire zones almost immediately and entered the cemetery on the first day of offensive operations. Commanders systematically decreased the diameter of the exclusion zone every few days until U.S. Army and Marine units entered, fought in, and held sacred space. U.S. forces fought within 250 yards of the Imam Ali shrine, which allied Iraqi security forces were prepared to storm.

What explains the difference in counterinsurgency operations in these two cases? Why did planners decide to conduct operations on sacred space in August but be unwilling to do so in April? This question is puzzling because the insurgents, counterinsurgency forces, and location are the same in both cases.

Variation in the Nature of the Iraqi Government

I argue that in August the vociferous support of an undivided interim Iraqi government under Prime Minister Iyad Allawi gave U.S. forces the legitimacy and cover they needed to undertake offensive operations on sacred space without alienating Iraqi Shi'ites. Official Iraqi government spokesmen and U.S. officials consistently portrayed operations as efforts to reassert the Iraqi government's authority in a lawless city held hostage by criminals. Many Shiite elites disagreed, but they did not have platforms to widely disseminate their opposition and mobilize opinion. In April and May, in contrast, the Coalition Provisional Authority was the highest sovereign authority in Iraq; no Iraqi government existed. The 25 members of the Iraqi Governing Council, appointed by the CPA, disagreed among themselves over counterinsurgency operations. Several Sunni Arab members had resigned or suspended their membership to protest the assault in Fallujah. Many Shi'ite members publicly opposed assaulting Najaf and may have threatened to resign if an assault occurred. Planners knew that insurgents and dissident IGC members would portray an assault as an attack by foreign infidels on Najaf and Islam.

Throughout the first uprising in April and May, Dan Senor and Brigadier General Mark Kimmitt, senior CPA advisor and deputy director for coalition operations, respectively, were the most public faces describing counterinsurgency operations to the Iraqi public. Senor and Kimmitt held almost daily press briefings in English from CPA headquarters in Baghdad's "Green Zone."[42] Iraqi, pan-Arab, and the international media attended and widely disseminated these press briefings, which were the main source of news about besieged Najaf. The U.S.-funded al-Iraqiya television network and al-Sabah newspaper were among Iraq's most watched and read media sources at the time, and their coverage of events in Najaf heavily concentrated on Senor's and Kimmitt's press briefings. Bremer and Sanchez also occasionally held press briefings, the latter appearing at press podiums wearing a holster and pistol. Iraqi officials, including Defense Minister Ali Allawi, played almost no role in publicly describing the Najaf uprising or operations. In April and May Kimmitt, an American general wearing camouflage fatigues and speaking in English, was the primary authority who explained and justified counterinsurgency operations in Najaf to the Iraqi public via translation.

Moqtada used Friday sermons in Kufa and press conferences in the Imam Ali shrine to describe himself as defending the city of Najaf, its religious institutions, and Islam from foreign invaders who threatened desecration. Immediately after seizing the shrine, Sadr declared, "I proclaim my solidarity with Ali Sistani, and he should know that I am his military wing in Iraq."[43] Sistani did not publicly respond. On April 16 Moqtada said in his sermon that he had liberated Najaf and that "we shall never permit their [U.S.'s] forces to enter this city of Najaf or the holy sites, for they are forbidden to them." On April 23 he said that Najaf would never fall to occupiers and claimed that the city had always been victorious in rebellions against the Ottomans and the British.[44] Although Iraqis remembered the 1991 Ba'ath assault on insurgents, which did more damage to the shrine cities than the Ottoman siege in 1843 and British blockades in 1918 and 1920 did, Sadr compared the United States to other foreign occupiers of Iraq more often than to the previous Iraqi regime. He also used Friday sermons, such as the one on April 30, to criticize IGC members and Shi'ite parties that did not support his defense of Najaf.

Many prominent Iraqi leaders condemned the threat of U.S. incursions in sacred space in April and May. Salama al-Khafaji, a Shi'ite member of the IGC, called the raid on al-Sahla Mosque "a violation of sanctity" that burdened Iraqi authorities working with the Americans. Her response would have been stronger if the assault had been on a more sacred site, such as Kufa's Grand Mosque or the Imam Ali shrine. Abdul Karim al-Muhammadawi, who had temporarily suspended his participation in the Governing Council, seemed prepared to call upon his tribesmen to support Sadr.

At that time Bremer and U.S. officials were committed to transferring sovereignty to an interim Iraqi government in three months at the end of June, but they had not yet selected a prime minister or Iraq's first new president since 1979. Although the IGC was relatively powerless administratively, the support of its 25 members was seen as critical to a smooth transfer of sovereignty. The threat of Shi'ite resignations over operations in Najaf greatly concerned U.S. officials. Pressure from Shi'ites cooperating with the coalition led Bremer to allow numerous mediation attempts, made successively by an Iranian delegation, Ibrahim Jaafari of the Da'wa Party, SCIRI leaders, Najaf officials, Mowaffak al-Rubaie, and tribal leaders. All failed.

U.S. planners sought support for potential operations from other Iraqi government officials, even creating some officials along the way. After U.S. forces retook the governor's office in May, Bremer appointed Adnan al-Zurufi governor of Najaf. Zurufi, who had lived in exile in Detroit, would play an important role in August when he authorized counterinsurgency operations in the Old City. It is possible that Bremer suddenly appointed him in May to counter Iraqi dissent regarding U.S. forces entering Najaf. Although Bremer had consistently referred to the insurgents in Najaf as criminals violating Iraqi law, Zurufi attempted to facilitate a resolution of the standoff., Immediately after assuming the governorship, Zurufi said the United States had backed off of demands to capture or kill Sadr and the Mahdi Army. Since the United States officially sought to arrest Moqtada on an outstanding Iraqi arrest warrant issued in Najaf, Zurufi, as governor of Najaf, suggested that the prosecution of Moqtada under that warrant would be delayed, possibly until after the American occupation ended.[45]

On June 30 the CPA turned sovereignty of Iraq over to an interim Iraqi government and dissolved. The IGC had dissolved itself a month earlier. The interim government was designed as an indigenous caretaker authority until National Assembly elections could be held, presumably in January 2005. The interim president and two deputy presidents held little authority, which was heavily concentrated in the hands of interim Prime Minister Iyad Allawi. No legislature existed during the interim government period, although a conference of Iraqi notables convened in mid-August to select a body that would organize January's elections and, at least on paper, hold veto power over Allawi's decrees.

Although many Iraqis considered the interim Iraqi government illegitimately appointed by U.S. officials, it nevertheless represented a centralized indigenous government that most Iraqis thought should have authority throughout the country. Immediately after the transition, Allawi's government sought to improve the security situation throughout Iraq, including passing a national security law during the first week of July. A month after the transition, 66.2 percent of respondents in an International Republican Institute public opinion poll felt that Prime Minister Allawi had been very or somewhat effective since the transfer of sovereignty.[46] When asked on what issue Allawi had been most effective, 45.2 percent of respondents said "improving security." "Improving outside relationships" was the next most common substantive response. at 13.3 percent. When asked which of varying degrees of decentralized authority would best serve your interests, 56.8 percent said "a strong central government in Baghdad." This evidence suggests that prior to August's uprising, Iraqis wanted a strong central government and saw Allawi as laying the foundations for it.

During August's counterinsurgency campaign, Allawi and other members of his cabinet prominently and repeatedly held press briefings to explain and justify operations in Najaf. In contrast to the numerous briefings U.S. officials held in April and May, U.S. officials rarely held press briefings in August on counterinsurgency operations in Najaf. It is difficult to identify when and where decisions were made by U.S. officials, partly because U.S. Ambassador John Negroponte and General George Casey, commander of Multi-National Force–Iraq, rarely addressed the situation publicly. Bremer, Sanchez, Senor, and Kimmitt were each much more prominent in the international, pan-Arab, and especially Iraqi media in April and May than either Negroponte or Kimmitt were in August. In April and May, Iraqis heard U.S. officials explain and justify U.S. operations in English. In August, Iraqis heard Iraqi officials explain and justify U.S. operations in Arabic. Allawi and his cabinet ministers announced developments in frequent press briefings, which the media relied upon for information. When U.S. officials did appear, they repeatedly emphasized that they undertook operations in the cemetery and near the shrines at the request of Iraqi authorities. A few weeks after the uprising ended, Negroponte said, "When it comes to calling the plays on the field, especially on sensitive military operations, there's only one quarterback, and his name is Allawi."[47] This media strategy allowed the United States to minimize the potential negative consequences of operations. U.S. spokesmen claimed that Allawi authorized each progressive intrusion on Najaf's sacred spaces (cemetery, Old City, shrine).

Allawi's statements were repeated by other ministers as well as Najaf's governor and chief of police. Counterinsurgent forces publicly stated that only Iraqi forces would enter shrines, and Iraqi security forces' capabilities were demonstrated in gradually more difficult operations. Iraqi negotiators and Allawi repeatedly stressed that they gave Moqtada multiple opportunities to stand down. On August 7 Interim Prime Minister Iyad Allawi held his first press conference since the fighting began and categorically rejected the possibility of a cease-fire. The following day Allawi flew to Najaf on an American Blackhawk helicopter, met with Marine commanders, and repeated his rejection of negotiations or a truce with insurgents in Najaf. He pledged generous reconstruction spending in Najaf after the militiamen leave.[48] As U.S. bombing in the cemetery and downtown Najaf continued, Iraqi newspapers reported that the governor of Najaf and Interim Prime Minister Iyad Allawi, both U.S. appointees, had even given permission for U.S. Marines to enter the Imam Ali shrine.

The Iraqi interim government described insurgents as criminals released in Saddam Hussein's pre-invasion general amnesty.[49] Counterinsurgency operations in Najaf were thereby portrayed to

Iraqis as a necessary step to reestablish law and order throughout the country and the insurgency was linked to the end of the Ba'ath regime. On August 8 Allawi reinstated the death penalty, which had been suspended since the fall of Saddam's regime. Iraqi governmental officials at the local, provincial, and national levels echoed Allawi and publicly sanctioned encroachment on sacred space to root out insurgents. Zurufi, still Najaf's governor, said during a press conference: "This operation will never stop before all the militia leave the city. The cemetery is now a field of terror in the city."[50]

The international media, particularly television stations from other Arab and Muslim-majority countries, often portrayed Allawi and his cabinet as a puppet regime. At the time, however, he was the caretaker of a strengthening but fragile Iraqi central government, one that fought the international media's portrayal of counterinsurgency operations. On August 7 he banned al-Jazeera from operating in Iraq for 30 days. Iraqi officials later threatened members of the international media that remained in Najaf.[51]

Throughout August U.S. forces repeatedly prepared and then backed off plans to assault the shrine. Privately, U.S. officers emphasized that they hoped public disclosure of assault plans and preparations would lead Sadr to back down. On August 18 Iraqi Defense Minister Hazim Shaalan flew to Najaf on a U.S. military helicopter and announced that an assault on the shrine was imminent and would be led by Iraqi troops. He stated:

> Breaking into the shrine and controlling it will be by the Iraqi National Guards and there will be no American intervention in this regard. The only American intervention will be aerial protection and also securing some of the roads which lead to the shrine. As for entering the shrine, it will be 100 percent Iraqis. Our sons of the National Guards are well-trained for the breaking-in operation and it will be easy within hours.[52]

In the Iraqi media, Shaalan appeared as a constant and public presence on U.S. bases in Najaf throughout August. Some accounts claim that Shaalan, and ultimately Allawi, really did hold the power to authorize incursions on sacred space. Karl Vick of the *Washington Post* wrote that Shaalan "set the tone" with Marine commanders.[53] U.S. officials emphasized that the decision to storm the shrine would be Allawi's, not the U.S.'s.[54] When U.S. forces finally entered the Old City on August 24, they were accompanied by several hundred members of the Iraqi 36th National Guard Battalion, which drew militia members from five major Iraqi former exile groups.[55]

Although the Battalion rarely engaged in fighting, their presence was a clear signal that the interim Iraqi government and other Iraqi political factions supported counterinsurgency operations inside the Old City. Iraq's largest political factions would be complicit in an assault on the shrine.

Compared with the earlier uprising and despite greater risk to the shrine, few prominent Iraqi Shi'ites criticized U.S. operations in August. In April and May, independent members of the Iraqi Governing Council had taken different positions on the uprising; the interim Iraqi government, by contrast, was unified behind Allawi's open support for decisive action in August. Mowaffak al-Rubaie, national security advisor in the interim administration, again served as an intermediary between Moqtada al-Sadr and coalition authorities. His August statements, however, clearly represented the Iraqi government's position. When cease-fire talks broke down on August 14, he stated: "The Iraqi interim government did not leave any stone unturned to lead to a peaceful conclusion. The government is resuming military clearing operations to return the city of Najaf to normal functioning and to establish law and order in this holy city."[56] The statements of other prominent Iraqi officials, such as Shaalan, Interior Minister Falah Naqib, and Minister of State for Military Affairs Qassim Dawood, are almost interchangeable with Allawi's.

The most public dissent to the operations by Iraqi officials came on August 15, when a conference of more than 1,100 Iraqi notables convened to select a 100-member commission that would organize elections in January 2005 and hold a veto power over the interim prime minister's decrees. Some Shi'ite members of the commission used the opening session to demand an end to military operations in Najaf. A letter demanding an immediate cease-fire was drafted, and a delegation met Allawi. Other members, however, supported the government's position that the uprising was a challenge to central authority. Ayatollah Hussein al-Sadr led a delegation from the commission to the shrine to mediate, but Moqtada refused to meet them, probably because he opposed the commission's goal of organizing elections under occupation. Meeting them might have implied that he recognized and endorsed the commission. If he had met them, however, he might have fractured the unity of the Iraqi government's support for U.S. operations. Further dissemination of dissenting voices from the commission might have pressured U.S. planners to limit offensive operations.

Alternative Explanations

Alternative explanations and factors may play a role in explaining the difference between the two counterinsurgency campaigns, but they appear less important than the above changes in the nature of the Iraqi government.

One possible alternative factor was the differing political contexts of the two operations. Yet both uprisings came at critical times in the transition process, and planners saw both uprisings as attempts by Sadr to delay or derail plans to establish democracy in Iraq. CPA officials in April were preparing for the planned June transfer of sovereignty, and Bremer continued with the selection of interim Iraqi government officials despite the violence in Najaf. The August uprising coincided with the convening of Iraqi notables to select a council that would organize the first post-invasion elections in January. Despite the uprising, the convention proceeded as planned.

A second possible factor was changes in the command structure of counterinsurgency forces. However, while the structure of multinational forces in Iraq changed in mid-May when Combined Joint Task Force 7 was replaced by Multi-National Force–Iraq, the chain of command for U.S. forces was similar in both operations. Generals Sanchez and George Casey both reported to U.S. Central Command, which General John Abizaid commanded from July 2003 until March 2007. The relevant national security advisors and decision makers in the White House did not change between the two operations.

A third possible explanation could be related to the fact that the U.S. Army led counterinsurgency forces in Najaf in April–June whereas the Marines initially did so in August. It is possible that different organizational cultures or doctrine help explain differences in operations. In a controversial article, Alex Berenson and John Burns of *The New York Times* claim that local Marine commanders in Najaf (presumably Colonel Anthony M. Haslam and Major David Holahan) acted without the approval of the Pentagon or senior Iraqi officials when they "decided to smash guerillas" loyal to Sadr.[57] They say the battle reflects "an age-old rivalry within the American military—between the no-holds-barred, press-ahead culture of the Marines and the slower, more reserved, and often more politically cautious approach of the Army."[58]

Details in Berenson's and Burns's article, however, do not support the assertion that a purported cultural difference in the

U.S. military explains the decision in August to discard exclusion and no-fire zones and fight on sacred space. The Marines skirmished with Sadr's militia almost immediately upon their arrival on July 31, but they did not enter the cemetery until after the insurgents' August 5 attack on Najaf's police station. Berenson and Burns cite an unnamed official who claims that after Sadr summoned reinforcements from around Iraq that day, U.S. Ambassador John Negroponte "decided to pursue the case."[59] It appears, therefore, that Negroponte or Allawi or both may have authorized the Marine entry into the cemetery. Berenson and Burns suggest that fighting drew U.S. troops farther onto sacred space. Yet the Marines' purported cultural dispositions cannot explain why incursions into the Old City occurred only after the cemetery was effectively secured and further incursions had been authorized. The fighting cannot be explained as a series of dominoes; the restraint shown in the earlier uprising strongly suggests that U.S. forces could have limited the fighting to the cemetery after August 8. The puzzle is why did operations continue farther onto sacred space?

Furthermore, Army units in August conducted some of the most aggressive and dangerous offensive operations on Najaf's sacred spaces. Alex Berenson later reported:

> In Najaf, two battalions of the Army's tanks did what a lighter Marine battalion could not, inflicting huge casualties on Mr. Sadr's insurgents while taking almost none of their own. The 70-ton tanks and 25-ton Bradleys pushed to the gates of the Imam Ali shrine at the center of the old city. Meanwhile, the Marines spent most of the fight raiding buildings far from the old city.[60]

Berenson and Burns ironically quote Lieutenant Colonel Myles Miyamasu, an Army commander in Najaf, as being disappointed that a cease-fire was signed before Sadr was militarily forced from the mosque. Army commanders were as eager to "press ahead" as were Marine commanders. U.S. newspapers quoted local Army and Marine commanders in Najaf more often in August than they did in April and May. This does not reflect local commanders' greater latitude; it reflects the fact that other U.S. officials, especially Negroponte and Casey, deferred to Iraqi authorities to explain unfolding events. Reporters talked to more local U.S. commanders in August because they were the only relevant U.S. "officials" willing to speak.

Marine and Army units operated similarly in Najaf in August, which suggests that doctrine does not explain the difference. In contrast, Army operations in Najaf in April and May differed considerably from concurrent Army operations elsewhere in Iraq and their later operations in August. No difference exists between Army and Marines operations in August. The difference to be explained is between Army operations in April–May and those of the Army and Marines in August.

Another alternative explanation for the willingness to assault sacred spaces in August might be the presence of more capable Iraqi security forces then. However, the Army used Iraqi counterinsurgency units in May to successfully assault al-Sahla Mosque. Although most Iraqi forces in Najaf from April to June were of limited counterinsurgency value, the same could be said of Iraqi forces available in August, with the exception of the Iraqi 36th National Guard Battalion. This battalion, which would have led the assault on the Imam Ali shrine, arrived in Najaf on August 24, long after U.S. forces had moved into the cemetery and Old City. The 36th Battalion deployed to Najaf because planners were willing to assault the shrine, not because their presence made doing so feasible.

Perhaps the cases are not independent. Maybe Negroponte and U.S. decision makers in Washington learned from the April campaign that repeating Bremer's gradual "anaconda strategy" would not pry entrenched insurgents out of Najaf. Knowing this, they instead opted for decisive offensive action in August. Unfortunately, little public information currently exists on key White House decision makers' perceptions of Bremer's strategy and how they affected later decisions. It is hoped that the release of military and political documents in the future will reveal if and how Washington decision makers and the military absorbed lessons. It remains unclear where, how, and when decisions to abandon exclusion and no-fire zones were made in August. The memoirs of Ambassador Negroponte and Colonel Haslam—when and if they are completed—could contain clues.

Many commentators believe that the absence of Grand Ayatollah Ali al-Sistani, Iraq's most prominent Shi'ite cleric, from Najaf throughout the August uprising gave U.S. forces a green light to assault Najaf's sacred spaces. Purportedly suffering from a heart ailment, Sistani flew from Baghdad to London on August 6, just as the uprising began. On August 12 he issued a statement from his hospital bed via his London office, saying that Najaf and other Shi'ite cities were "experiencing tragic circumstances now, in which sanctities are violated, blood is shed, and properties destroyed, with no deterrence.... His eminence calls on all factions to work seriously to end this crisis soon, and lay principles to ensure that it does not occur again."[61] The following day he underwent surgery at Harefield Heart Hospital, 20 miles northwest of London, to unblock a coronary artery.

Some analysts suggest that Sistani decided to leave Najaf after fighting began. This scenario seems unlikely. Arranging the reclusive Grand Ayatollah's trip from Najaf to London required logistical planning that probably began weeks earlier. Although Sistani did not go straight to the hospital upon arrival, he was clearly sick. Sistani's office in London released an extraordinary video of the Grand Ayatollah in his hospital bed. Although most Iraqis had come to recognize Sistani's visage by August 2004, the images broadcast on Arab satellite television were the first televised images most Iraqis saw of him and showed a clearly weak patient.

His absence simplified some tactical challenges for U.S. commanders in August because they did not need to worry about harming him, but his absence was not the key factor that explains why the United States launched aggressive counterinsurgency operations in August. Sistani remained relatively quiet during the April and May uprising, although he did condemn Sadr's threat to use suicide bombers to protect Najaf. Senior Iraqi Shi'ite clerics warned the United States to stay outside of Najaf after U.S. forces launched an offensive against insurgents in Karbala in April, but they did little publicly after the United States began limited operations in May. If Sistani had been present in Najaf in August, he likely would have remained relatively quiet, because he would have known that his authority would decrease if the Allawi government and U.S. forces ignored a demand from him for restraint.

There are other factors that are constant across both cases and therefore do not explain the difference in outcomes. In both uprisings, opinion leaders throughout the Shi'ite world put pressure on Sistani and other senior clerics in Najaf to halt the fighting. Demonstrations routinely occurred after Friday prayers in urban Shi'ite communities in Iran, Bahrain, Lebanon, and Pakistan.[62] Senior Shi'ite clerics outside of Iraq publicly pressured Najaf's clerical establishment. Grand Ayatollah Hussein Fadlallah in Lebanon, in particular, repeatedly called on Shi'ite leaders in Iraq to draw a "red line" for counterinsurgency forces. By not issuing clear red lines, he argued, clerics in Najaf effectively gave counterinsurgency forces a "green light" to desecrate sacred space. Fadlallah's criticism was aimed at Sistani and Najaf's other three preeminent Grand Ayatollahs and implicitly questioned their willingness and ability to protect Iraq's shrines.

Many Shi'ite clerics outside of Iraq wanted Najaf's clerics to issue a statement—any statement. It could have been for or against a counterinsurgency assault, but they feared that the institutions of Shi'ite clerical authority, and hence their authority, would be harmed if such important actions occurred without comment by Najaf's preeminent clerics.

Some Shi'ite clerics outside of Iraq tried and failed to define the limits of counterinsurgency operations. Grand Ayatollah Kadhim al-Haeri in Qom has a long history in Najaf and remains, at least nominally, the supreme religious guide for many of Sadr's followers. In August he issued a statement condemning to perdition any Muslim who participates in an assault on the Imam Ali shrine. Issued far from Najaf, these rulings from a purportedly authoritative religious source had little or no influence among Iraqi Shi'ites. No reports exist of Shi'ite Iraqi security forces abandoning their post because of Haeri's statement.

Since Sunnis respect Ali as the fourth "Rightly-Guided Caliph," his shrine could be a sacred space for all Muslims. However, just as during the Ba'athist assault in 1991, threats to the shrines of Najaf and Karbala in 2004 triggered little unrest in Sunni communities in Iraq or elsewhere.[63] Shaykh Harith al-Dhari of the Association of Muslim Scholars, one of the most influential organized Sunni Arab political factions in Iraq at the time, openly supported Moqtada. But this support was widely seen as an opportunistic ploy to unite nationalist factions and never developed into a significant alliance. When media or leaders outside of Iraq protested or commented on fighting in Najaf, their criticisms tended to focus on the killing of Iraqis and the morality of U.S. operations. Najaf's sacred space appeared less important to Sunnis than the loss of life. In contrast, the concurrent U.S. assault on Fallujah triggered tremendous unrest and protest in Sunni communities throughout the Muslim world.

Conclusions and Implications

No clear winners or losers emerged from either uprising in Najaf in 2004. Moqtada al-Sadr and the Mahdi Army survived both uprisings and can claim to have defied U.S. political and military authority. However, up to 1,000 insurgents were killed in the August uprising. The deaths of many key Mahdi Army officials may have undermined Sadr's control over the organization that he had created. Rogue elements of the Mahdi Army would later be implicated in sectarian violence. Sadr strengthened his claim to be the most prominent Shi'ite leader resisting occupation and, superficially, his popularity soared. In late April, during the first uprising, an Iraqi public opinion survey found that 81 percent of respondents felt they had a better or a much better opinion of Moqtada al-Sadr than they had three months earlier, and 67 pecent said they somewhat (35 percent) or strongly (32 percent) supported him.[64] Yet this increased popularity did not translate into open support. A survey a month later found that only 22 of 1,093 respondents named Moqtada when asked, "If you could vote for any living Iraqi for president, who would it be?"[65] In comparison, the Hashemite claimant to the throne of Iraq received 27 "votes." Saddam Hussein, imprisoned and disgraced at the time by his capture, received 37. Sadr's uprisings failed to attract new allies or derail planned political transitions. A sustained nationwide urban insurgency by Shi'ites against the occupation did not occur. Instead he further alienated Najaf's religious and business establishments and failed to attract a senior clerical patron for his movement, something rival factions that claim leadership of his father's social movement have successfully done.

Coalition officials can claim that Sadr's uprisings did not delay the planned June transition to sovereign Iraqi rule or August's convening of Iraqi notables and subsequent elections. Only a handful of U.S. soldiers and marines were killed in the uprisings.Counterinsurgency operations successfully avoided significant damage to the Imam Ali shrine and Kufa's Grand Mosque. Although offensive operations leveled a large swath of the Valley of Peace Cemetery and damaged numerous buildings, counterinsurgency operations did not permanently alienate other Shi'ite political and religious factions. Yet Moqtada and the Mahdi Army survived. The established Shi'ite Islamist parties cooperated with one another more than ever after the August uprising, partly out of fear of a centralized security state led by the secularist Allawi.

Iraq's interim cabinet ministers, especially Prime Minister Iyad Allawi, paid the highest political costs in the two uprisings. In an International Republican Institute public opinion survey immediately before the August uprising, 66.2 percent of Iraqis felt that Prime Minister Iyad Allawi had been very (30.6 percent) or somewhat (35.6 percent) effective since the handover of authority on June 28.[66] Two months later only 13.6 percent considered him very effective and 32 percent viewed him as somewhat effective.[67] The percentage of respondents viewing him as very ineffective increased from 8.9 to 28.3 percent. Defense Minister Shaalan's and Interior Minister Naqib's promises to decisively defeat the Mahdi Army in Najaf branded them enemies of the Sadr trend. Most important, Iyad Allawi's strong stance against insurgents in Najaf renewed Shi'ite Islamists' fears of a strengthened centralized security state.[68] For many Iraqis, Allawi's handling of the crisis seemed heavy-handed. Some Iraqis respected and applauded his action; others feared it. Da'wa and SCIRI would soon electorally ally with Sadr's supporters and actively campaign against Allawi in January and December 2005.

Most analyses portray Grand Ayatollah Sistani as the clearest winner in both uprisings, especially after he successfully mediated a resolution in August before the Imam Ali shrine was raided.[69] He upheld the traditional Shi'ite clerical establishment's reputation as ultimate protectors of the shrine. In the eyes of American decision makers, he emerged as a "moderate" Shi'ite cleric capable of checking Sadr's influence. In the eyes of Iraqi Shi'ites, he returned to save Najaf at the last possible moment. Yet the crises revealed limits to Sistani's influence. Although Moqtada nominally deferred to the authority of the clerical establishment, Iraqis again saw Moqtada manipulate his relationship with senior clerics in pursuit of his goals—an end to the occupation and U.S.-dictated political processes.

This analysis of the 2004 uprisings offers some preliminary implications for method, theory, and policy. Studies of insurgency and counterinsurgency on sacred space often focus on single cases, yet within these cases they rarely compare how those same insurgent and counterinsurgency forces operated on nonsacred space. Without such explicit comparisons, it is difficult to assess reliably the effect of sacred space on operations. This chapter compared U.S. counterinsurgency operations in Iraq in April across cities and found that operations in Najaf differed considerably from concurrent operations in other southern cities and in Fallujah. The chapter also highlights the analytic value of comparing different operations on the same sacred space, thereby holding constant a number of possibly confounding factors. Comparing the two operations in Najaf in 2004, for example, holds constant the insurgents, counterinsurgency forces, spatial and spiritual geography, and other contextual factors.

Although the interim Iraqi government was appointed by a foreign occupier it had an ability to authorize controversial counterinsurgency operations on sacred space in a way that prevented the insurgency from spreading. For foreign occupiers, this fact suggests that indigenous governments, even those perceived as puppets, could offer important legitimizing influence. In other words, "legitimate" messages can come from illegitimate sources.

The Iraq cases, however, also suggest that the unity of the Iraqi government was a key factor. It was important that the interim Iraqi government consistently authorized and supported offensive operations. This unity of voice was possible because no legislative body existed to check or balance Iyad Allawi's cabinet. The interim president and deputy presidents lacked a willingness or ability to challenge the prime minister yet even a semi-official temporary convention of elites in mid-August seemed sufficient to crack the perception of unity in the Iraqi government. The effects of the convention's opposition suggest that authoritarian indigenous governments should be more effective than democratic indigenous governments at sanctioning counterinsurgency on sacred space by occupation forces. Iraqi governments after January 2006, for example, would probably have been less effective than the interim government in authorizing U.S. operations in Najaf, because some Shi'ite members of the Transitional National Assembly and, after December 2006, the Iraqi National Assembly would almost certainly have dissented. Therefore, efforts to promote democracy could undermine efforts by occupiers or foreign troops to conduct counterinsurgency operations on sacred space.

Notes

1. Iraq has 18 governates, established in 1976, which are further subdivided into districts. See Humanitarian Information Center (HIC), "Iraq Governorates and Districts." humanitarianinfo.org/iraq/maps/ 103%20A4%20laminated%20map%20governorate%20and%20district.pdf.

2. Most Muslims believe that the Mahdi will lead the Believers in the climactic battle between good and evil on the Day of Judgment. (Twelver) Shi'ite Muslims believe that the son of the Eleventh Imam was and is the Mahdi, hidden by God since 874.

3. Twelver Shi'ites recognize twelve imams as the rightful successors to the Prophet Muhammad. They compose, by far, the largest faction in contemporary Shi'ite Islam.

4. Abdulaziz Sachedina, 'Najaf,' in *The Oxford Encyclopedia of the Modern Islamic World 3* (New York: Oxford University Press, 1995),. 223–24.

5. Yitzhak Nakash, *The Shi'is of Iraq* (Princeton, N.J.: Princeton University Press, 1994), p. 185.

6. This idea is consistent with David Lake's deductive work on rational extremism. Lake argues that terrorists seek to provoke targets into disproportionate responses in order to radicalize their own moderates and build support for their goals in the long run. David A. Lake, "Rational Extremism:

Understanding Terrorism in the Twenty-first Century," *Dialog-IO* 1, no. 1 (Spring 2002), 15–29.

7. Anthony Shadid, "In Iraqi Gypsy Village's Fate, An Omen of Frontier Justice. Raid by Cleric's Militia Went Unchallenged, Witnesses Say," *The Washington Post*, April 3, 2004, A18.

8. Anthony Shadid, *Night Draws Near: Iraq's People in the Shadow of America's War* (New York: Picador, 2005), p. 440.

9. The United States claimed that it detained Yacoubi and sought 27 others on ten-month-old arrest warrants issued by an Iraqi judge for the April 2003 murder of Ayatollah Abd al–Majid al–Khoei. Coalition Provisional Authority Briefing with Brigadier General Mark Kimmitt, Deputy Director for Coalition Operations; and Dan Senor, senior advisor, CPA. Baghdad, Iraq, April 5, 2004. www.iraqcoalition.org.

10. Sadr's followers also tried to seize the Imam Husayn and Abbas shrines in Karbala but were unsuccessful. From available evidence, it is unclear if the Badr Corps helped Bulgarian and Polish coalition troops prevent insurgents from occupying Karbala's shrines.

11. Lieutenant Colonel Thomas Isom. Interview by Operational Leadership Experiences Project team with Combat Studies Institute, digital recording, December 14, 2005. Fort Leavenworth, Kansas. (Digital recording stored on CD-ROM at Combined Arms Research Library, Fort Leavenworth, Kansas.)

12. The Spanish general quickly fell out of favor with Bremer after he attempted to negotiate with insurgents, issued a statement that the Spanish had nothing to do with Yacoubi's arrest, and offered to replace Najaf's governor with a Badr Corps official. L. Paul Bremer, *My Year in Iraq: The Struggle to Build a Future of Hope* (New York: Simon & Schuster, 2006), pp. 319, 323–24.

13. In response to a question during his April 7 press conference, Kimmitt replied:

> Najaf is one of those cities that we do have some concern about. We do have a fairly strong coalition presence on the outskirts of the city. But we've got to recognize the time and the number of pilgrims inside of Najaf city right now. We are weighing our options, thinking very carefully about the way to restore order to Najaf. But at the same time, doing it in such a manner that does not alienate the pilgrims who are celebrating one of the most important observances of the Muslim calendar.

Coalition Provisional Authority briefing with Brigadier General Mark Kimmitt, deputy director for coalition operations, and Dan Senor, senior advisor, CPA. Baghdad, Iraq. www.iraqcoalition.org.

14. Bremer, *My Year in Iraq*, p. 324.

15. Sanchez is reportedly writing his memoirs, which could shed considerable light on counterinsurgency operations in Najaf. Reports suggest that the exclusionary zone was two miles, but it is unclear what its exact dimensions were in April 2004.

16. Major Barry Wiltcher. Interview by Operational Leadership Experiences Project team with Combat Studies Institute, digital recording, November 18, 2005. Fort Leavenworth, Kansas. (Digital recording stored on CD-ROM at Combined Arms Research Library, Fort Leavenworth, Kansas.)

17. Bremer, *My Year in Iraq*, p. 326.

18. Thom Shanker and Edward Wong, "Waiting for Change in Najaf, Preparing to Force It in Falluja," *New York Times*, April 27, 2004. www.nytimes.com.

19. For details on the uprising in al-Kut, see the memoirs of the head of the CPA in Wasit. Mark Etherington, *Revolt on the Tigris: The Al-Sadr Uprising and the Governing of Iraq* (Ithaca, N.Y.: Cornell University Press, 2005).

20. Coalition Provisional Authority briefing with Brigadier General Mark Kimmitt, Deputy Director for Coalition Operations, and Dan Senor, senior advisor, CPA. Baghdad, Iraq. April 9, 2004. www.iraqcoalition.org.

21. Rajiv Chandrasekaran, *Imperial Life in the Emerald City: Inside Iraq's Green Zone* (New York: Alfred A. Knopf, 2006), p. 274.

22. Major Peter Zike. Interview by Operational Leadership Experiences Project team with Combat Studies Institute, digital recording, March 23, 2006. Fort Leavenworth, Kansas. (Digital recording stored on CD-ROM at Combined Arms Research Library, Fort Leavenworth, Kansas.)

23. Pat White, "Task Force Iron Dukes Campaign for Najaf," *Armor*, November–December 2004. http://findarticles.com

24. Major Peter Zike.

25. Bremer, *My Year in Iraq*, p. 342.

26. CJTF7 Release #040523b, "TF 1st Armored Division Conducts Offensive Operations," May 23, 2004. Press release by Combined Joint Task Force 7, Baghdad, Iraq.

27. Hadi Mizban, "Forces Raid Iraq Mosque, Kill 32 Fighters," *Associated Press*, May 23, 2004. No weblink for this wire report.

28. Ahmed Mukhtar, "Al-Sadr's Demise?" *Al Ahram Weekly*, Cairo, June 1, 2004. http://weekly.ahram.org.eg/2004/692/re14.htm The witness cited in the al-Ahram piece is probably mosque employee Radhi Mohammed, quoted in the previous week's Associated Press Report.

29. White, "Task Force Iron Dukes Campaign for Najaf."

30. Luke Harding, "Sacred Shia Site Damaged as Tanks Move into Najaf," *The Guardian*, May 15, 2004. www.guardian.co.uk.

31. Bremer, *My Year in Iraq*, p. 355.

32. Ali A. Allawi, *The Occupation of Iraq: Winning the War, Losing the Peace* (New Haven, Conn.: Yale University Press, 2007), p. 274.

33. Sergeant Jason McManus. Interview by Operational Leadership Experiences Project team with Combat Studies Institute, digital recording, February 8, 2007. Fort Leavenworth, Kansas. (Digital recording stored on CD-ROM at Combined Arms Research Library, Fort Leavenworth, Kansas.)

34. Sergeant Jason McManus.
35. Sergeant Jason McManus.
36. Sergeant Jason McManus.
37. Sergeant Jason McManus.
38. Hal Bernton, "Courage Amid Chaos: How One Battle Unfolded," *The Seattle Times*, September 18, 2004. http://archives.seattletimes.nwsource.com
39. Allawi, *The Occupation of Iraq*, p. 328.
40. Michael Georgy, "Iraq's Sistani Returns, Plans to End Najaf Crisis," Reuters, August 25, 2004.
41. Dexter Filkins, "Insurgents Quit Mosque in Najaf after Peace Deal," *New York Times*, August 28, 2004. www.nytimes.com.
42. Transcripts of CPA press briefings are available at www.iraqcoalition.org.
43. Allawi, *The Occupation of Iraq*, p. 230.
44. See Juan Cole, "Muqtada's Friday Sermon: Marines Should Surrender," *Informed Comment*, posted April 17, 2004. juancole.com.
45. Edward Wong and Dexter Filkins, "U.S. Strikes Mosque Held by Iraqi Cleric's Militia," *New York Times*, May 12, 2004. www.nytimes.com/.
46. International Republican Institute (IRI), "Survey of Iraqi Public Opinion, July 24–August 2, 2004." IRI successfully interviewed 2,846 Iraqis across all 18 governorates. The overall margin of error for the survey is +/–2.57%. Similarly, 62 percent thought the Interim Government as a whole had been very or somewhat effective. www.iri.org.
47. Robin Wright and Rajiv Chandrasekaran, "U.S. Now Taking Supporting Role in Iraq, Officials Say. Concern Surrounds Whether Power Shift Is Too Late," *The Washington Post*, September 22, 2004, A 01.
48. John F. Burns and Alex Berenson, "Iraq's Premier Takes Hard Line Against Rebels," *New York Times*, August 9, 2004. www.nytimes.com.
49. Sabrina Tavernise and John F. Burns, "U.S. Officers Say Two-Day Battle Kills 300 Iraqis," *New York Times*, August 7, 2004. www.nytimes.com.
50. Chago Zapata, "11th MEU battles anti-Iraqi forces in An Najaf," *Marine Corps News*, August 11, 2004. www.globalsecurity.org.
51. Scott Baldauf, "Najaf Police: A Thin Blue Line Between Foes," *The Christian Science Monitor*, August 23, 2004. www.csmonitor.com.
52. Karl Vick, "For Iraqis Preparing to Invade Shrine, First an Internal Battle," *The Washington Post*, August 20, 2004, A 10.
53. Karl Vick, "In Najaf, Iraqi Politics Dictate U.S. Tactics," *The Washington Post*, August 24, 2004, A 01.
54. John F. Burns, Sabrina Tavernise, and Alex Berenson, "Iraq Chief Gives 'Final Warning' to Rebel Cleric," *New York Times*, August 20, 2004. www.nytimes.com.
55. By August, half of the battalion's men had come from the two Kurdish parties, with the rest mostly from the Iraqi National Congress and the Iraqi National Accord. Troops provided by the Supreme Council for the

Islamic Revolution in Iraq had reportedly stepped down from the battalion. Vick, "For Iraqis Preparing to Invade Shrine, First an Internal Battle."

56. Alex Berenson and John F. Burns, "Talks Fall Apart for Shiite Rebels and Iraq Leaders," *New York Times*, August 15, 2004. www.nytimes.com.

57. Alex Berenson and John F. Burns, "8-Day Battle for Najaf: from Attack to Stalemate," *New York Times*, August 18, 2004. www.nytimes.com.

58. Ibid.

59. Ibid.

60. Alex Berenson, "Hand-to-Hand Combat: Fighting the Old-Fashioned Way in Najaf," *New York Times*, August 29, 2004. www.nytimes.com.

61. Alex Berenson and John F. Burns, "U.S. Switches Tactic in Najaf, Trying Isolation," *New York Times*, August 13, 2004. www.nytimes.com.

62. For some protests, see Nazila Fathi, John Kifner, and Hari Kumar, "Shiite Muslims Condemn U.S. for Attacks on Holy Cities," *New York Times*, August 13, 2004. www.nytimes.com.

63. Although Harith al-Dhari, spokesperson for the Sunni Arab Association of Muslim Scholars, publicly supported Moqtada and attempted to ally with his cause during the uprising.

64. Iraqi Centre for Research and Strategic Studies, "Public Opinion in Iraq, April 20–29, 2004." ICRSS polled Iraqis in Baghdad, Basrah, Mosul, Babel, Diyala, Ramadi, and Sulaymaniyah. Unpublished public opinion poll.

65. Independent Institute for Administration & Civil Society Studies (IIACSS), "Public Opinion in Iraq: First Poll Following Abu Ghraib Revelations." IIACSS polled Iraqis from May 14 to May 23, 2004 in Baghdad, Basrah, Mosul, Hillah, Diwaniyah, and Baqubah. Unpublished public opinion poll.

66. International Republican Institute (IRI), "Survey of Iraqi Public Opinion, July 24–August 2, 2004."

67. International Republican Institute (IRI), "Survey of Iraqi Public Opinion, September 24–October 4, 2004." IRI successfully interviewed 2,004 Iraqis across all 18 governorates. The overall margin of error for the survey is +/–2.5 percent. www.iri.org.

68. Allawi, *The Occupation of Iraq*, p. 325.

69. For example, Visser sees Sadrism as a doctrinal challenge to contemporary Shi'ism. He writes: "In the sphere of religious doctrine, it was Sistani who emerged unscathed. Just as their nineteenth-century colleagues had fended off Shaykhism and Babism, the traditionalist clergy of post-war Najaf with Sistani at the helm dealt a decision blow to the Sadrists—at least as far as the question of religious renewal and Shiite doctrine was concerned." Reidar Visser, "Sistani, the United States and Politics in Iraq: From Quietism to Machiavellianism?" *NUPI Paper* no. 700. Oslo: Norwegian Institute of International Affairs, March 2006.

7

Iron Fists without Velvet Gloves

The Krue Se Mosque Incident and Lessons in Counterinsurgency for the Southern Thai Conflict

Joseph Chinyong Liow

On April 28, 2004, insurgents in Thailand's restive southern provinces mounted a string of coordinated attacks against eleven police and military outposts. In the province of Pattani, rather than scattering into the nearby villages and jungles for refuge after perpetrating their attack, a unit of 32 militants retreated to the historic Krue Se Mosque.[1] A subsequent nine-hour standoff between them and Thai security forces culminated in the launch of a full-scale attack on the mosque that resulted in the killing of all 32 militants and one civilian. The siege and assault at the mosque is significant on several counts for the study of counterinsurgency in southern Thailand. Mainly it speaks to the increasing salience of religion in the southern Thai conflict, which has already been raging for a century as the Malays from the predominantly-Muslim southern provinces wrestle autonomy and independence from the central Thai state.

Against this backdrop, the desecration of the mosque by Thai security forces threatened not only to further polarize relations between the local community and the Thai government, but also to increase sympathy for the cause of the insurgents. Second, the fact that the Thai government was caught by surprise by the events of April 28 is a severe indictment of flaws in their counterinsurgency campaign, which were only aggravated by the manner in which tactical operations were conducted by security forces at the mosque.

With these observations borne in mind, this chapter assesses the events surrounding April 28 and its aftermath from the broader perspective of the Thai government's counterinsurgency effort against a resurgent separatist insurgency in the southern provinces. The chapter begins by briefly identifying the contours of the combustible combination of religion, ethnic identity, and local historical narrative in southern Thailand. It next outlines how these issues converged and dramatically erupted by assessing what took place on and immediately after April 28, 2004, focusing primarily on events that unfolded at Krue Se Mosque. The chapter then critically examines the tactical operation at Krue Se conducted by counterinsurgency forces and discusses how it relates to more pressing strategic concerns with the broader counterinsurgency campaign in southern Thailand.

In essence, the chapter argues that, in the first instance, the Krue Se operation and its aftermath clearly contravened some core principles of counterinsurgency and demonstrated a lack of tactical and strategic awareness. More disconcerting, however, is the fact that the shortcomings of the operation reveal deeper problems with the broader counterinsurgency effort in southern Thailand. At a more general level, the discussion also sheds light on the larger concern of this volume, namely, the particular strategic and tactical care that is required in the conduct of counterinsurgency operations in "sacred spaces."

In the final analysis, I argue that because of both the symbolic significance of Krue Se Mosque for the Malay-Muslim community as well as the whole range of problems that have stemmed from the April 28 operation on its premises (problems that were compounded by flaws in counterinsurgency capabilities of Thailand's security apparatus that by and large have not been rectified since the Krue Se incident), the desecration of the mosque by Thai security forces has polarised relations between the local community and the Thai government. Moreover, the Krue Se incident is likely to have also increased sympathy for the insurgent cause. In other words, the Krue Se incident will fuel a new historical narrative of repression and resistance which Bangkok will have to deal with for many years to come.

Religion and Conflict in Southern Thailand

Since January 2004, when militants launched an audacious raid on an army camp in Narathiwat, Thailand has witnessed a surge of violence in its restive southern provinces of Pattani, Yala, and Narathiwat that has reached unprecedented levels.[2] To be sure, violence in this region is not new. Indeed, the past four decades or so have witnessed intermittent armed conflict between the Thai state and a number of separatist organizations. At the heart of the conflict remains the struggle for self-determination along ethnocultural lines, though others have suggested alternative causes.[3] The population of southern Thailand is predominantly ethnic Malay-Muslim. Historically, the provinces, at one time collectively known as Pattani Darussalam, enjoyed various degrees of autonomy despite being forcefully incorporated into the sphere of influence of Siamese suzerainty in 1786. As a tributary of Siam, though, Pattani was obliged to send Bunga Mas (Flowers of Gold) to the Siamese courts every two and a half years in a gesture of respect.[4] On several occasions leaders of Pattani refused to perform this gesture of obeisance. This refusal led to Siamese recriminations that resulted in wars between Siam and Pattani, which in local Pattani folklore were known as wars of resistance. Because of this historical legacy, relations between the central state in Bangkok and the provinces in the south have been marked by tension and mutual distrust.

Historical and geopolitical considerations were further aggravated by Bangkok's repeated disregard for local cultural and religious identity and practices during their administration of the southern provinces. As was noted earlier, the population in Pattani, Yala, and Narathiwat are predominantly ethnic Malay-Muslims. Additionally, neighboring provinces of Satun and Songkhla also have a significant proportion of Malay-Muslims. The difference between them and the three southern provinces, however, is that while the Malay-Muslims in the latter speak Malay, by and large those in Satun and Songkhla do not. The salience of this distinction is consequential, since the "survival" of the Malay language has long been, and continues to be, a major raison d'être of the struggle against Bangkok. Generations of Malay-Muslims from the south have resisted the implementation of assimilationist policies that aim to eliminate vestiges of Malay culture and language in the name of national identity-building. This distinction explains, at least in part, why Satun, which has a far larger ethnic Malay population than Songkhla, has found itself insulated from the violence that has raged in the south over the past few years.

Along with language, religion has also been a major source of friction between the central state and the southern provinces. In southern Thailand there is an intimate correlation between Malay ethnicity and the Islamic religion, to the extent that Jawi (the traditional Malay written script), and not Arabic, is considered the "language of Islam" in the region. Various policies enacted by the Thai government over the years to curb Malay cultural and religious expression have contributed to the mood of resistance against the state. These policies include forcing Malay-Muslims to attend national rather than Islamic schools, as well as the forcing implementation of Thai civil law in place of *shari'a* (Islamic religious law) and *adat* (Malay customary law).

Resistance to the central state peaked in the 1960s with the formation of organized armed separatist groups. Among the most prominent were the *Barisan Revolusi Nasional* (National Revolutionary Front), formed in 1963, and PULO (Pattani United Liberation Organization), formed in 1968. Notably, the founding leaders of these two groups were both Islamic religious teachers. Groups such as BNPP (Barisan Nasional Pembebasan Pattani, or National Liberation Front of Pattani) and GMIP (*Gerakan Mujahideen Islam Pattani,* or the Mujahideen Movement of Pattani) would later emerge as the separatist movement expanded. An attempt in the 1990s to form an umbrella organization to bring these disparate groups together through the formation of Bersatu (also known in some sources as the United Front for the Liberation of Pattani) was essentially stillborn, a victim of factionalism and competition both across its constituent groups as well as within some of them.[5]

Given the pertinence of creed, culture, and language to the grievances that the Malay-speaking Muslims of southern Thailand harbor toward the Thai government, it should not be surprising to find that religion has always been a major ingredient in the conflict in southern Thailand. It is by virtue of this background that the desecration of the historically symbolic Krue Se Mosque on April 28, 2004 is freighted with significance.

Sacred Symbolisms: The Krue Se Mosque

In Malay-Muslim folklore, the 400-plus-year-old Krue Se Mosque is emblematic of Malay-Muslim identity. Legend tells of a Chinese lady of noble birth, Lim Ko Niew, who had come to southern Thailand

400 years ago in search of her brother, Lim Ko Thiam. Upon hearing that he had married a local Muslim woman (daughter of the governor of Pattani) and had converted to Islam and refused to return to China, she committed suicide, but not before laying a curse on the mosque then being constructed at the site of Krue Se that it would never be completed. In 1935 Krue Se was rendered an official historical site, and its unfinished dome roof perpetuated the legend of the Lim Ko Niew curse. With this declaration, no repairs or changes were allowed to be made to the site without permission from the Department of Fine Arts.

As a historical site, the mosque has become a public space for visitors and tourists, who watch as the curse of Krue Se is repeatedly reproduced as a commodity through advertisements and onsite walking tours.[6] To Muslims, however, the mosque is a sacred place to be used for prayer. The reproduction of the curse placed upon Krue Se, expressed in the commercialism surrounding it, is viewed by Muslims as untruthful and an insult to Islam. Local protests were registered through a series of demonstrations and rallies that took place in 1989–1990, when Muslims of all sects (including Shi'a Muslims) demanded that the mosque be reverted to its original status as sacred communal space and that the Lim Ko Niew shrine, which was located next to the mosque, be removed. The Malay-Muslims felt that removing the official status of Krue Se would allow them to complete the mosque, thereby directly disproving the curse. Others, though, opined that the fact that the mosque remains intact today despite the curse demonstrates the resilience of Pattani Islam in the face of persecution. Chaiwat Satha-Anand makes the argument that the curse rose in prominence in a time when Thai-Chinese had control of a large portion of Pattani's economy. In these changed circumstances, the Muslims rallied "trying to expand the cultural space of their own identity by contracting the Chinese space."[7]

Whatever the interpretation, the point to stress is that local understandings of the history of Krue Se are associated with negative foreign influences, whether Siamese or Chinese. Because of the folklore surrounding the Krue Se curse as well as the role of the mosque as a stage for showcasing Muslim identity, one must recognize the grave importance of the historic mosque and the totemic place it occupies in the hearts of the local Muslim community. From the perspective of this local history, then, the choice of Krue Se Mosque as the site of a defiant stand on the part of the insurgents against the Thai government was hardly coincidental.

There is a further significance to the Krue Se incident that needs to be registered as well. The decision by militants to mount attacks on April 28 was also striking in that several other incidences of rebellion against the Thai state have been recorded in the Malay-Muslim provinces on or around that date, the most prominent of which was the Dusun Nyor rebellion of April 28, 1948.[8] The significance of both time and space in the militants' choice of Krue Se as the site of resistance to the Thai state points to a calculated attack, meticulously orchestrated and executed in order to maximize symbolism and arouse Malay-Muslim fervor.

The April 28 Attacks

On April 28, 2004, more than 100 militants,[9] many thought to be religious teachers and students from Islamic private schools across the region, conducted 12 devastating coordinated predawn attacks and suicide operations (sometimes called "martyrdom operations") on a series of police posts and security installations in Yala, Songkla, and Pattani (leading to 108 militants and 5 police and military officials being killed and 17 arrested).[10] These attacks broke the prevailing pattern of separatist violence in southern Thailand, which until then had never witnessed suicide operations. The attacks culminated in the siege of the historic Krue Se Mosque in Pattani, to where a number of militants had retreated, and its eventual assault by Thai security forces.

According to eyewitness accounts, a number of men had streamed into Krue Se Mosque on the evening of April 27 at about eight o'clock, some clad in the distinctive all-white garments characteristic of missionaries from the Jemaat Tabligh movement.[11] In the mosque, the men conducted prayers and Qur'anic recitation throughout the night. At the same time, militants across the southern provinces were also reportedly engaging in various religious rites in preparation for the following day.[12]

At four o'clock the following morning the men in Krue Se proceeded to change from their all-white garments to black t-shirts, camouflage pants, and headbands. A call to *jihad* was issued to the town through the mosque public address system in an (ultimately failed) attempt to incite a mass uprising against "Siamese invaders." Next the group set out with machetes, knives, and a few handguns and attacked police posts and government installations in surrounding villages. Similar attacks took place in other provinces at about the same time, suggesting that the Krue Se militants were part of a larger, coordinated operation. Despite having ample time and opportunity to disperse into the surrounding villages and jungles, the militants in Pattani chose to return to Krue Se, knowing full well that they would easily be surrounded. In hindsight, it is apparent that they were already prepared to become *shahid*, martyrs for Islam, for in the tradition of Muslim martyrdom many among them had specifically instructed family members not to wash their bodies after death.[13]

Though taken entirely by surprise, Thai security forces reacted swiftly to the attacks. By six o'clock in the morning, security forces consisting of the Pattani Special Task Force, troops from the Anti-Riot division and Special Forces, and snipers had already been mobilized and encircled the mosque. The impasse, with militants dug in and security forces deployed outside the mosque, was punctuated by intermittent exchange of gunfire. The first fatality in Krue Se, however, was not a militant but a civilian who was in the mosque performing prayers during this time. This incident would prove to have considerable repercussions on how the entire operation would be viewed by the local community in the aftermath.

Between nine and ten o'clock in the morning security forces attempted to overwhelm the militants with a barrage of tear gas, but this effort was unsuccessful, since the mosque was heavily barricaded. The limited scope of tactical operations at this time was due to the fact that Deputy Prime Minister and Director of the Internal Security Operations Command (ISOC) Chavalit Yongchaiyudh had issued standing instructions that force was not to be used and that food and water were to be supplied to the militants. Commanders on the ground were further instructed to attempt negotiations with the insurgents. This view, however, was not shared by Chavalit's deputy, Panlop Pinmanee, ISOC deputy director and the highest ranking official on the ground in Pattani on that day. Instead Panlop favored the use of military force to end the standoff. Meanwhile a crowd had begun to build up around the mosque, further increasing the pressure on security forces. By the time security forces launched their assault, the crowd had swelled beyond a thousand people.

At two o'clock in the afternoon, Panlop decided to overrule Chavalit's instructions to exhaust all means of negotiation and ordered the mosque to be seized by force. Five teams of 17 soldiers each launched a pincer operation against the militants, covered by snipers who took out militants attempting to return fire. Heavy weaponry such as rocket launchers and M-16 assault rifles were used against the militants. By the end of the six-minute-long operation at Krue Se, all 32 militants and one noncombatant were dead. Police officers who were interviewed described the standard operating procedure (SOP) of the security forces as "shoot to kill," opining that the emergency decree imposed in some parts of the three southernmost provinces permitted them to do so.[14] By the end of the operation, curious onlookers had transformed into angry protestors remonstrating against the inordinate amount of force that had been brought to bear on the mosque and those taking refuge within it. In order to prevent a possible riot, officers quickly removed the bodies of the militants from the scene.

The Salience of Religious Motifs

Notwithstanding this careful orchestration of violence to resonate with historical memories of victimization, the events of April 28 also heralded a new and disturbing dimension to the southern Thai conflict. For the first time in recent history the traditionally ethnonationalist struggle had assumed a patently discernible religious flavor. The sight of bloodstained floors and holy books in Krue Se Mosque no doubt resonated with the Muslim population in the south and further fed resentment as Islam served as an increasingly potent avenue to comprehend, rally, articulate, and express resistance against the central state.

During an inquiry launched immediately after the attacks in the Thai senate, Kraisak Choonhavan, chairman of the Foreign Affairs Committee, revealed that some of the militants who carried out attacks in other locations on April 28 were evidently found with a single bullet through the head and rope marks on the wrists, indicating that summary executions might have taken place.[15] It was further reported that some of the people captured in the other attacks that day carried prayer beads and consumed holy water prior to their offensive in the belief that doing so rendered them invisible.[16] According to one source, these militants also admitted to partaking in elaborate mystical rituals prior to the operations, including meditation, *ilmu kebal* (self-defense, invincibility training), chanting of holy verses and *zikir* (recitation of the name of Allah), and use of *gacabek* or prayer beads (which, according to *tarekat* practice, assist followers in meditation).[17] This evidence raised the possibility that a new group with cultish, if not millenarian, religious inclinations might have surfaced in southern Thailand's kaleidoscope of conflict.[18]

A six-member government investigatory commission was subsequently appointed to look into the conduct of the Krue Se operation. In its report, the commission found that although violence was initiated by the insurgents, security forces acting under orders from Panlop had used excessive force and heavy weapons disproportionate to the threat posed by the assailants.[19] Citing United Nations standards for the use of force and firearms, the report further concluded that "Because the deaths of the insurgents were inflicted by actions of state officials who claimed they were fulfilling their official duties, the process of verifying this must be conducted through the justice system."[20] Beyond the reassignment of Panlop, however (ostensibly as part of a "rotation plan"), no other action was taken against security officials involved in the decision to take the mosque by force. Further attempts at investigation of possible abuses by security forces at Krue Se as well as the other sites of the coordinated attacks of April 28 were stonewalled. Lawyers for relatives of the insurgents reported that prosecutors used

> delaying tactics to avoid serious investigations or bringing charges against military and other officials. Soldiers and police officers summoned in civil suits have not appeared, claiming that they had to work on other assignments or had been relocated to other provinces. Public prosecutors have delayed proceedings, using excuses such as not having documents ready.[21]

Notwithstanding the reluctance on the part of then-Prime Minister Thaksin Shinnawatra or others in his administration to sanction any official investigation or trial of officers involved in Krue Se, the Thai government did undertake a number of measures in an attempt to assuage local resentment. Immediately after the release of the investigatory commission's findings, the government moved to offer compensation to the families of all those killed at Krue Se. Bangkok further undertook to repair the damages to the mosque suffered in the military action, to the sum of USD 218,000.[22]

Perhaps the most significant and symbolic gesture from the Thai government, but one that took place only after the fall of Thaksin more than two years after Krue Se, was Prime Minister Surayud Chulanont's public apology for the government's policy missteps in recent years. While targeted specifically in response to the Tak Bai Massacre of October 25, 2004, when the Thai military caused the deaths of 85 Muslim protesters in Narathiwat province, allusions were also made to other events such as Krue Se.[23] Similar to the Indian government's predicament after the Golden Temple operations in 1984, discussed in greater depth by Christine Fair in chapter 2, the Thai government came to a realization that such efforts were necessary to make amends for major flaws in counterinsurgency operations. That said, in Thailand's case these efforts were necessary but not sufficient in and of themselves, and this fact has become patently clear with the intensification of insurgency in the south since April 28, 2004.

Assessing the Krue Se Operations

The demands of counterinsurgency operations are not unfamiliar to the operational culture of Thailand's security forces. In point of fact, we should note that, prior to the outbreak of this most recent cycle of separatist insurgency in its southern provinces, Thai security forces had enjoyed an admirable reputation as relatively competent practitioners of counterinsurgency. The Maoist communist rebellions that plagued North, Northeast, and Southern Thailand from the 1950s to 1983 were effectively managed, and eventually quelled, through a combination of textbook "carrot and stick" counterinsurgency premised on the identification and rectification of root causes such as poverty and local political representation on the one hand, and the creation of an effective, trained counterguerrilla warfare unit on the other.[24]

Much in the same vein, earlier permutations of the ethnonationalist separatist movement in the southern provinces that had been waging organized armed resistance against the Thai government since the early 1960s, and from which the current movement spawned, were eventually whittled down when counterinsurgency operations underwent some major restructuring in the early 1980s. This restructuring included the creation of the Southern Border Provinces Administrative Centre (SBPAC), which played a major role in overseeing the introduction of economic and infrastructural development into the southern provinces as well as serving as a bridge between the local community and the central Thai government, and the Civilian-Police-Military Task Force 43 (CPM-43), which coordinated security operations in the south in tandem with the SBPAC.[25] Given this background and experience, the seeming ineptitude of Thailand's security establishment and its inability to conduct a properly calibrated counterinsurgency campaign today, as the Krue Se operation demonstrates, is glaring.

What Went Wrong?

To understand what went wrong at Krue Se, we first need to appreciate the fact that as of April 2004 the Thai government was still unclear as to the nature of the intermittent violence that had surfaced in the restive southern provinces since 2001; they certainly had no idea of the identity of the enemy at the time. Even though a discernible spike in violent acts such as arson, shootings, and the occasional bombing was evident by 2002, the upper echelon of the Thai government remained in denial of the fact that an erstwhile dormant separatist insurgency had been reignited. In fact, then Prime Minister Thaksin Shinnawatra famously dismissed the April 28 attacks as the acts of drug addicts and bandits funded by criminal gangs.[26]

This statement prompted widespread criticism both from local community leaders, who did not appreciate the dismissive attitude reflected in the prime minister's ill-informed suppositions, and from the community of concerned analysts and observers who had discerned disturbing trends in the violence that spoke of the possible existence of deeper motivations than simple drug addiction or conspiratorial political machinations. To be fair, it should be noted that some members of the security establishment were prepared in private to countenance the possibility of a resurgence in separatist activity. Nevertheless, it was only the discovery of a booklet entitled *Berjihad di Pattani* (The Waging of a Holy Struggle for Pattani), the first and thus far clearest attempt at articulating religious impetus to violence and conflict in southern Thailand, that prompted Bangkok to admit publicly that it had a resurgent separatist insurgency confronting it.

Second, there were major problems with the tactical chain of command and the state of professionalism in the Thai security establishment that became evident in the manner in which the operations were conducted. This issue was captured most clearly in Panlop's direct contravention of the instructions of his superior, Chavalit, when he ordered the full-scale assault on the mosque and jettisoned the latter's standing directive for ground commanders to refrain from the use of force and to pursue negotiations. Furthermore, though Panlop was deputy director of ISOC, the Krue Se operation itself was not in his immediate jurisdiction but in that of the Fourth Army, which operated in the south. The clash between Panlop and Chavalit prompted the former's immediate transfer out of the ISOC after the incident.

Third, there was clearly no tactical blueprint for the operations at Krue Se beyond the use of force. Because of this void, it was not surprising when the measure of force brought to bear on the militants was blatantly excessive. The hurling of a total of eight grenades into the mosque even before serious attempts at negotiations were made was telling of the security establishment's tactical priority. As a matter of fact, according to the report of a government-appointed fact-finding commission, no attempts were made to initiate negotiations at all during the siege. The only communication between the security forces and the militants holed up in the mosque were demands by the former for unconditional surrender, failing which a full-scale assault on the mosque would ensue.

To be sure, there were mitigating factors. The fact that the militants were armed and had in fact fired upon security forces, killing three soldiers in the process, was clearly one of them. Moreover, their arsenal, while paltry in size compared with what the security forces that had encircled them possessed, did include several automatic weapons and a grenade launcher. On balance, however, given the fact that the tactical advantage lay with the security forces, the lack of any significant supplies and resources in the hands of the militants, and the absence of any hostages, a convincing case can be made that the initiative lay in the hands of those outside the mosque.

Moreover, even if the use of force was deemed inevitable, security forces did not appear to take into consideration universally accepted norms that dictate operations of this nature, whereby, according to the U.N. Basic Principles on the Use of Force and Firearms by Law Enforcement Officials, "Whenever the lawful use of force and firearms is unavoidable, law enforcement officers shall exercise restraint in such use and act in proportion to the seriousness of the offence and the legitimate objective to be achieved...(and to) minimize damage and injury, and respect and preserve human life."[27] These injunctions were plainly contravened at Krue Se.

Finally, there did not appear to have been situational awareness or serious thought given to larger strategic contexts or possible repercussions. A number of issues were at stake in this regard. No doubt, a crowd had gradually built up. Because of this fact, there were concerns that, at the very least, a protest might have taken place even as the militants remained in the mosque, which would have impeded operations. To that effect, Panlop had defended his decision to order the assault by countering: "I had no choice. If I had delayed my decision by two or three hours there would have been more catastrophe."[28] Similarly, field commanders on the ground had opined that "we did all we could."[29] These protestations notwithstanding, it appears that little thought was given to the larger issue of the sanctity of the mosque as a religious and cultural site, or the message that an assault on the mosque would convey. The ground sentiments of those who were there and witnessed the attack on the insurgents at the mosque were captured in the opinions of one bystander:

> It would have been much better if they [the insurgents] were captured alive. But the officials chose to purge them once and for all. I don't think the state has the right to kill people even if they have stirred up troubles. The officials did not really understand why more and more people joined the crowd since the late morning. When the officials' shooting started, many people booed and some even threw stones at the army officers.[30]

Considering that such a view would likely have been shared by the majority of the crowd who had witnessed the operation unfold, it is possible to surmise that the notion that security forces "had no choice" simply cut no ground with the local community.

Furthermore, as was suggested earlier, there were no attempts to initiate dialogue with the insurgents. In fact, religious leaders on the ground who had offered to speak with the insurgents were brushed aside by security forces.[31] Given that the militants intended theirs to be "martyrdom operations" calculated to inspire a larger uprising, the fact that the Thai military's assault on Krue Se was met with a sea of protests among locals and threats of retaliation from militant groups is hardly surprising. A statement posted on the Internet immediately after the massacre and attributed to the Pattani United Liberation Organization, a separatist group whose leaders are in exile in Sweden, Libya, and Indonesia, urged all Malay-Muslims to rise up and warned that the slayings by security forces will be paid "with blood and tears." Local Muslims whose family members were among those killed on April 28 (whether in Krue Se or other theaters on the day) were reported to have expressed a desire for revenge. For instance, a *Time* magazine article on the attack quoted a local averring: "I am so angry now that I will kill to defend my family and my faith.... I want revenge."[32] Much in the same vein, two *ustaz* (religious teachers) interviewed on the matter had expressed to the author that they would have taken up arms in *jihad* against the Thai state after that incident if only they knew where to obtain weapons.[33]

Tactical missteps were further compounded when the fallout from the Krue Se operation was mishandled by the security establishment. Notwithstanding the public disagreement between Chavalit and Panlop, which resulted in the latter's transfer out of the region, rather than distance themselves from Panlop's unilateral decision to raid the mosque, across the entire Thai security establishment desultory attempts were made to justify the use of force, which did little more than fan public anger in the south over the actions. Feelings of injustice were further stoked by separatist propaganda, which on the second anniversary of Krue Se decried the lack of accountability and absence of an acceptable explanation on the part of the Thai government for how the operation was handled.[34] Yet perhaps the greatest affront to the local community was what took place two and a half years after Krue Se, when General Panlop Pinmanee returned to the Internal Security Operations Command (ISOC) in the capacity of "public relations advisor" after the September 2006 coup.

Challenges to Counterinsurgency Operations in Southern Thailand

Though violence had already begun escalating in southern Thailand by April 2004, very little was known about its source, nature, and motivations. Concomitantly, explanations bandied about by various government agencies sought to link violence to criminal activities, drug addiction, revenge killings, and turf wars. As was suggested earlier, it was only with the devastating attacks on April 28 that security forces, and the nation at large, caught a startling glimpse of the nature of the enemy, and the reality of the threat they were facing.

The fact that the militants who perpetrated the attacks on that day had political objectives reminiscent of the old separatist movements was clear from the content of the booklet *Berjihad di Pattani*, which essentially exhorted local Malay-Muslims to wage war for their homeland lost to the "Siamese colonizers."[35] Despite this continuity, there were also disturbing signs pointing to new developments in the age-old conflict. The most telling of these signs was the fact that Krue Se was the first instance in the long history of separatist violence in the southern provinces that witnessed large-scale suicide attacks.

The nature of the recruitment and the ideological indoctrination involved in the buildup to Krue Se was further indicative of the challenge confronting the counterinsurgency effort. According to Abdullah Akoh, a militant who was initially part of the April 28 operation but who had pulled out at the last minute, the recruitment of militants for the operation was a lengthy process that centered on a key figure who possessed "great persuasion skills."[36] This key figure was Ismail Yusof Rayalong, the leader of the *Hikmatallah Abadan* (Brotherhood of the Eternal Judgment of God). Also known as Ustaz Soh, he apparently took up to five years to assemble his network of militants responsible for the April 28 attacks.[37]

Ismail's recruitment modus operandi was based on persuasion and the cultivation of trust. According to Abdullah, once the *ustaz* had ascertained that he shared the same views about the predicament of the Malay community in southern Thailand and that he could be sworn to secrecy, he proceeded to divulge details of his secret life as an Islamist nationalist and "freedom fighter" and his goal of forming a network of militants "to liberate *Pattani* from the invading Siamese." Soh premised his ideology on a version of folk Islam, which among other things involved rituals believed to impute to adherents supernatural powers which would make them invisible to the enemy and invincible to his bullets.[38] This preparation culminated in the dramatic events of April 28, 2004, when well over 100 young men, intoxicated from Abdullah's ideological cocktail of Islam, *jihadism*, and mysticism, followed through with his instruction by charging into storms of machinegun bullets in the belief that they would be unscathed.

A number of observations that bear heavily on our understanding of the nature of at least some aspects of the insurgency and the counterinsurgency effort itself can be distilled from Abdullah's disturbing account. First, given the painstaking but careful recruitment process described, it should be clear that the insurgency had been incubating for a number of years, something of which Thai intelligence was unaware.[39] Second, and more disconcerting, such was the secrecy and effectiveness of the covert buildup of an insurgent network that even today it remains unclear how many similar cells or combinations of cells exist. Finally, the attacks of April 28 are a harbinger of a new dimension to the old phenomenon of ethnonationalist armed separatism.

I have argued elsewhere that there have been significant trends of continuity in the long-standing conflict in southern Thailand, chief of which is the local historical narrative of subjugation and colonialism that informed the genesis of organized armed separatism decades ago and continues to underscore the continuation of resistance today.[40] Nevertheless, I have also noted that perhaps more so than in the case of previous generations of separatist militancy in southern Thailand, it is evident that today religious referents are being used more frequently and effectively to provide further meaning and purpose to the ethnonationalist rebellion.

In sum, the insurgent in Thailand today has both a "head-start" in the current insurgency over Thai security forces owing to the low-key but effective buildup of the existing decentralized cell structure, as well as a wide ideological arsenal that draws on local cultural and religious grievances. The failure to realize that a new generation of insurgents was in the making speaks to the urgent problems of the poor state of the intelligence apparatus as well as the need for capacity building.

Structural Weaknesses

Considering the instrumental role that various security institutions played in the conduct of effective counterinsurgency—such as the SBPAC and CPM-43 mentioned earlier, it follows that the premature dismantling of these structures could have had an impact on the continued efficacy of wider counterinsurgency operations over the years. In hindsight, this was exactly what transpired in southern Thailand. Upon becoming prime minister in 2001, Thaksin Shinnawatra made a cryptic declaration of victory over separatism in the south, arguing that the security problem had been whittled down to a mere "law and order" issue. Following this "triumphant" declaration, Thaksin proceeded to dismantle the SBPAC and CPM-43.

This, as we now know, proved to be a major policy miscalculation. Here we need to note that the SBPAC not only played an important role in fostering closer relations and mutual trust between the local community, security forces, and government officials, it served a critical intelligence function as well. Over the years the SBPAC had labored to put in place a region-wide intelligence network premised on informants who fed crucial information on the remnants of the insurgents to the CPM-43. By dismantling both, the Thaksin administration in effect took apart the only institutions with a proven track record in counterinsurgency.

The intelligence "gulf" created by the dismantling of the SPBAC and CPM-43 has been compounded by endemic interagency rivalry between the military and police (and at times within the military itself) and to a large extent contributes to the inability of the Thai government to craft a consistent and coherent policy on the conflict in the south.[41] As was suggested earlier, previous counterinsurgency operations were anchored on carefully spun webs of human intelligence. The dismantling of the SBPAC and CPM-43 effectively unraveled these webs and created mayhem for counterinsurgency.

Moreover, by transferring command of operations in the south from the local army command to the police, what the government effectively did was import endemic interagency tension between these two organizations into the arena of conflict management. The transition period from the military to the police witnessed the piecemeal dismemberment of the intelligence network that the former had developed over the years, as informants started to be killed in shootings reminiscent of earlier periods of violence in the conflict even as the military retreated from active command. The situation was not helped by the constant rotation of commanders in the south that took place during the Thaksin administration.

Similarly, the closure of the CPM-43 disrupted a delicate balance and division of labor in tactical operations that, while not perfect, nevertheless served the counterinsurgency effort well for more than a decade. At another level, tensions between hardliners in the security forces, who favor more aggressive tactics and the injection of more boots on the ground, and those who stress the need for a more balanced campaign to win the hearts and minds of the local community continue to be played out in a way that has stymied counterinsurgency operations and stonewalled any attempt at substantive policy recalibration.

A third glaring weakness of the broader counterinsurgency effort that the Krue Se operations illuminated was the inability of the security forces to appreciate the tactical theater of operations and strategic constraints. Insofar as the militants were concerned, their objectives were both clear and carefully calculated: they wanted to drive a wedge between the Thai state and local communities by mobilizing symbolism and provoking an overreaction by the security forces. Few would argue that they failed in this venture. The insurgents killed at Krue Se are now treated as martyrs by the local community. If indeed the insurgents were intent on martyrdom, then the question that would weigh heavily on the minds of security officials even before the dust settled at Krue Se is how widespread and deep-seated is the hatred and sense of alienation among the young Malay-Muslim men in southern Thailand to the extent that, to them, the independence of Pattani is something worth sacrificing their lives for.

To be fair, it seemed that the Thai government was aware of the need for a more measured and conciliatory approach to counterinsurgency immediately following the events of April 28. After the bloodbath, the government announced a three-year "road map" to restore peace in the region. According to its pronouncement, this "road map" would be premised on respect for religious differences and public participation in policy-making in the region. Bangkok also sanctioned an investigation into the Krue Se incident, the findings of which were discussed above. By then, however, the sentiments of the local community had already shifted significantly toward the insurgency and against the Thai state. Matters were not helped by further tactical missteps such as the Tak Bai incident of October 25, 2004, and the persistence of heavy-handed policies sanctioned by an Emergency Decree that endorsed detention without trial and the implementation of "shoot-on-sight" tactics. The net result was sobering. In the words of a former separatist, "They [the insurgents] had planned this for years. But they were pleasantly surprised by Thaksin's policies which helped us create a pool of recruits."[42]

Conclusion

Immediately following the Krue Se massacre a *Bangkok Post* editorial postulated:

> The high death toll among the insurgents, compared with the relatively low casualties on the government side, is a disaster for the insurgents. The government at last can claim a major victory in the war on terror.... Yesterday should mark a huge setback for the insurgents and could result in a scaling back of the violence.[43]

Events that have transpired since indicate that if Krue Se is to be considered a victory, it was a pyrrhic victory.

Viewed three years after Krue Se, there is no denying that the security operations carried out at that mosque that fateful day reopened deep historical wounds. Yet notwithstanding a mounting casualty rate, various changes in field commands in the south, and a coup in Bangkok, little has changed in terms of the Thai security forces' readiness to adopt more holistic approaches to counterinsurgency. Intelligence gathering remains weak, interservice rivalries continue to persist and to some extent have been aggravated by politicking and factionalism following the coup, and relations with the local community continue to be strained by mutual distrust and suspicion. The Surayud administration's apology for abuses perpetrated by the previous government, while initially welcomed in the local community, has not been followed by any move to hold the field commanders accountable, thereby calling into question the sincerity of the apology and causing further disillusionment. As a consequence, even though the battle at Krue Se might have been won, the war continues, marked by an escalation of violence and references to the April 28 event as one of the most recent examples of the security forces' reliance on the use of force as its chief tool of counterinsurgency and a rallying point for local grievances that fan the flames of insurgency.

To be sure, the unprecedented nature of the April 28 attacks has thus far not been repeated. Nevertheless, even though there have not been any signs of *Hikmatallah Abadan* activity, neither the full extent of Ismail Rayalong's (Ustaz Soh) network nor its relations with other organizations known to be involved in the current violence, such as *Barisan Revolusi Nasional*—Coordinate (BRN-C or the National Revolutionary Front—Coordinate) can be ascertained conclusively. The point to note, however, is that the psychological impact of April 28 and Krue Se continues to linger even as violence has become an almost daily occurrence. Meanwhile the Thai government and its security forces continue to demonstrate appalling insensitivity in their conduct of the counterinsurgency campaign.

When pressured to explain the crackdown on protestors on October 25, 2004, in which 85 Malay-Muslims died, most of them while in custody, security forces inflamed tensions by suggesting that the deaths were the fault of the protestors themselves because they were fasting.[44] Similarly, security forces continue to raid mosques and schools with impunity, and the much criticized disappearance of locals remains for the most part the only outcome of the aggressive counterinsurgency campaign. Most alarmingly, these tactics persist despite the weak intelligence obtained.

From a careful analysis of security operations that unfolded at Krue Se, and more broadly what has transpired in southern Thailand since, it is clear that what is urgently needed is a carefully thought-out, assiduously conducted counterinsurgency campaign in southern Thailand that relies as much on persuasion and sound human intelligence as it does on the use of force. It other words, what is required is a major paradigm shift in counterinsurgency thinking, tactics, and strategy in the Thai security establishment. In light of the track record of the security forces over the past three years, however, such a paradigm shift is not likely to materialize anytime soon.

Notes

1. The Krue Se Mosque (known as Krisek in local Malay parlance) is located in the Muang district of Pattani province in southern Thailand. The mosque, believed to have been built circa 1578–1599, is a major symbol of local culture and identity for the Malay-Muslims of southern Thailand. As the chapter will discuss in greater detail, there is major folklore attached

to the history of Krue Se, which resonates with the local people to this day.,Indeed, it is because of the symbolism of the mosque that the April 28 military operation at Krue Se warrants close scrutiny in the context of the objectives of this volume.

2. This section provides only a brief sketch of the roots of conflict and violence in southern Thailand. Detailed studies of the history behind the violence can be found in Surin Pitsuwan, *Islam and Malay Nationalism: A Case Study of Malay-Muslims of Southern Thailand* (Bangkok: Thai Khadi Research Institute, 1985); Ibrahim Syukri, *History of the Malay Kingdom of Pattan,* trans. C. Bailey and J. Miksic. (Athens, Ohio.: Center for International Studies, 1985); Wan Kadir Che Man, *Muslim Separatism: The Moros of Southern Philippines and the Malays of Southern Thailand* (Singapore: Oxford University Press, 1990); Thanet Aphornsuvan, "Origins of Malay Muslim 'Separatism' in Southern Thailand. Asia Research Institute," Working Paper Series No.32. (Singapore: Asia Research Institute, 2004); Joseph Chinyong Liow, "The Security Situation in Southern Thailand: Towards an Understanding of Domestic and International Dimensions," *Studies in Conflict and Terrorism* 27, no. 6 (2004), 531–48.

3. Duncan McCargo, "Thaksin and the Resurgence of Violence in the Thai South: Network Monarchy Strikes Back?" *Critical Asian Studies* 38, no. 1 (2006), 39–71; Marc Askew, *Conspiracy, Politics, and a Disorderly Border: The Struggle to Comprehend Insurgency in Thailand.* Policy Studies No.29. (Washington D.C.: East-West Centre Washington, 2007).

4. Pitsuwan, *Islam and Malay Nationalism*, p. 33.

5. For more information about the separatist movements that are active in southern Thailand, see International Crisis Group (ICG), *Southern Thailand: Insurgency, Not Jihad.* ICG Asia Report no. 98, May 18, 2005.

6. Chaiwat Satha-Anand, *The Life of This World: Negotiated Muslim Lives in Thai Society* (Singapore: Marshall Cavendish, 2005), pp. 71–72.

7. Satha-Anand, *The Life of This World*, p. 76.

8. Malay peasants had clashed with police forces of the Phibun Songgkram government in Kampung Dusun Nyor in the Rang-ae district of Narathiwat, a conflict allegedly resulting in 400 Malay-Muslim and 30 police deaths. This was not the only violence associated with April 28. On April 29, 1980, a noodle shop in Pattani was bombed, resulting in 14 injuries. On April 28, 2003, a guerrilla unit armed with automatic rifles raided an armory of Thaksin Pattana 2 outpost in Narathiwat's Sukhirin district at 2:30 A.M., killing four soldiers before stealing more than 30 machine guns. Half an hour later an outpost in Tharn Toh district, Yala, was raided, with 20 more guns stolen and many soldiers wounded.

9. Because of space constraints, what is provided here is a sketch of the events that transpired on April 28, 2004. For more details see International Crisis Group, *Southern Thailand*, pp. 21–27.

10. Discerning whether or not the attacks described herein are "suicide operations" or high-risk missions hinges upon knowledge of the attacker's

intent. To my knowledge, most of the militants involved in this siege who died in the conduct of operations were prepared not to return home alive. In other words, they appear to have been fully intent on becoming martyrs that day. (Suicide missions are distinguished from high-risk missions by whether the attacker intends to die in the conduct of a suicide mission. The latter leaves open the possibility of living to fight another day.) Their intent to become *shahid* was evidenced in the notes that they had left behind at home the morning they set out for their respective missions. The community also recognized them as martyrs by burying them as *shahid*. These operations were executed in the hope of sparking a wider uprising among the people through the use of the symbolism of martyrdom.

11. The Jemaat Tabligh is a transnational Islamic missionary movement that originated in South Asia. It has a significant presence in southern Thailand that is epitomized by the Markaz Dakwah Yala, the Tabligh center in Yala province that is arguably the largest complex of its kind in Southeast Asia. The Jemaat Tabligh is generally thought to be an apolitical movement that shuns the pursuits of this world (including politics and political allegiances) and focuses on asceticism and purification of Islamic practice in preparation for the afterlife. The Jemaat Tabligh welcomes all Muslims to join them in the conduct of their mission work, which usually takes the form of either seven-day or four-month trips. In this respect, it has a "revolving door" membership. In southern Thailand the Jemaat Tabligh has in fact been credited by the government for "turning" separatist militants and encouraging them to abandon their violent struggle for a more peaceful, spiritually focused life.

12. For instance, the government fact-finding team reported that instigators had conducted a religious ceremony at the Na Thawi district in Songkhla province, which included the release of consecrated sand in the surrounding areas.

13. I was informed that many of these youths had left these instructions in the form of notes to their family members before they departed for the mosque the night before. Interview with Ahmad Somboon Bualuang, Pattani, August 15, 2004. This information was confirmed by Chaiwat Satha-Anand in Bangkok, August 17, 2004. I was also informed that in Narathiwat province there are tombstones with the word *shahid* written on them, where the bodies were buried after April 28, 2004.

14. "The New Face of Militancy in the South," *The Nation*, May 19, 2004.

15. "Killings at Pattani's Krue Se Mosque and a Cover Up Enquiry," www.countercurrents.org, May 6, 2004. www.countercurrents.org.

16. International Crisis Group, *Southern Thailand*, pp. 21–22.

17. See "The (Un)making of a Militant," *New Straits Times*, September 12, 2005; Nidhi Aeusrivongse, "Understanding the Situation in the South as a 'Millenarian Revolt,'" *Kyoto Review of Southeast Asia* 6 (2005), 7.

18. See "Imam Admits Contact with Separatists," *The Nation*, September 1, 2004.

19. See "Krue Se Report." www.nationmultimedia.com/specials/takbai/p2.htm.

20. See "Thailand: Investigate Krue Se Mosque Raid: No Justice Two Years After Deadly Clashes in the South," *Human Rights News*, April 28, 2006. hrw.org.

21. "Thailand," *Human Rights News*, April 28, 2006.

22. The mosque reopened on January 21, 2005.

23. "Surayud Apologizes for Government Abuses in the South," *The Nation*, November 3, 2006.

24. For studies on the communist rebellion in Thailand, see Kanok Wongtrangan, *Change and Persistence in Thai Counter-Insurgency Policy* (Bangkok: Institute of Security and International Studies, Chulalongkorn University, 1983); Gawin Chutima, *The Rise and Fall of the Communist Party of Thailand (1973–1987)* (Canterbury: Centre of Southeast Asian Studies, University of Kent at Canterbury, 1990); Tom Marks, *Making Revolution: The Insurgency of the Communist Party of Thailand in Structural Perspective* (Bangkok: White Lotus, 1994).

25. For more information on the SBPAC and CPM-43, see International Crisis Group, *Southern Thailand*, pp. 11–12.

26. "112 Killed in Southern Thailand Gunbattles," *The Associated Press*, April 28, 2004.

27. See Office of the High Commissioner for Human Rights, "Basic Principles for the Use of Force and Firearms by Law Enforcement Officials." www.unhchr.ch/html/menu3/b/h_comp43.htm.

28. Quoted in "Thai Mosque Killings Criticised," BBC News, July 28, 2004. news.bbc.co.uk.

29. This was articulated by a senior police officer who was at the scene on April 28, 2004,during a discussion I had with members of the National Security Council, Singapore, December 22, 2004.

30. "Media for Peace," *Bangkok Post*, May 9, 2004.

31. This point was shared during my interview with religious teachers, Pattani, January 11, 2005.

32. Simon Elegant and Andrew Perrin, "The Road to Jihad?" *Time*, May 3, 2004.

33. Author interview, Pattani, December 13, 2004.

34. See "*Dua Tahun Tragedi Masjid Krisek* (Two Years After the Krisek Mosque Tragedy," www.puloinfo.net, undated. puloinfo.net/? Show=ReadArticles&ID=28.

35. For an analysis of the content of this document see Joseph Chinyong Liow, *Muslim Resistance in Southern Thailand and Southern Philippines: Religion, Ideology, and Politics*. Policy Studies No.24. (Washington D.C.: East-West Center Washington, 2006), pp. 39–42.

36. Abdullah said he decided to stay out of the April 28 operation because it did not make any sense to use knives against guns. Researcher interview with Abdullah Akoh, Pattani, transcribed on May 5, 2006.

37. According to Abdullah, Ustaz Soh was a friendly religious teacher who made his students and those around him feel at ease. Abdullah said they would play football together, go out for meals in public places, and share desserts.

38. Abdullah related how these rituals included the drinking of holy water that would make their bodies impervious to bullets and knives, and the recitation of repetitive prayers until the militants entered a state of trance.

39. This fact was further confirmed in interviews with former militants who claimed to have ties and communications with the current generation of militants. Telephone interview with Wan Kadir Che Man, September 20, 2005; interview with PULO officials, Gothenburg, September 6, 2006.

40. For a further discussion on this, see Liow, *Islam and Resistance in Southern Thailand and Southern Philippines*, pp. 34–36.

41. For example, the police operating in the south continue to report to national headquarters in Bangkok while the military comes under the command of the fourth army stationed in Pattani.

42. Telephone interview with Wan Kadir Che Man, September 20, 2005.

43. "Southern Insurgents Dealt a Heavy Blow," *Bangkok Post*, April 29, 2004.

44. This incident took place during the Muslim fasting month of Ramadan.

8

Conclusion

Counterinsurgency in Sacred Spaces

Nora Bensahel

Why Do Insurgents Use Sacred Spaces?

Sacred spaces clearly offer some advantages to insurgents, since the chapters in this volume demonstrate that this is a fairly common tactic. The reasons often have little to do with the religious beliefs of any particular denomination, since as the cases show, insurgents have taken over Christian churches, Sikh temples, and Muslim mosques. Instead, sacred spaces appear to offer a number of advantages to insurgents that help them achieve their objectives, including attracting new recruits and cultivating popular support, conferring logistical and tactical advantages, reducing the chances of a direct attack, and undermining symbols of the state's authority.

Recruiting and Garnering Popular Support

Insurgency and counterinsurgency are fundamentally a struggle for support of the population who are frequently alienated and/or aggrieved. Using sacred spaces can help build support for an insurgent movement by providing what Fair refers to as "the façade of fighting a 'holy war' " (chapter 2, p. 44). Operating out of sacred spaces brings a religious dimension to the insurgent movement, even if that movement has largely secular or political goals. This action can help build support among religious followers and help convert them to the insurgent cause. As Pardesi's chapter 4 on the Red Mosque demonstrates, in some cases the institution in question had long-standing ties to militant groups that were not in contest with the state until quite recently. Rather, in that case, the Pakistani security establishment knowingly cultivated such madaris and mosques as sources of militant manpower for deployment in Kashmir and Afghanistan. As most of the cases in this volume demonstrate, covering an insurgent movement with a religious veneer can also widen its potential base of supporters by appealing to members of the broader religious community who would otherwise have no direct interest in that movement.[1] Sites that attract large numbers of people—either because of their religious significance or because they are part of larger complexes—offer particular advantages in this regard, since they provide a constant influx of potential recruits and supporters.

In some cases insurgents may be able to appropriate religious institutions, structures, and even symbols to expand their base of supporters, especially in those religions with some tradition of martial valor and martyrdom. For example, militants ensconced within the Golden Temple in Amritsar occupied a building (the Akal Takht) that was built by a Sikh guru named Hargobind. Hargobind, along with Guru Gobind Singh, is strongly associated with introducing and strengthening martial elements within some variants of the Sikh tradition. By utilizing the Akal Takht, the militants aptly inserted their own causes and leaders into the Sikh traditions of hagiography and martyrdom. However, at the same time this move alienated other Sikhs who were offended by the hubris of the militants taking over this important and indeed sacred building. Furthermore, because the militants took residence above the Sikh scripture resident in the building, some Sikhs were outraged at behavior that was tantamount to sacrilege.

Similarly, the Red Mosque case demonstrates a particularly lethal example of appropriation of religious as well as religio-political structures. The Red Mosque was an important Deobandi[2] institution with strong political ties to the Jamiatul Ulema-e-Islam (JUI) as well as the Pakistani intelligence agencies and the army. Pakistan's first military ruler, Ayub Khan, appointed its first imam Maulana Abdullah. Similarly, General Zia ul Haq was personally close to Abdullah because of his firm support of the *mujahideen* in Afghanistan and his anti-Shia sectarian agenda. (Abdullah was slain in 1998 in a sectarian attack.) In 1992 Abdullah established the Jamia Hafsa madrassa with ISI patronage. While its connection to military and Islamist political leadership is well established, so was its connection to Islamist militants. With their cultivated ties to Islamist politicians, military and intelligence contacts, and established militant groups, these clients gone awry proved to be formidable. Moreover, their Islamist networks facilitated a backlash far from Islamabad following Operation Silence.

Logistical and Tactical Advantages

Sacred spaces can provide logistical and tactical advantages for insurgents who anticipate a military reaction from state authorities. As Hassner notes in chapter 1, these advantages can "offer insurgents an opportunity for leveling the playing field with the counterinsurgency forces outside the shrine" (p. 21).

The physical layout of the site can provide a number of advantages. Some sacred spaces are designed to be closed off from their surroundings in order to offer protection against invaders. The resulting perimeter walls, observation and sniper posts, and storage areas make it easier for insurgents to defend themselves within such sites and to repel military actions against them. The Golden Temple in Amritsar, the Imam Ali shrine in Najaf, the Red Mosque, and the Church of the Nativity in Bethlehem all offered these sorts of advantages.

Sacred spaces that are open or integrated into cities offer a different set of tactical advantages. An open layout makes it much easier for insurgents to enter and exit the site without being observed and makes it much harder for counterinsurgency forces to cordon off the site and control movements in and out of the area. As Ganguly notes, the openness of the Hazratbal mosque in Srinagar was one reason why the Indian security authorities decided against a counterinsurgency strategy that involved overwhelming force. Open sites also increase the chances that civilians and worshippers who are constantly flowing in and out of the site will be held as hostages or killed during counterinsurgency operations, as was a concern in Bethlehem and in the seizure of the Holy Mosque in Mecca. In the case of the Red Mosque, its location in the heart of Islamabad posed a particular set of challenges. Because Islamabad is the capital city, the Pakistani government risked appearing out of control and hostage to the Islamists. As a consequence, Pakistan's security elite came under international pressure to restore the writ of the law. Beijing, which came to tolerate the death of its citizens in Pakistan's Baloch hinterland, was unwilling to countenance such recklessness in the nation's capital. President Musharraf received accolades from global capitals on restoring law and order in the city. While the militants' stronghold at the Red Mosque was particularly embarrassing for Musharraf for numerous reasons, the large numbers of worshippers and students at the complex challenged state action. It was unclear who was there by way of active support and who was there because of coercion. In the aftermath of the operation, many Pakistanis viewed the slain as innocent victims of Pakistani state excesses.

The cases in this volume also reveal that insurgents often have more detailed knowledge of the layout of the site than state security forces do. Insurgents are therefore able to craft strategies that take full advantage of hidden rooms and storage sites, and they often stockpile food, water, and armaments so that they can withstand an extended siege. For example, Bhindranwale used his extensive knowledge of the Golden Temple complex to amass extensive stockpiles before Operation Blue Star. And the militants who took over the Holy Mosque in Mecca used the basement to store weapons and facilitate their movement throughout the mosque. In principle, state security forces should be able to learn enough about the layout of these sites through reconnaissance and intelligence activities to offset these advantages, but for reasons to be discussed below, they did not do so in any of the cases examined in this volume.

Reducing the Chances of a Direct Attack

There are at least three reasons why state security forces might refrain from conducting offensive counterinsurgency operations against militants in sacred spaces. First, sacred spaces often provide a right of sanctuary to all who enter and prohibit the use of violence within the site.[3] Violating this prohibition through offensive counterinsurgency operations may provoke a popular backlash against the state and strengthen support for the insurgents.

Second, the state faces strong pressures not to harm worshippers or religious structures while conducting counterinsurgency operations. This is a particular concern when worshippers are taken hostage or become trapped in a site, as was the case at the Hazratbal mosque, the Red Mosque, and the Golden Temple. But even when worshippers are not directly at risk, there can be grave concern about the negative political consequences of ordering an attack on a sacred site. Killing innocent worshippers or damaging shrines can quickly turn the population against the state and increase popular support for the insurgent cause—particularly if such operations occur during holy periods or on religiously significant dates. In Najaf, for example, U.S. military forces ruled out a direct attack against the Imam Ali shrine because they understood that public support for their mission would plummet if they damaged the structure in any way, even inadvertently. They therefore used great tactical restraint, relied heavily on indirect fire and use of nonlethal munitions, and proceeded more slowly than their capabilities would have allowed. In Bethlehem, Israeli decision makers chose to avoid a direct confrontation with the militants inside the Church of the Nativity because, as Hassner notes, they "realized early on that the public relations costs of a hot pursuit into one of Christianity's primary sacred sites would be prohibitive" (chapter 1, p. 31).

Third, offensive counterinsurgency operations may undermine command and control arrangements in state security forces and increase the risk of insubordination. This possibility is most likely to be a problem for sites of primary religious importance and for religions with a specific prohibition against violence in sacred sites. Religiously observant members of the security forces may choose to disobey the orders of their commanders if they believe that those orders violate the laws of god. The Holy Mosque in Mecca provides a notable example of this dynamic. The Saudi Arabian army and National Guard demanded to see fatwas (religious decrees) authorizing an attack against the mosque before they would follow such orders. Even after such fatwas were produced, more than a third of the 3,000 members of the security forces refused to follow the order to attack and joined the militants instead. The resignation of many Sikh officers and soldiers following the attack at the Golden Temple also exemplifies this problem and likely contributes to India's unwillingness to engage in military action on such sites. States without robust and established command and control mechanisms may be even more likely to avoid direct attacks on sacred spaces because of fears of insubordination and desertion.

Undermining Symbols of the State

In some cases, specific sacred sites are so deeply linked with the ruling regime that they become the focus of the insurgents' objectives. They are no longer instrumental: they are a direct symbol of state power and therefore offer insurgents a powerful platform from which to advance their agenda. This situation is most obvious in the case of the Grand Mosque in Mecca, since religion and the state are so inextricably linked in Saudi Arabia. The insurgents chose to take over that mosque precisely because they opposed the role of the ruling family in religious affairs. As Ménoret notes in chapter 5, the insurgents "justified the occupation in political terms.... The mosque was the very symbol of the subservience of religion and the religious to the Al Saud dynasty.... The insurgents rendered it a means and site of resistance against the dynasty itself" (p. 126).

Even where state power is less closely identified with religion, some sacred sites can have political significance which makes them ideally suited for insurgent operations. The Hazratbal mosque in Srinagar, for example, had been a center of opposition to monarchical rule in the 1930s and was an important political platform for the state. The militants who took it over were thus challenging the role of the state as well as using the tactical advantages it provided. In southern Thailand, the Krue Se mosque is a symbol of Malay-Muslim identity and therefore of resistance to the state. According to Liow, "The choice of Krue Se mosque as the site of a defiant stand on the part of the insurgents against the Thai government was hardly coincidental.... The militants' choice of Krue Se as the site of resistance to the Thai state points to a calculated attack, meticulously orchestrated and executed in order to maximize symbolism and arouse Malay-Muslim fervor" (pp. 181–82). Similarly, as Pardesi's work shows (chapter 4), the militant siege at the Red Mosque in the seat of the Pakistan government simultaneously exposed Islamabad's ambivalence about its relationship with militants and humiliated the Musharraf regime for its incapacity to reinstate law and order in the capital.

Counterinsurgency and the Additional Demands of Sacred Space

Countering an insurgency is difficult under any conditions, but counterinsurgency operations in sacred space pose additional challenges that planners need to anticipate and prepare for accordingly. Yet the cases in this volume show that this does not always happen, and even when it does, the outcomes of the operations are often affected by dynamics that might have been anticipated. Even the recently released U.S. counterinsurgency manual, which was drafted by a team of experts from the Army and the Marine Corps, mentions religion only in passing—and those references only note that religion can help contribute to conflict and soldiers are advised to show respect for local religions and traditions.[4] Several principles of counterinsurgency have important additional dimensions when sacred spaces are involved.

The Battle for Public Perceptions

Since support of the population is such a crucial element of counterinsurgency operations,[5] planners must always be mindful of the ways in which such operations will be perceived. Sacred spaces pose additional challenges for the battle of perceptions, because as Hassner notes, they both deepen and widen the public relations costs of taking military action. Counterinsurgency operations on sacred space can deepen these costs, because people often react viscerally to the desecration of religiously important sites. It can also widen those costs, by appealing to members of that religious community around the world. An attack on a school may upset those in the local community, but it will probably not inflame the passions of students around the world. An attack on a mosque, by contrast, may well spark indignation and resentment among Muslims who live thousands of miles away. Therefore counterinsurgency operations must be even more sensitive to the ways in which they will be perceived and whether they will strengthen or weaken public support for the insurgents.

Most important, governments need to be able to counter the insurgents' claims to religious legitimacy and to convincingly demonstrate that it is the insurgents—not state security forces—that are responsible for violating the sacredness of the site. Without an effective information campaign, any ensuing damage will likely be blamed on the state, regardless of who started shooting. Indian security forces learned this lesson the hard way after Operation Blue Star. Media were not allowed to cover the operation, and when they were allowed to enter the temple, they largely held the army responsible for the massive damage to the temple. The army was never able to counter this perception, despite later releasing pictures of the arms caches and the sacrilegious behavior of Bhindranwale and his followers. A similar situation occurred after the siege of the Holy Mosque in Mecca. The Koran makes an important distinction between those who initiate violence and those who respond to it, and as Ménoret notes, "the shrine could be a formidable tribune for the group's opposition to the royal family, [but] the Koranic verse could become a trap if the insurgents were the first to open fire, shed blood, or use their weapons in any way" (pp. 124–25). After the siege, the group that took over the mosque and the Saudi opposition claimed that army forces had fired the first shots, despite claims from authorities on the scene that the insurgents had breached the sanctity of the mosque by firing first and taking hostages. As Pardesi notes of the Red Mosque episode, while the military operation was a tactical success, its failure to manage the public opinion fallout fostered widespread criticism of the operation throughout the country and galvanized militants in Pakistan's tribal areas.

If done well, a good information campaign can decrease popular support for the insurgents by holding them responsible for the initiation of violence. It can also encourage the state to pursue a strategy of restraint which, as will be discussed below, can often be more successful. Indian authorities learned the lesson of Blue Star, and Operation Black Thunder was fully televised from the very beginning. This exposure enabled audiences around the world to see the depravity and sacrilegious behavior of the insurgents inside the Golden Temple and gave the police strong incentives to honor their commitments, act in accordance with the law, and clearly explain the reasons for their actions. In Bethlehem the restraint of the Israeli military and government outreach to religious elites around the world led the Palestinian leadership to be blamed for provoking the incident at the Church of the Nativity.

The Primary Importance of Intelligence

Successful counterinsurgency operations require accurate and timely information about the identity, location, and activities of insurgents.[6] Insurgents, after all, are not easily distinguishable from the population, since they do not wear uniforms and do not amass weapons and materiel on a large scale. Gathering such intelligence and ensuring its reliability is a continual challenge for all counterinsurgency operations, but it can become even more difficult when sacred spaces are involved. Sacred spaces, especially those of primary importance, may draw large numbers of visitors from around the country, the region, or even the world, enabling insurgents and foreign fighters to hide in plain sight among the crowds. Open complexes or those situated in urban areas make it even more difficult to identify insurgents, since these areas cannot easily be cordoned off through access controls.

Hassner identifies several crucial pieces of information that counterinsurgency forces need to collect in order to understand how a religious community will respond to an attack on a sacred site. Religious elites are often the best source of this information, but they are likely to be coerced or threatened by the insurgents to prevent them from sharing what they know. He concludes that "counterinsurgency forces would do well to conceive of religious authorities as assets that need to be protected before they can be expected to cooperate" (p. 29). Insurgents may also threaten members of the security forces who enter sacred spaces to collect information as basic as the spatial layout of the site. Indian operatives did not enter the Golden Temple to collect this information, even though the site is quite open, because of fears that they would be tortured or killed. This possibility may be one of the reasons why all of the cases in this volume show that insurgents knew much more about the geography and layout of the sites that they occupied than did the counterinsurgency forces charged with removing them.

Restraint and the Use of Force

Counterinsurgency operations rely on restraint in the use of force, not the indiscriminate use of force, in order to achieve success.[7] Killing and capturing insurgents may temporarily alleviate the violence, but the civilian casualties and damage that almost inevitably result can further alienate the population and strengthen the insurgency in the long run. As a result, police forces are generally seen as more effective at counterinsurgency than are standard military forces, since they are specifically trained to use force only when necessary and to avoid indiscriminate killing. The cases in this volume suggest that police forces are particularly valuable for counterinsurgency operations on sacred space, where the proper calibration of force is critical to ensure minimal damage to worshippers and religious structures.

Police forces may also be particularly helpful for such operations because, unlike military forces, they are usually recruited from and based in the communities where they operate. This connection may make them more sensitive to the religious and symbolic aspects of the sites and enable them to better judge how the local population will react to different types of operational approaches. In India, for example, one of the key lessons of Operation Blue Star was that local security forces would have much more legitimacy for such operations than national forces. For Operation Black Thunder, according to Fair, decision makers "hoped that the Punjab police, with their local ethnic and religious ties, could be an effective counterinsurgency force without rekindling the belief that the central government was using non-Sikh forces to occupy an important Sikh shrine" (p. 52).

Using police forces for counterinsurgency operations does carry risks. The very qualities that make them an attractive option—being a part of the community in which they serve—also make them more prone to being biased and potentially to being infiltrated by the insurgents. Armies may be a better option when local police forces are considered too unreliable or partisan, as Ganguly notes in chapter 3. These problems reinforce the need for effective tactical command and control of all counterinsurgency forces, whether local or national. The attack on the Krue Se mosque was ordered by a deputy who deliberately contravened his superior's directive not to use force, a decision that had disastrous consequences not only at the site but, as Liow argues, helped strengthen the insurgency in southern Thailand. And as was noted above, insubordination and desertion are particular risks for operations in sacred spaces.

The Role of Foreigners

Foreign forces face a somewhat paradoxical role in countering insurgencies. They are almost always at a disadvantage, since they cannot know the terrain, language, culture, and political issues at stake as well as the locals do.[8] Furthermore their very presence can often intensify the insurgency by provoking a violent nationalist backlash among those who would otherwise not support the insurgents. Patel in chapter 6 shows how Moqtada al-Sadr was able to rally support by comparing the U.S. damage to shrines to the damage caused by the Ottoman and the British empires, even though the Ba'athist assaults on shrine cities in 1991 actually did more damage. He also argues that foreign counterinsurgency operations require legitimacy from some sort of indigenous authorities, for otherwise they risk being held responsible for repressing dissent and desecrating sacred spaces.

Foreigners make for much better insurgents than they do counterinsurgents. They can help strengthen insurgencies by providing materiel, knowledge, and support that local groups might not otherwise be able to access. They may also be less restrained in using force, which poses particular challenges in sacred spaces. Ganguly describes how the foreign insurgents at Charar-e-Sharief were more than willing to destroy a shrine to which they felt no sense of connection, and he concludes that security forces may have to adopt harsher techniques against foreign insurgents. Sometimes foreign insurgents can overstep their bounds and lose support among local populations, which may have been one of the reasons why Sunnis in Iraq stopped cooperating with Al Qaeda in Iraq in early 2007 and have gradually started cooperating with U.S. and coalition forces in the country.

Winning the Battle but Losing the War

One of the most frustrating aspects of counterinsurgency is that tactical victories do not automatically aggregate into strategic success.[9] Achieving narrow military objectives in a particular engagement with insurgents may not appreciably improve popular support for the state or the overall level of violence—and it might even make these trends worse. Although this is true for all counterinsurgency operations, the difficulties of operating on sacred space make this possibility a particular concern. The attack on the Krue Se mosque succeeded in killing all of the insurgents inside but powerfully strengthened the overall insurgency in southern Thailand. Saudi Arabia was able (with help from the United States and France) to retake the Holy Mosque in Mecca, but the operation undermined the legitimacy of the state and strengthened many Islamic groups in the country. Indian authorities killed Bhindranwale during Operation Blue Star, but his movement grew stronger after his death, and the Golden Temple was once again taken over by militants only four years later. It is too early to ascertain the full range of impacts of the Red Mosque standoff in July 2007, but preliminary evidence suggests that it precipitated the expansion of Islamist cum Pashtun militancy in the Swat Valley in Pakistan's Northwest Frontier Province.

The cases analyzed in this volume starkly demonstrate that strategic consequences of counterinsurgency operations on sacred space can be quite negative even if the operations are considered to have been militarily successful.

Lessons for Operational Planning

Although the cases in this volume differ from each other dramatically in many respects, they do offer a few lessons for planning counterinsurgency operations in sacred spaces. These include assessing the degree of sacredness of a site, assessing the support of the local population, and the relative strengths of direct and indirect strategies.

Assessing Degrees of Sacredness

Not all sites are equally sacred. Different sites mean different things to different people, so their reactions to military operations on sacred space will vary as well. Sacredness tends to vary along two dimensions. The first is the hierarchy of importance that Hassner describes in chapter 1. Sites of primary importance are located on sacred ground, where a divine revelation has taken place or a religious movement has been formed. Sites of secondary importance are located on consecrated ground, at locations chosen by religious actors instead of by gods. Sites of tertiary importance—which constitute the vast majority of sacred sites—are designed for routine community use. Hassner argues that the more important the site, the more widespread and intense the public reaction will be against any damage or desecration. This means that commanders planning counterinsurgency operations on sacred sites, particularly those of primary or secondary importance, should minimize or prepare to mitigate some of the negative public relations fallout of their operations in the regional and perhaps even global community in addition to the local community.

The cases in this volume also indicate that there can be different degrees of sacredness within a single site. Some sites are open complexes that include many structures, streets, and activities. Here the degree of sacredness tends to increase as one moves from the outer edges of a site in toward the most sacred inner sanctum. This was an important lesson learned from Operation Blue Star in India, for example. When Operation Black Thunder occurred four years later, planners explicitly assessed how operating in different parts of the complex would be interpreted by the Sikh community. They concluded that entering the *serai* and the *langar* (residential buildings and a communal kitchen, respectively) would be less provocative than entering the inner temple, so they focused their initial operations on these outer areas. Their assessment proved largely correct: they were able to dislodge the insurgents without ever having to enter the sacred temple and thus provoking a strong counterreaction by the Sikh community.

Support of the Local Community

All counterinsurgency operations rely on the support of the local community. The people who live and work in the immediate environs of such operations can tip the balance toward success by providing assistance and information to the counterinsurgent forces, or they can tip the balance toward failure by providing clandestine information, resources, and other forms of support to the insurgents. Operational planners may choose different strategies according to the degree of support within the local community. In the case of Charar-e-Sharief (chapter 3), for example, military planners decided to pursue a siege rather than more direct military action because they knew that there were many insurgent sympathizers in the local community.

Furthermore, eyewitnesses from the community will play a crucial role in developing the narrative of the operation. Many people will believe these narratives, whether or not they accurately represent the events that occurred. This circumstance further underscores the importance of developing and executing a public relations strategy that proactively shapes the ways that these narratives will unfold. Several of the cases here—including Operation Blue Star, Charar-e-Sharief, and the Krue Se mosque—indicate that media blackouts usually backfire, since eyewitnesses will provide their own interpretations of events which will affect public opinion before the state can provide an adequate response. By contrast, the successes of Operation Black Thunder and operations at the Hazratbal mosque are at least partly attributable to a transparent media strategy that enabled people to see how events unfolded in real time.

Direct versus Indirect Strategies

The cases do not provide a clear finding as to whether direct attacks on insurgents operating in sacred space are more or less likely to be successful than indirect attacks or prolonged sieges. Indirect strategies were successful in Operation Black Thunder, where Indian authorities effectively deprived the insurgents of food, water, power, and other supplies, and in Hazratbal, where the general in charge explicitly refused to authorize the use of force at the advice of the principal negotiator, Wajahat Habibullah. Yet they were unsuccessful in the case of the Charar-e-Sharief shrine, which, according to Ganguly, "revealed the limits of armed restraint and negotiation" (chapter 3, p. 77). And Fair offers an important warning about the limits of indirect strategies by noting that if Operation Black Thunder had failed, "then this approach could have been criticized for being 'soft on the insurgents'" (chapter 2, p. 59).

One theme that does seem to hold across the cases, though, is that it may be important to try mediating with the insurgents before escalating into the use of force. If state security forces engage in violence without first having tried mediation, public opinion may well hold them responsible for not having done enough to avoid bloodshed. This is particularly true if the state forces actively reject an offer to attempt mediation, as occurred with the Krue Se mosque.[10] This finding has more to do with the battle for public perceptions than with the viability of mediation as a counterinsurgency strategy, since refusal to mediate makes it more difficult for insurgent groups to completely blame the state for the outbreak of violence.

A Final Word on Counterinsurgency in Sacred Spaces

Counterinsurgency operations rarely succeed or fail solely because of the sacredness of the site on which they take place. Counterinsurgency is inherently difficult, and the cases in this volume show that there are many other factors that affect success—including differences in terrain and geography, tactical choices, the legitimacy of the national government, and the training and capabilities of both the insurgents and the counterinsurgency forces, among others. But the cases do demonstrate that counterinsurgency in sacred spaces presents a number of additional issues that operational planners must address in order to be successful. Sacred spaces resonate powerfully among religious populations, a reaction that may make it difficult for counterinsurgency forces to maintain the popular support that is so vital for their success. Simply put, counterinsurgency is hard, but counterinsurgency on sacred spaces is even harder. Operational planners must account for these additional demands and prepare to mitigate them in order to increase the chances of success.

Notes

1. Hassner refers to this in chapter 1 as widening the audience costs involved in an operation.

2. Deobandi is a Sunni school of Islam that emerged from a Muslim religious revival movement in the South Asian subcontinent during British rule. It originated in the town of Deoband in modern-day India as a puritanical movement to uplift Muslims by purifying Islamic practices through, among other things, discouraging mystical beliefs, such as intercession by saints and propitiation at graves and shrines.

3. As Hassner notes in chapter 1, all traditions that offer the right of sanctuary in some form "must grapple with the difficult question of whether this right should be extended to armed insurgents" (p. 28).

4. United States Army, *The U.S. Army/Marine Corps Counterinsurgency Field Manual: U.S. Army Field Manual no. 3–24: Marine Corps Warfighting Publication no. 3–33.5* (Chicago: University of Chicago Press, 2007), pp. 6–13 and B-7.

5. David Kilcullen, one of the foremost scholars of counterinsurgency, defines counterinsurgency as "fundamentally a competition between each side to mobilize the population in support of its agenda." See "'Twenty-Eight Articles': Fundamentals of Company-level Counterinsurgency," *Military Review*, May–June 2006, p. 103.

6. For more on the crucial role of intelligence in counterinsurgency, see *Field Manual 3–24: Counterinsurgency*, chapter 3.

7. Kilcullen provides the following advice to deploying counterinsurgency forces: "You have more combat strength than you can or should use in most situations. Injudicious use of firepower creates blood feuds, homeless people, and societal disruption that fuel and perpetuate the insurgency." Kilcullen, "'Twenty-Eight Articles,'" p. 103. See also *Field Manual 3–24: Counterinsurgency*, pp. 1–25 and 1–27.

8. *Field Manual 3–24: Counterinsurgency*, p. 1–23.

9. *Field Manual 3–24: Counterinsurgency*, p. 1–28.

10. Liow writes in chapter 7 in this volume that religious leaders offered to mediate with the insurgents, but this offer was rejected by the security forces.

Index